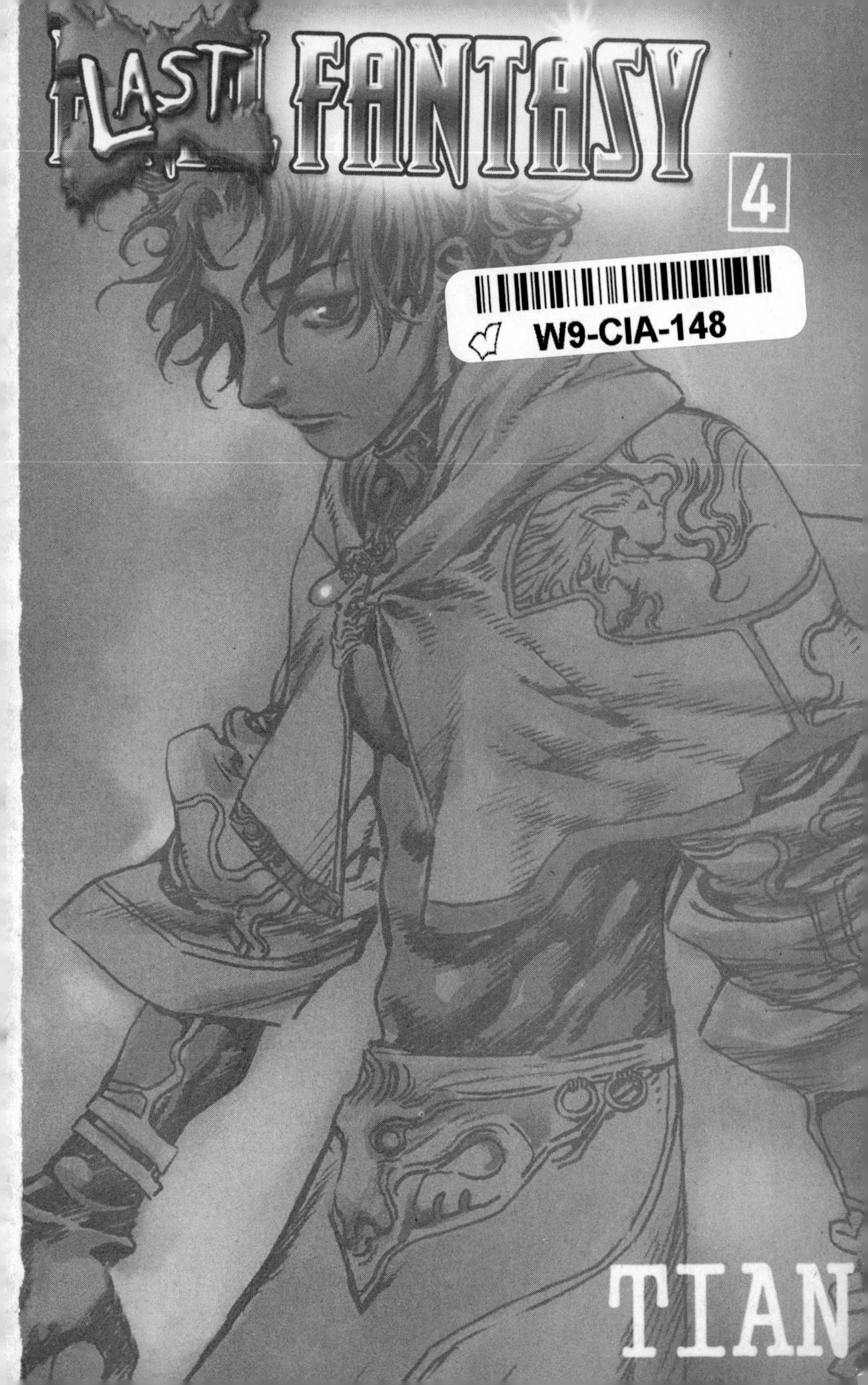
LAST FANTASY
4
TIAN

Last Fantasy Vol. 4
Story By Creative Hon
Art By Yong-Wan Kwon

Translation - Sora Han
English Adaptaion - Mike Wellman
Retouch and Lettering - StarPrint Brokers
Production Artist - Jennifer Carbajal
Graphic Designer - Fawn Lau

Editor - Luis Reyes
Digital Imaging Manager - Chris Buford
Pre-Production Supervisor - Erika Terriquez
Art Director - Anne Marie Horne
Production Manager - Elisabeth Brizzi
Managing Editor - Vy Nguyen
VP of Production - Ron Klamert
Editor-in-Chief - Rob Tokar
Publisher - Mike Kiley
President and C.O.O. - John Parker
C.E.O. and Chief Creative Officer - Stuart Levy

A  Manga

TOKYOPOP and  are trademarks or registered trademarks of TOKYOPOP Inc.

TOKYOPOP Inc.
5900 Wilshire Blvd. Suite 2000
Los Angeles, CA 90036

E-mail: info@TOKYOPOP.com
Come visit us online at www.TOKYOPOP.com

ISBN: 978-1-59532-529-7

First TOKYOPOP printing: March 2007
10 9 8 7 6 5 4 3 2 1
Printed in the USA

VOLUME 4

STORY BY CREATIVE HON
ART BY KWON YONG-WAN

HAMBURG // LONDON // LOS ANGELES // TOKYO

STORY THUS FAR

Tian--a low level under-experienced magic user whose only effective spell is Fireball--and Drei--an exceptionally strong, exceptionally dumb warrior for whom the obvious is a complex understanding-are best friends and partners in a quest to gain as much gold as possible. However, every moment of financial prosperity is usually quickly followed by a succession of financial disasters, which usually leaves the duo clambering for food, shelter and the tools necessary to take on the big, wide, rich world yet again. However, when they arrived in the town of Yekacherin not too long ago, they found what they had never thought possible...gainful employment. Working as virtual slaves for Anna, the commander of the town's militia who prefers to be called its Queen, they are earning their keep, which is fortunate in a town that is being slowly taken over by a corporate retail conglomerate known as rain emblem. Rain emblem is a convenient, one-stop shopping bazaar that is driving all of the small business in yekacherin away. And as if that wasn't annoying enough, mariel, the holy lady, is the liaison of a religious organization charged with helping the poor and destitute throughout the lands of sobeetrook. Capitalism on your left, socialism on your right, a near fascist sheriff with a royalty complex in the middle...What are our heroes to do? Fall in love, perhaps? Tian finds that his heart flutters for a young prostitute by the name of perina, which is made heartbreaking by the fact that he eventually finds her dead in an alley. And all the evidence he finds points to the infamous nagi, the thief, a man wanted by all.

CONTENTS

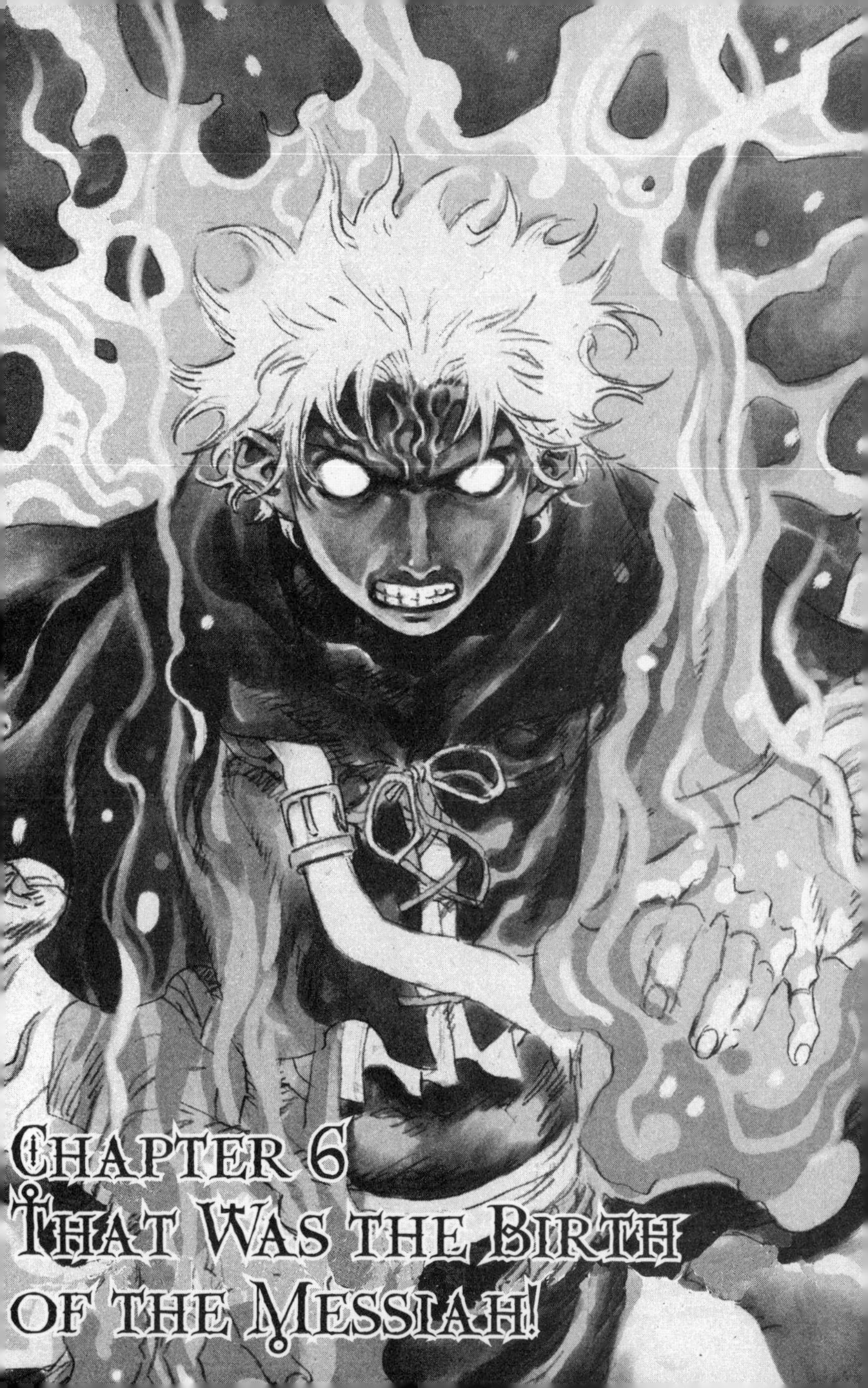
Chapter 6
That Was the Birth
of the Messiah!

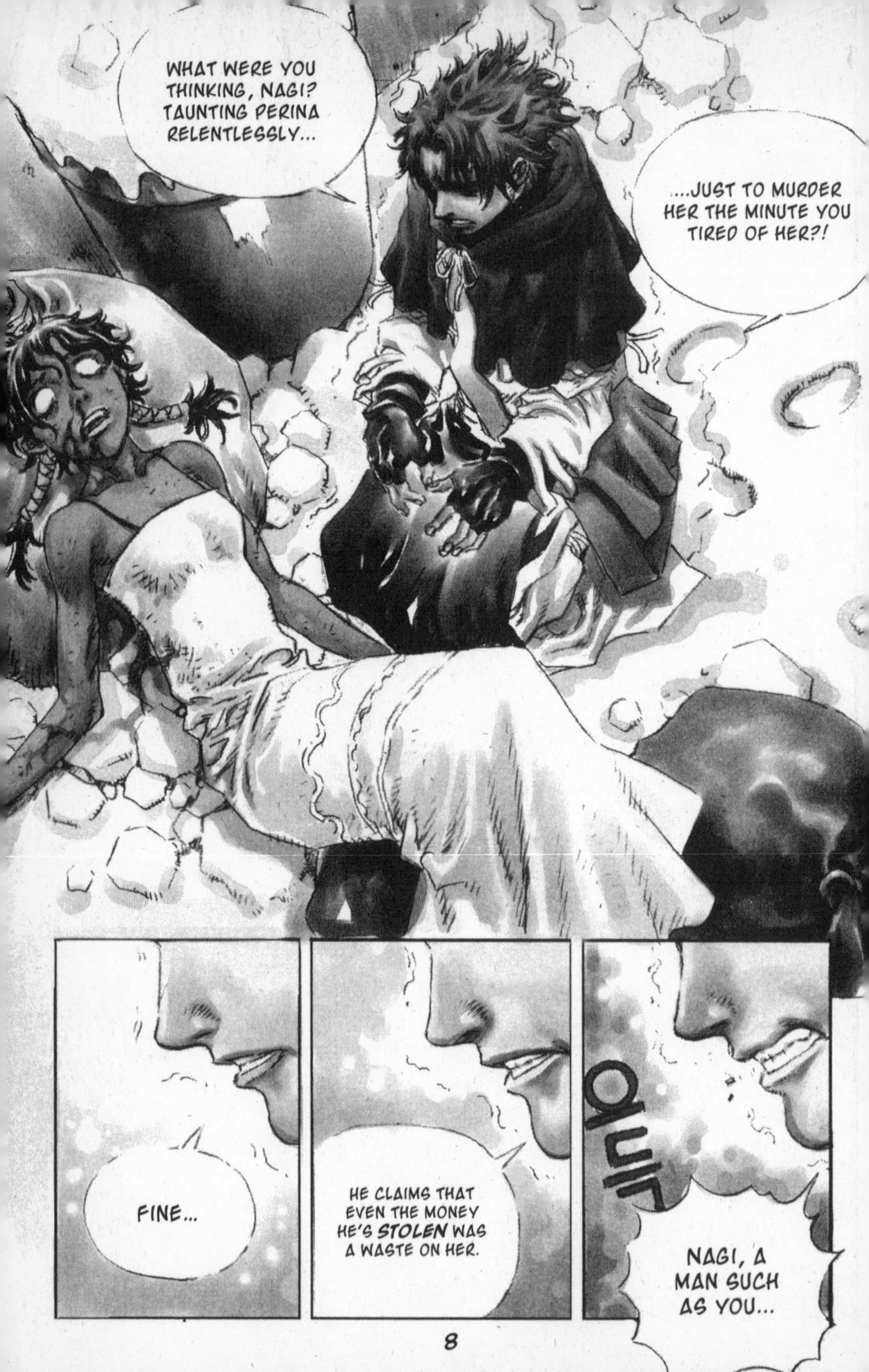
WHAT WERE YOU THINKING, NAGI? TAUNTING PERINA RELENTLESSLY...
....JUST TO MURDER HER THE MINUTE YOU TIRED OF HER?!
FINE...
HE CLAIMS THAT EVEN THE MONEY HE'S STOLEN WAS A WASTE ON HER.
NAGI, A MAN SUCH AS YOU...

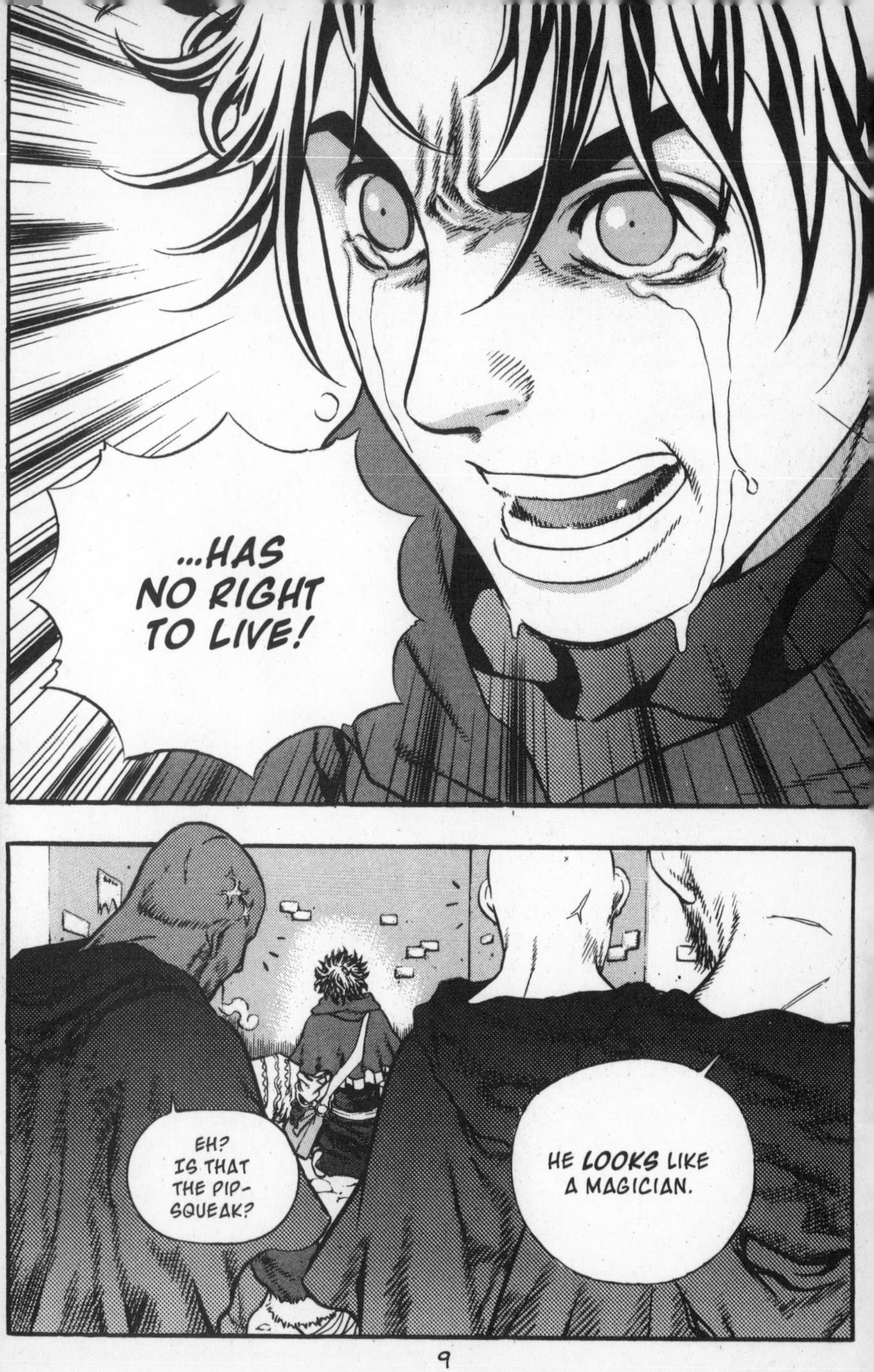
...HAS NO RIGHT TO LIVE!
EH? IS THAT THE PIP-SQUEAK?
HE LOOKS LIKE A MAGICIAN.

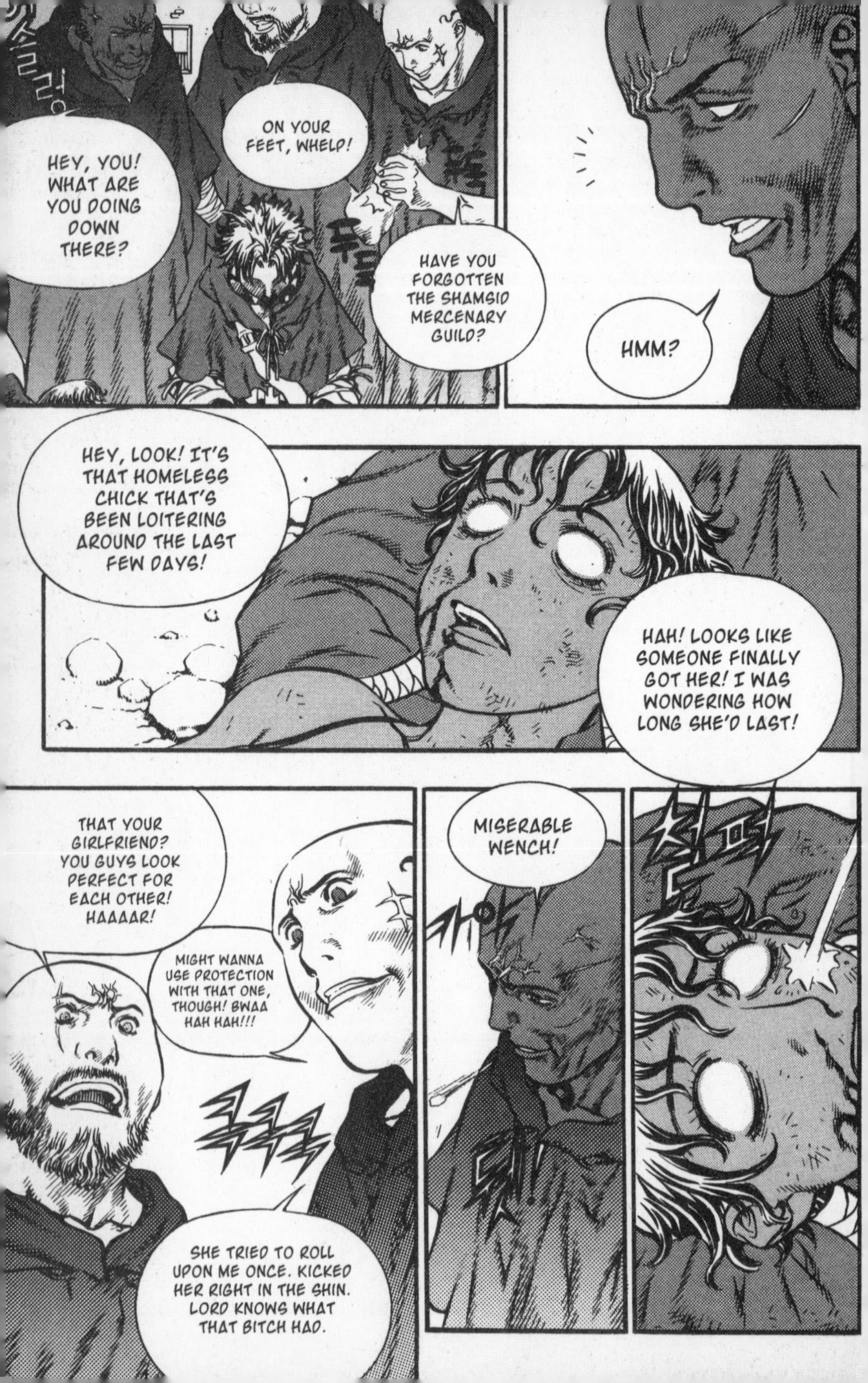
HEY, YOU! WHAT ARE YOU DOING DOWN THERE?
ON YOUR FEET, WHELP!
HAVE YOU FORGOTTEN THE SHAMSID MERCENARY GUILD?
HMM?
HEY, LOOK! IT'S THAT HOMELESS CHICK THAT'S BEEN LOITERING AROUND THE LAST FEW DAYS!
HAH! LOOKS LIKE SOMEONE FINALLY GOT HER! I WAS WONDERING HOW LONG SHE'D LAST!
THAT YOUR GIRLFRIEND? YOU GUYS LOOK PERFECT FOR EACH OTHER! HAAAAR!
MIGHT WANNA USE PROTECTION WITH THAT ONE, THOUGH! BWAA HAH HAH!!!
SHE TRIED TO ROLL UPON ME ONCE. KICKED HER RIGHT IN THE SHIN. LORD KNOWS WHAT THAT BITCH HAD.
MISERABLE WENCH!

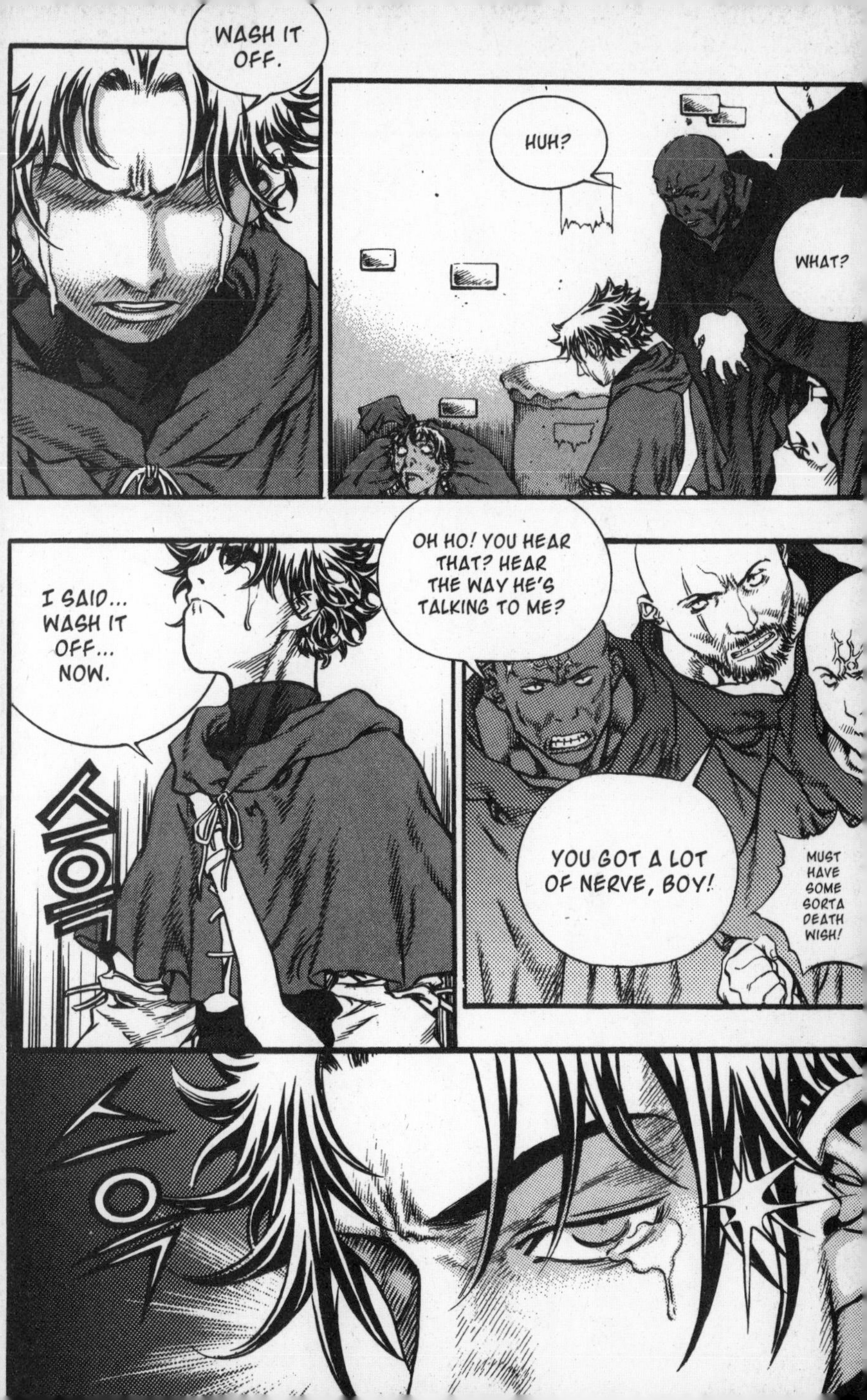
WASH IT OFF.
HUH?
WHAT?
I SAID... WASH IT OFF... NOW.
OH HO! YOU HEAR THAT? HEAR THE WAY HE'S TALKING TO ME?
YOU GOT A LOT OF NERVE, BOY!
MUST HAVE SOME SORTA DEATH WISH!

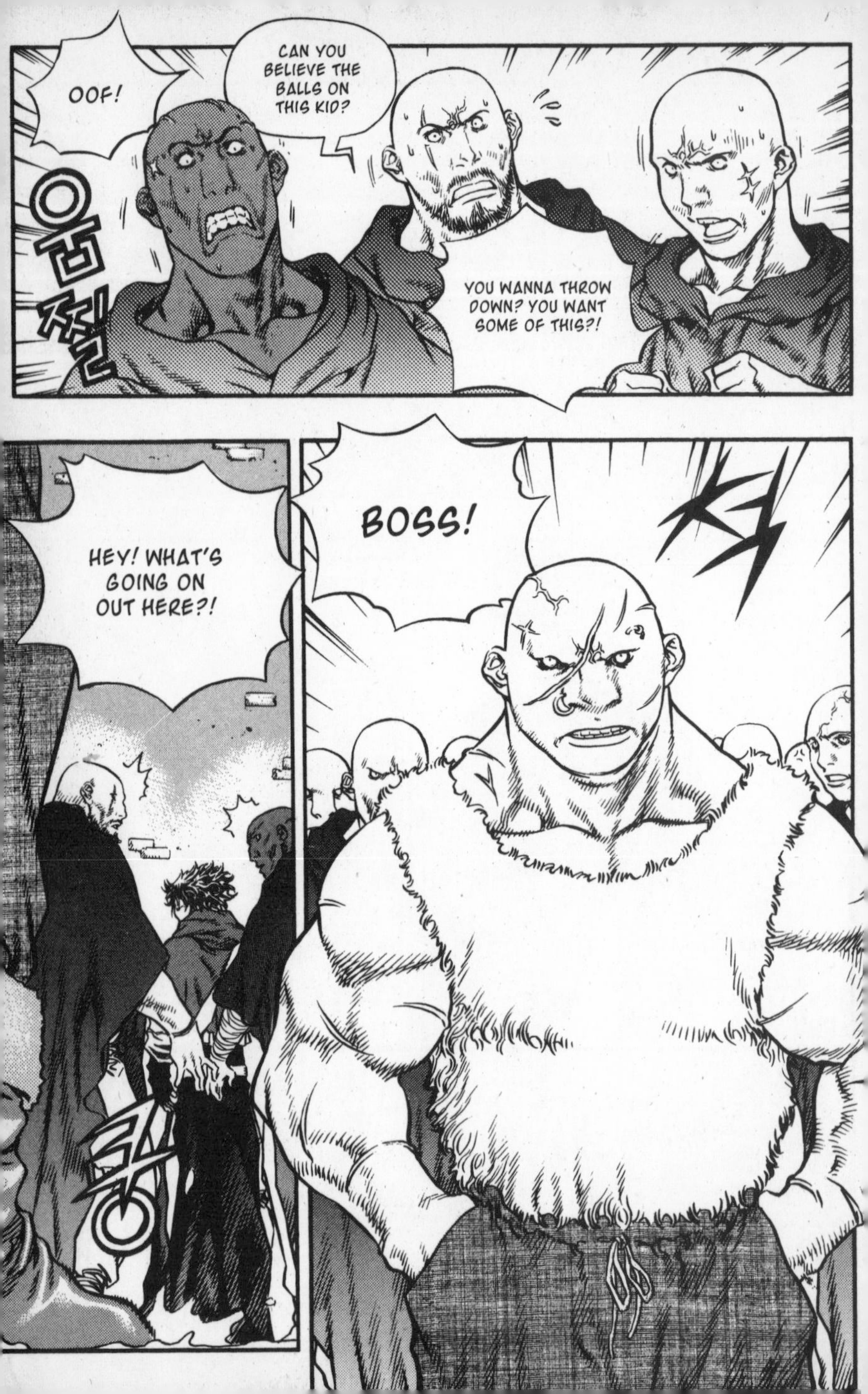
OOF!
CAN YOU BELIEVE THE BALLS ON THIS KID?
YOU WANNA THROW DOWN? YOU WANT SOME OF THIS?!
HEY! WHAT'S GOING ON OUT HERE?!
BOSS!

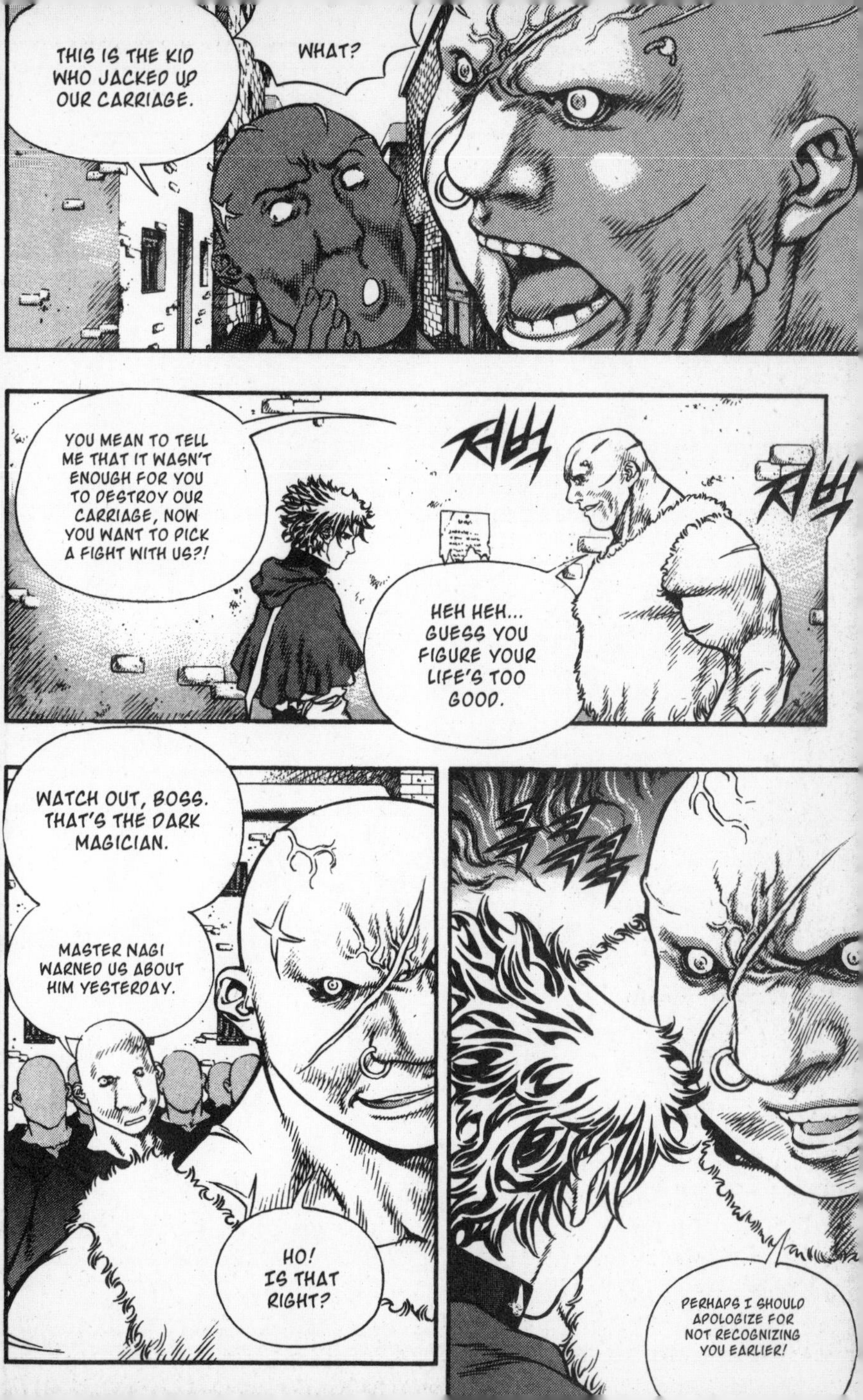
THIS IS THE KID WHO JACKED UP OUR CARRIAGE.
WHAT?
YOU MEAN TO TELL ME THAT IT WASN'T ENOUGH FOR YOU TO DESTROY OUR CARRIAGE, NOW YOU WANT TO PICK A FIGHT WITH US?!
HEH HEH... GUESS YOU FIGURE YOUR LIFE'S TOO GOOD.
WATCH OUT, BOSS. THAT'S THE DARK MAGICIAN.
MASTER NAGI WARNED US ABOUT HIM YESTERDAY.
HO! IS THAT RIGHT?
PERHAPS I SHOULD APOLOGIZE FOR NOT RECOGNIZING YOU EARLIER!

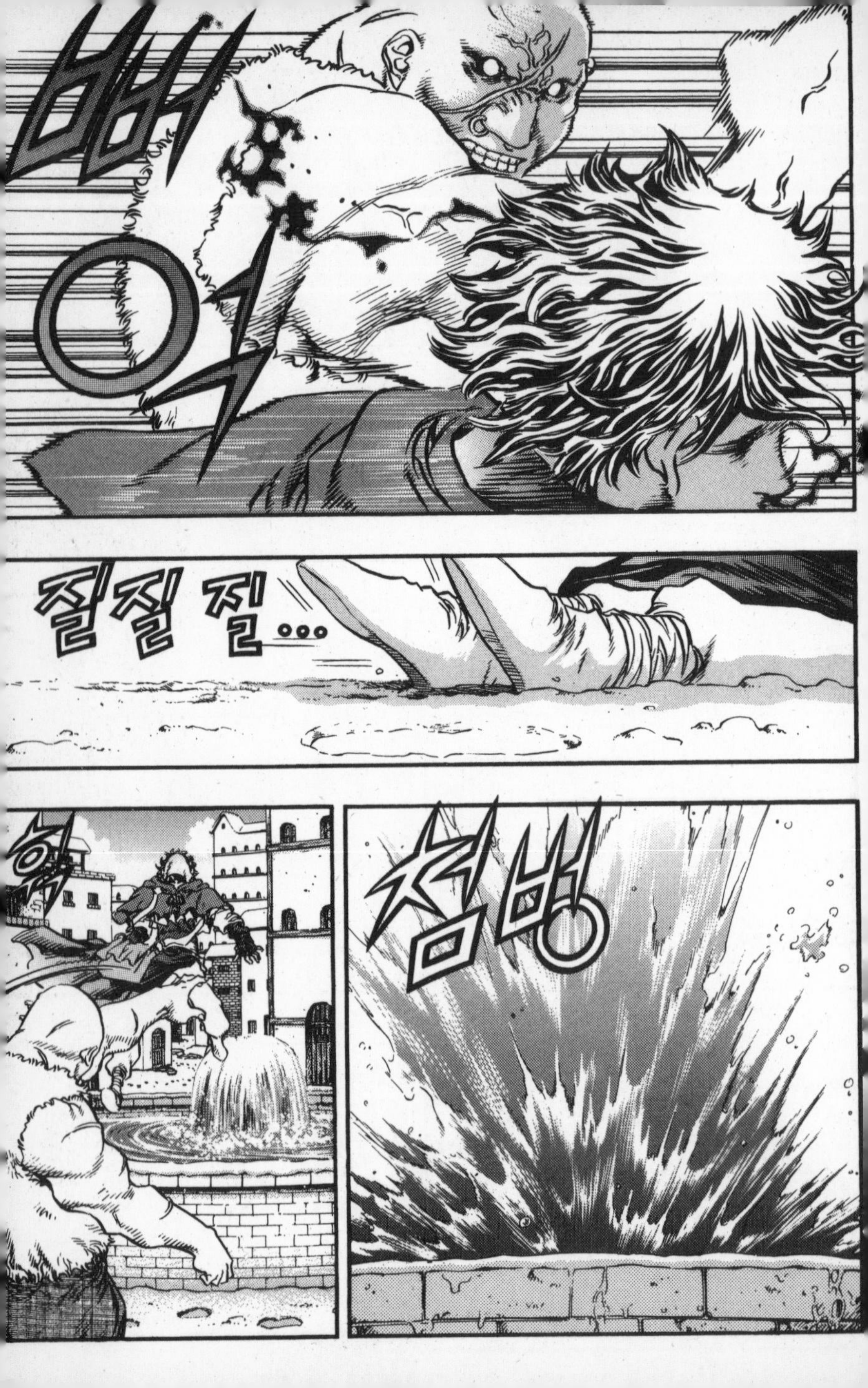
뻐억
질질질...
휙
첨벙

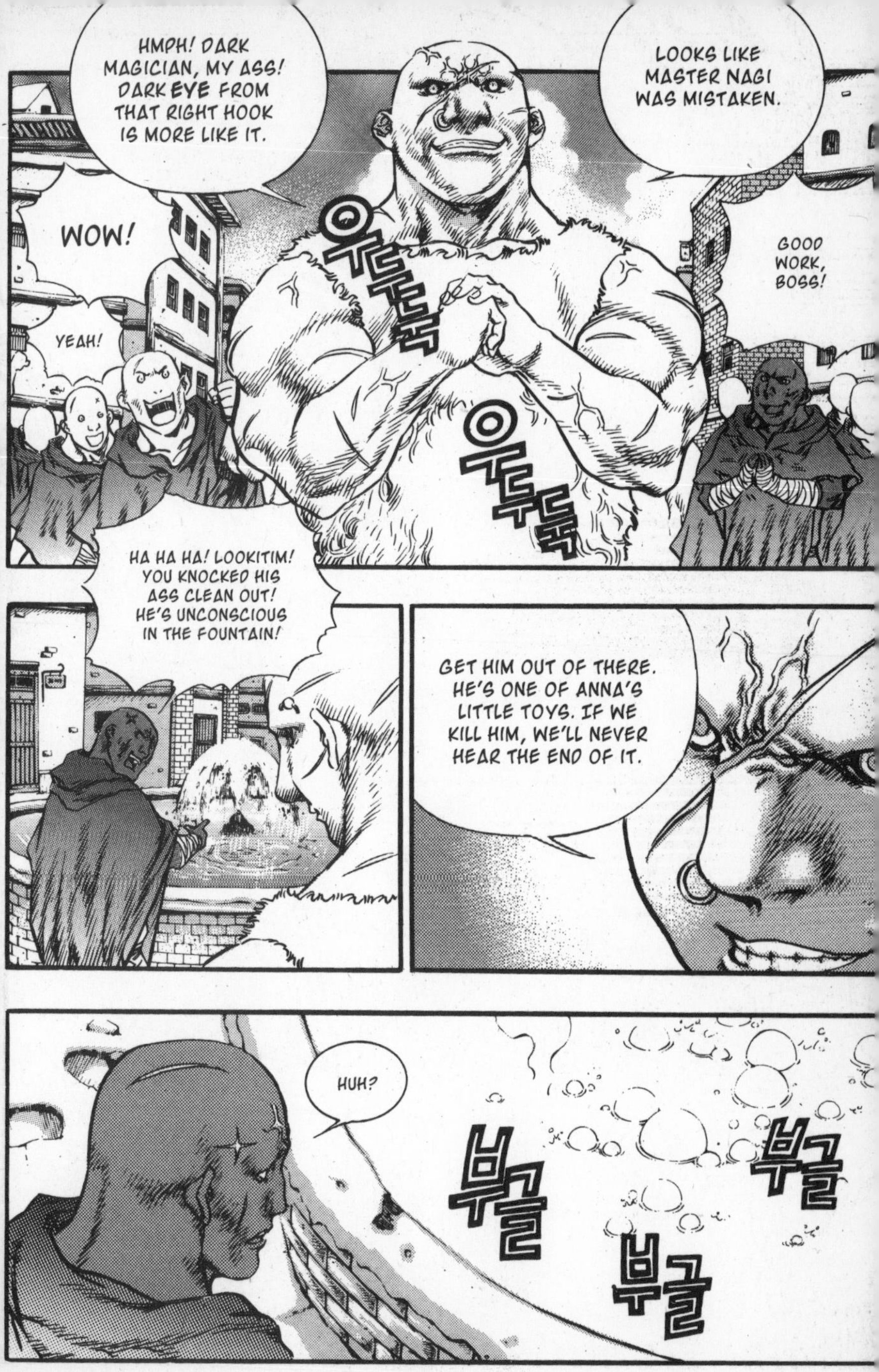
HMPH! DARK MAGICIAN, MY ASS! DARK EYE FROM THAT RIGHT HOOK IS MORE LIKE IT.
LOOKS LIKE MASTER NAGI WAS MISTAKEN.
으드득
으드득
WOW!
GOOD WORK, BOSS!
YEAH!
HA HA HA! LOOKITIM! YOU KNOCKED HIS ASS CLEAN OUT! HE'S UNCONSCIOUS IN THE FOUNTAIN!
GET HIM OUT OF THERE. HE'S ONE OF ANNA'S LITTLE TOYS. IF WE KILL HIM, WE'LL NEVER HEAR THE END OF IT.
HUH?
부글
부글
부글

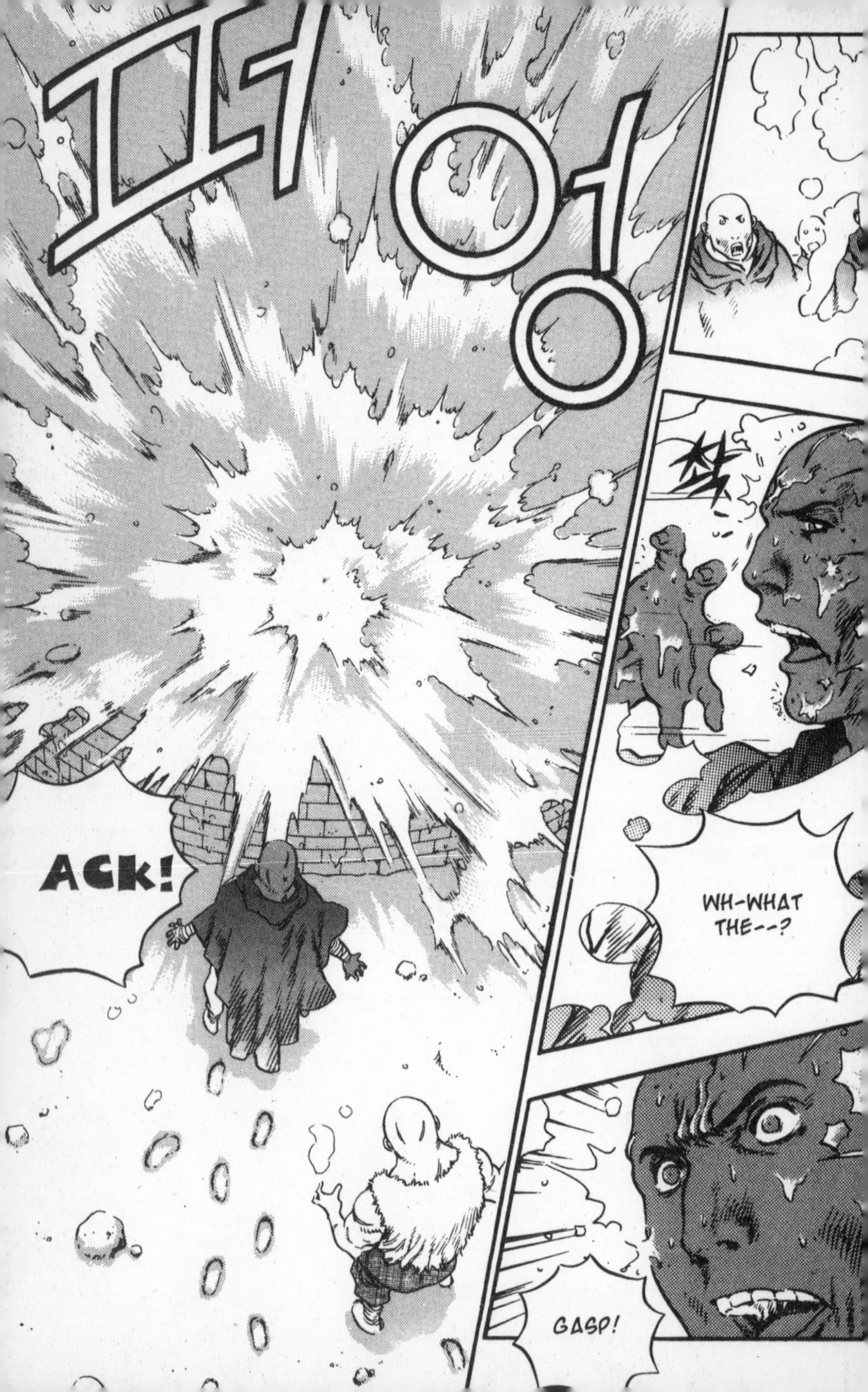
ACK!
WH-WHAT THE--?
GASP!

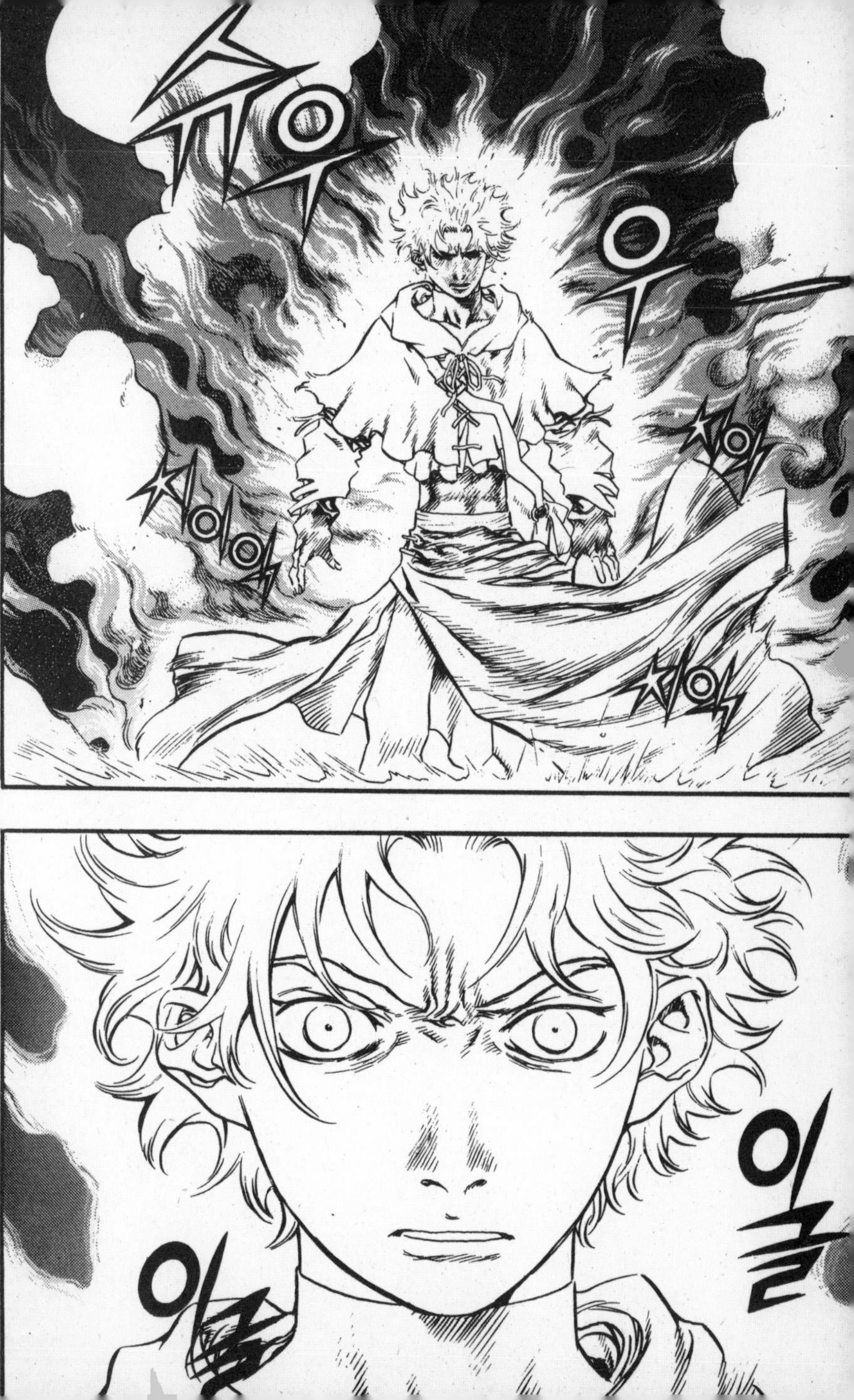
이글

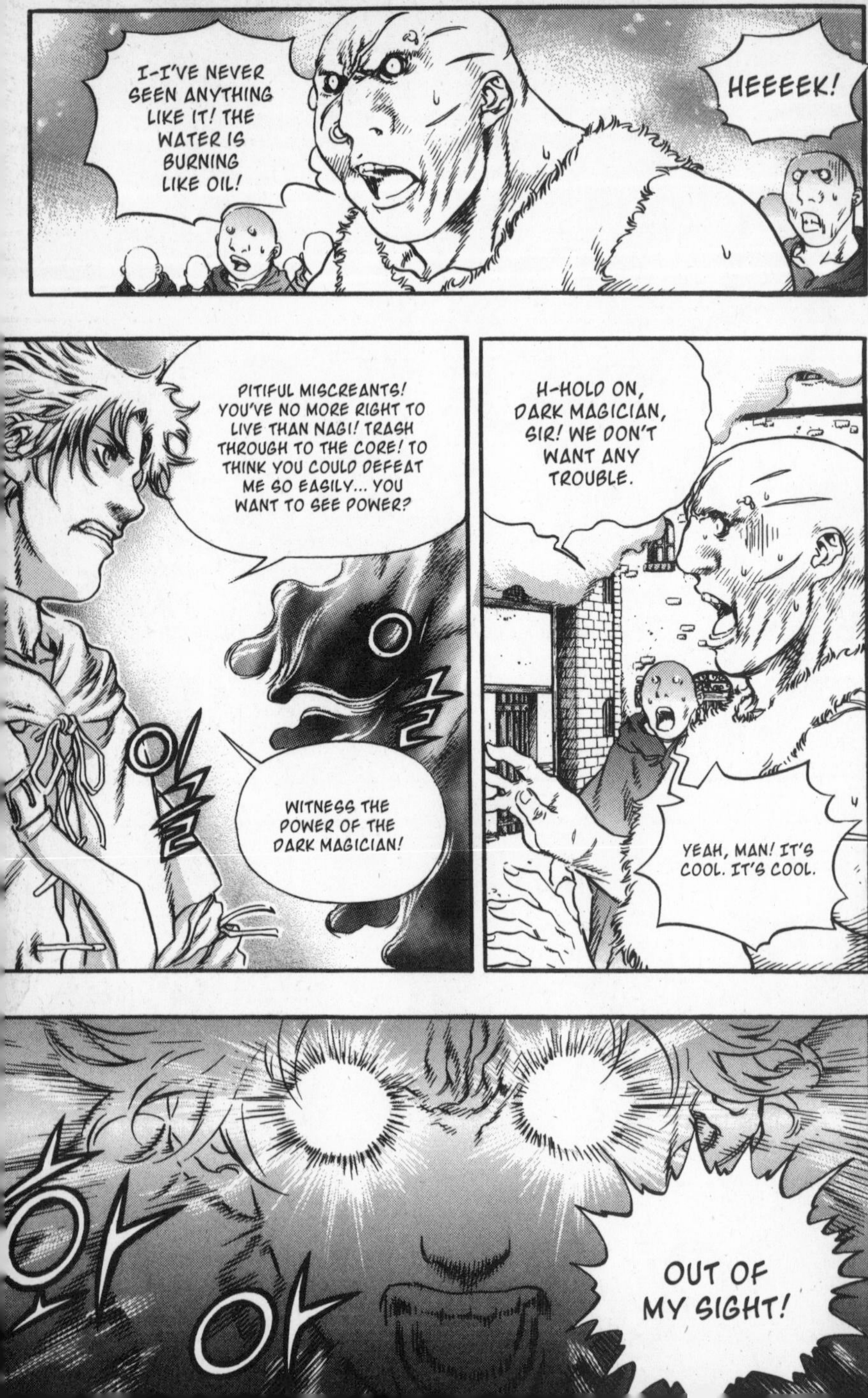
I-I'VE NEVER SEEN ANYTHING LIKE IT! THE WATER IS BURNING LIKE OIL!
HEEEEK!
PITIFUL MISCREANTS! YOU'VE NO MORE RIGHT TO LIVE THAN NAGI! TRASH THROUGH TO THE CORE! TO THINK YOU COULD DEFEAT ME SO EASILY... YOU WANT TO SEE POWER?
WITNESS THE POWER OF THE DARK MAGICIAN!
H-HOLD ON, DARK MAGICIAN, SIR! WE DON'T WANT ANY TROUBLE.
YEAH, MAN! IT'S COOL. IT'S COOL.
OUT OF MY SIGHT!

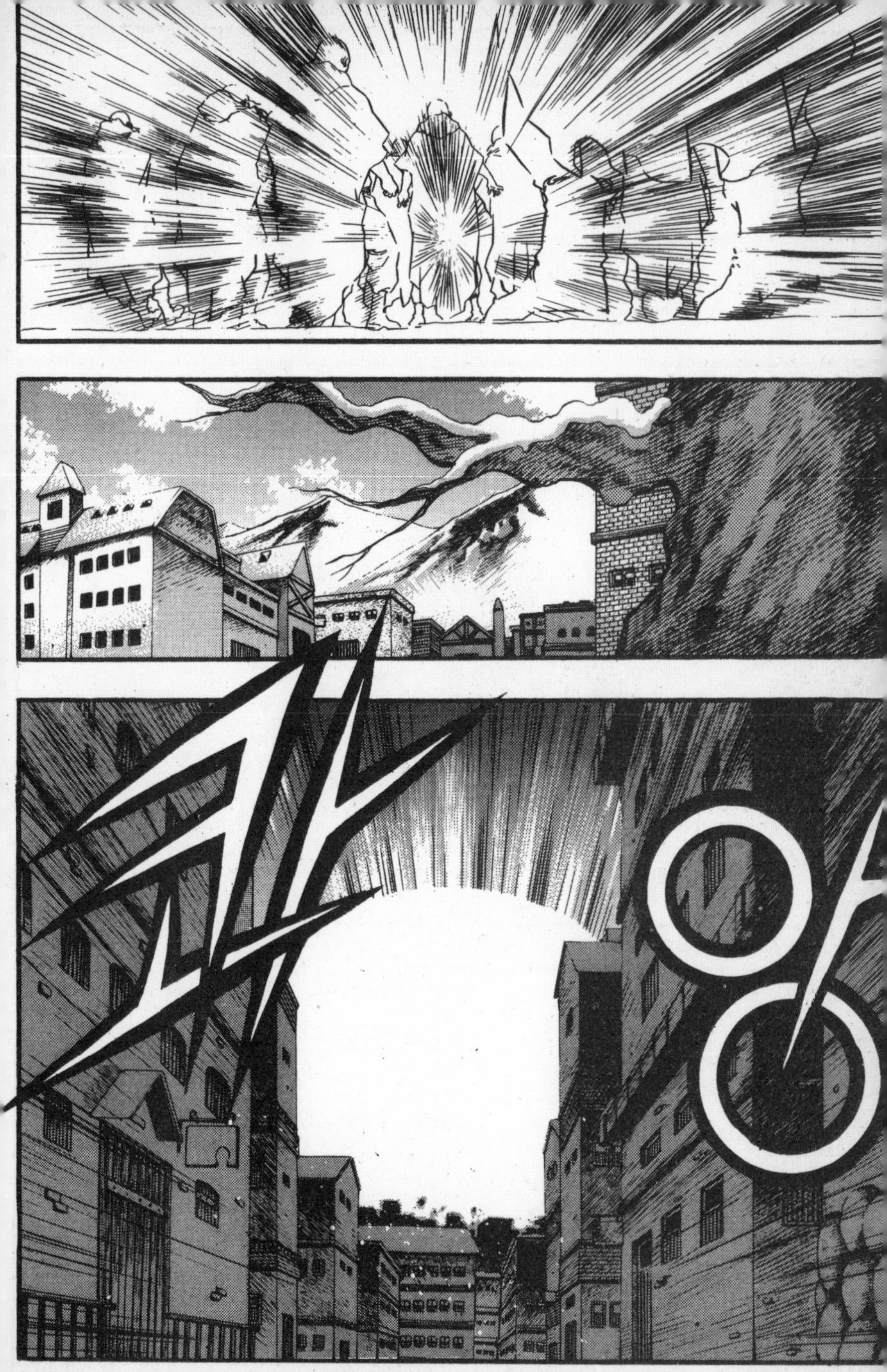

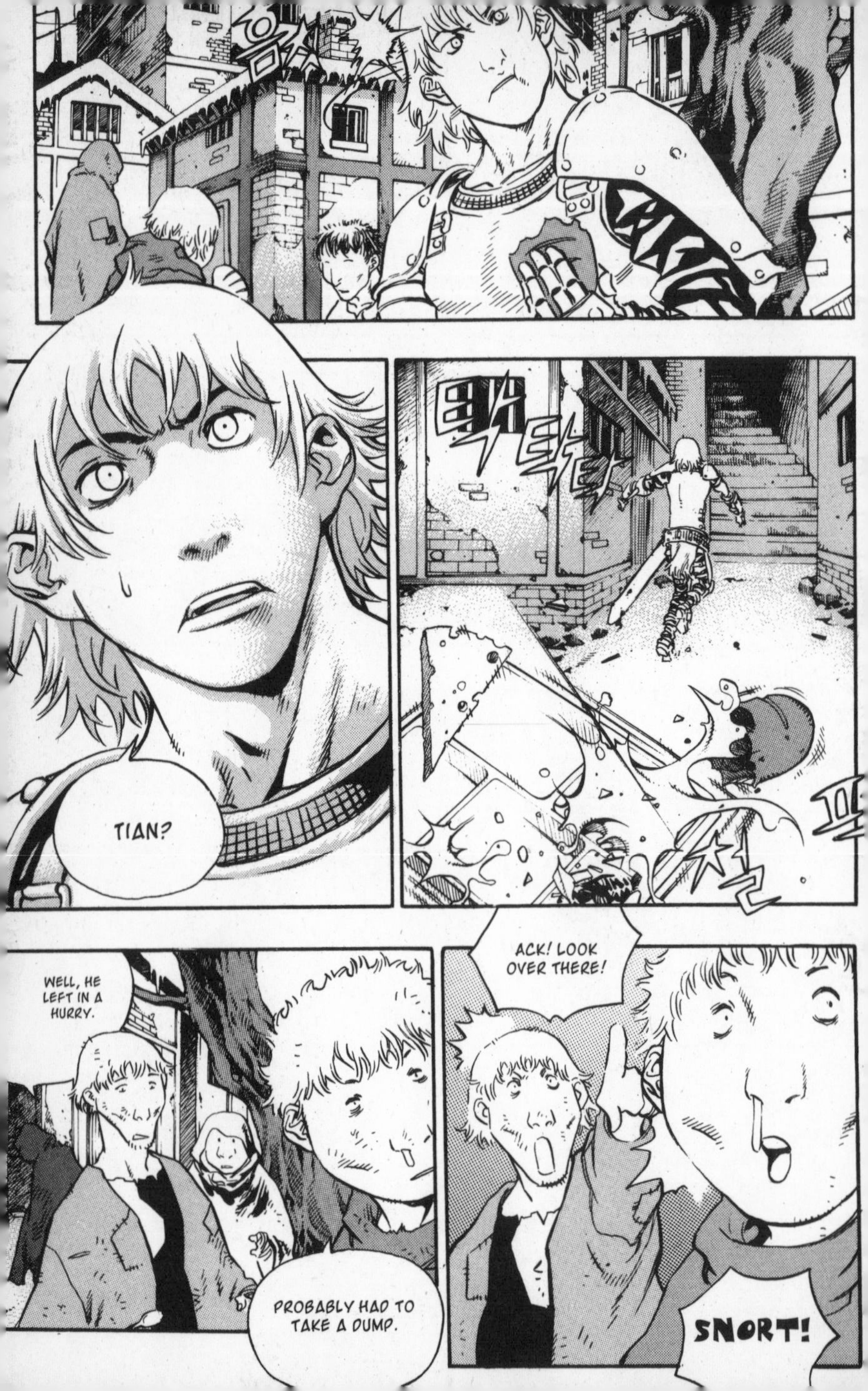
TIAN?
WELL, HE LEFT IN A HURRY.
PROBABLY HAD TO TAKE A DUMP.
ACK! LOOK OVER THERE!
SNORT!

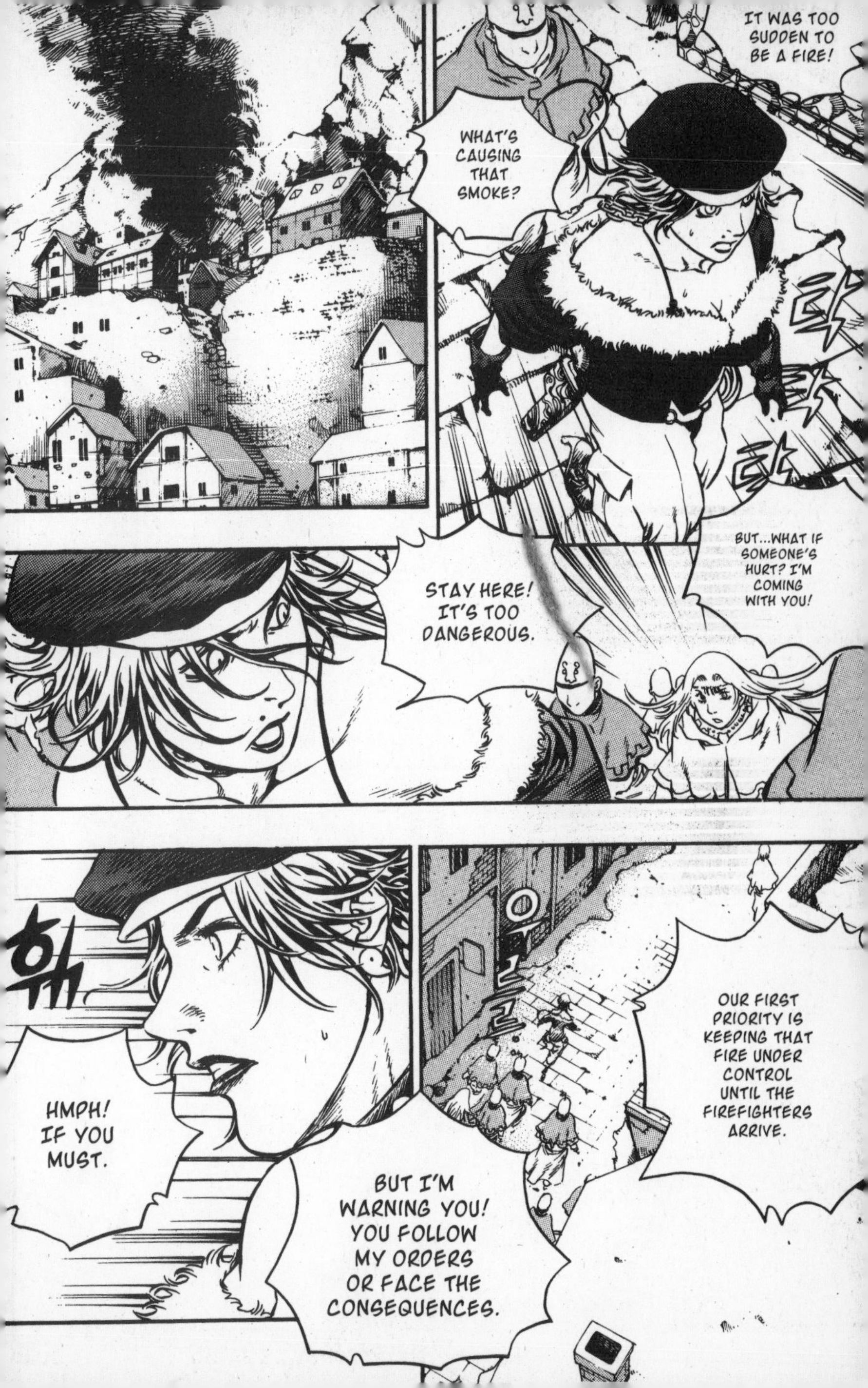

WHAT'S CAUSING THAT SMOKE?
IT WAS TOO SUDDEN TO BE A FIRE!
STAY HERE! IT'S TOO DANGEROUS.
BUT...WHAT IF SOMEONE'S HURT? I'M COMING WITH YOU!
HMPH! IF YOU MUST.
BUT I'M WARNING YOU! YOU FOLLOW MY ORDERS OR FACE THE CONSEQUENCES.
OUR FIRST PRIORITY IS KEEPING THAT FIRE UNDER CONTROL UNTIL THE FIREFIGHTERS ARRIVE.

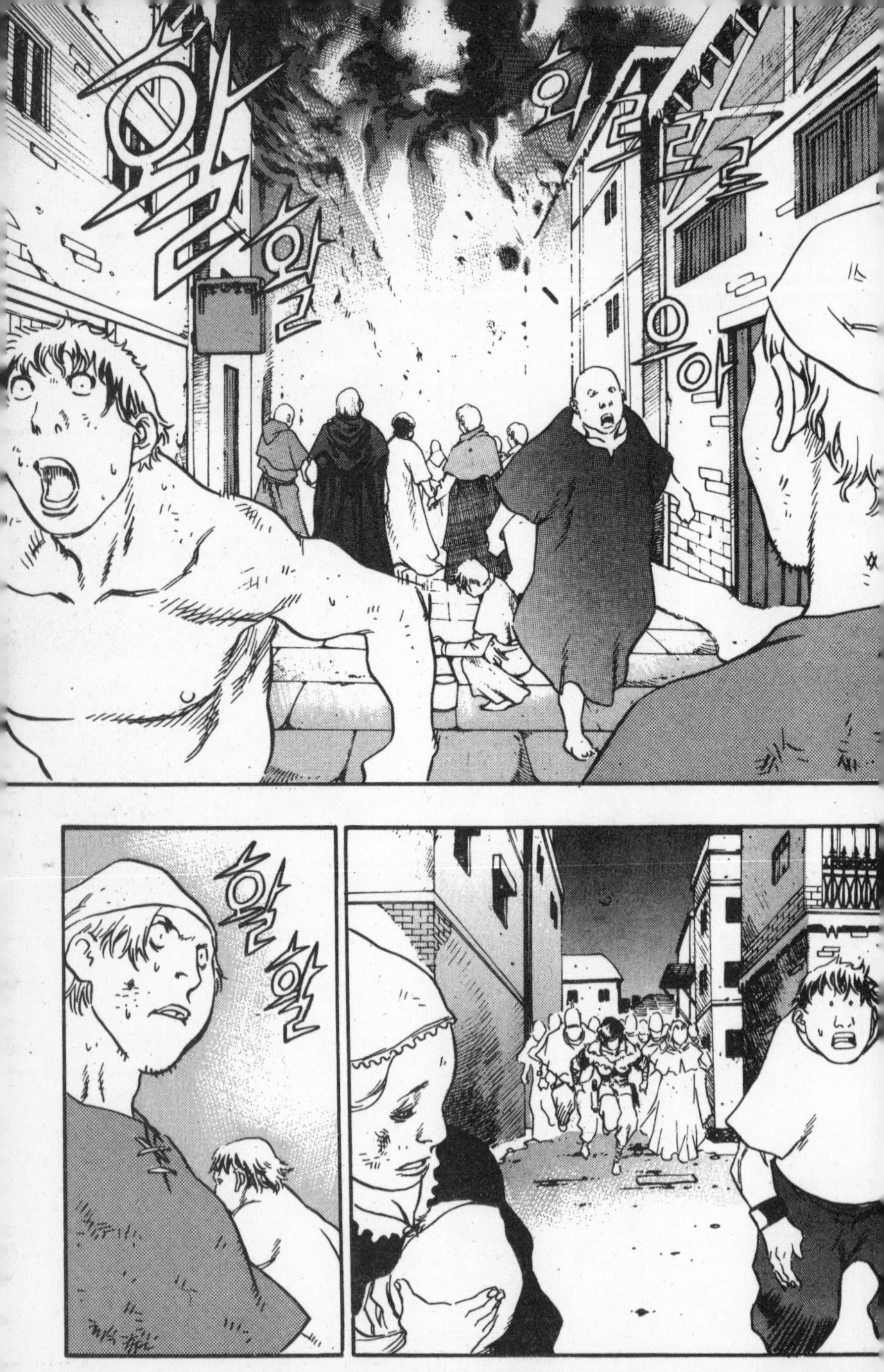
와글와글
와르르르
으아

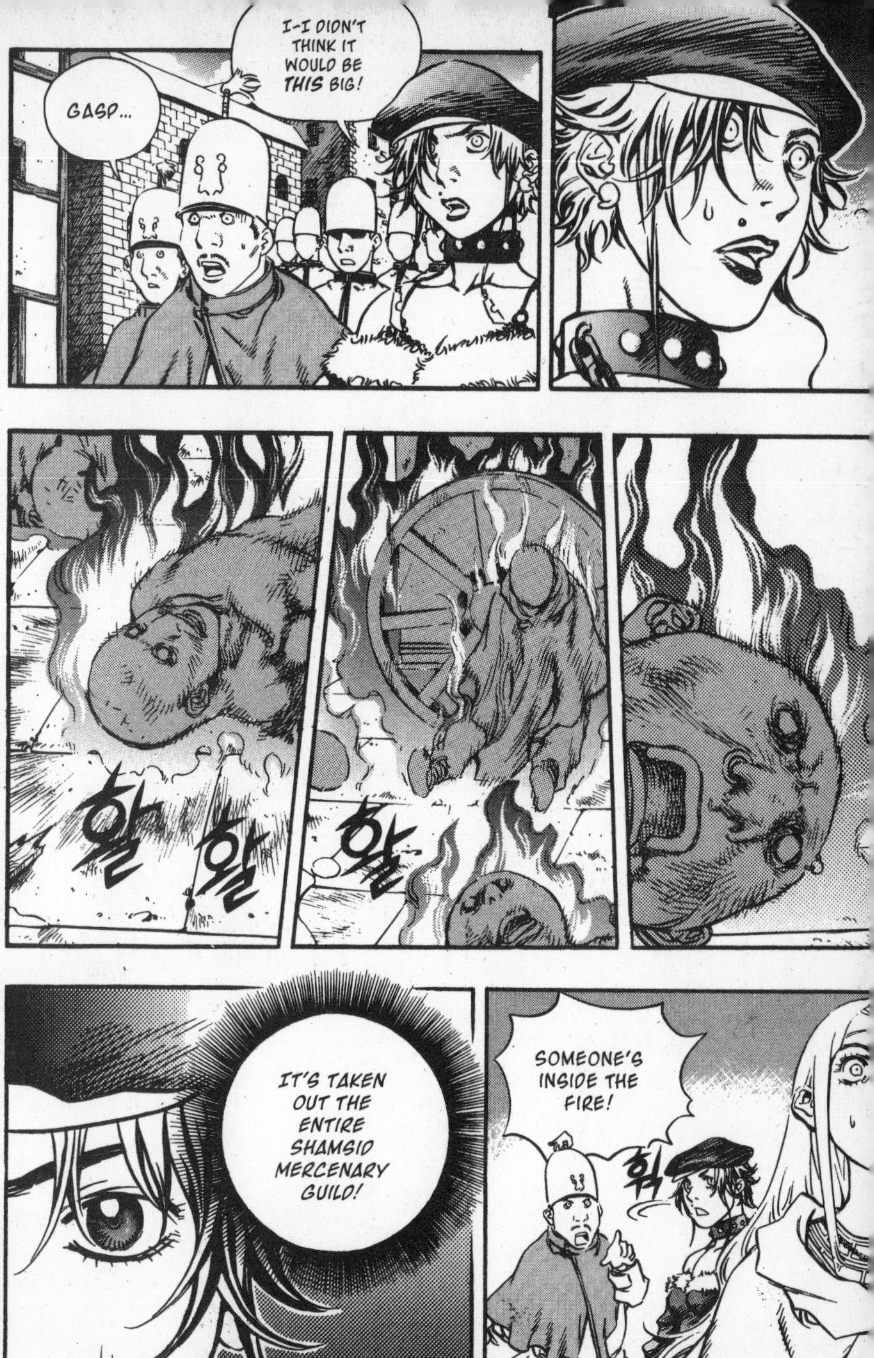
GASP...
I-I DIDN'T THINK IT WOULD BE THIS BIG!
활
활
활
IT'S TAKEN OUT THE ENTIRE SHAMSID MERCENARY GUILD!
SOMEONE'S INSIDE THE FIRE!
휙

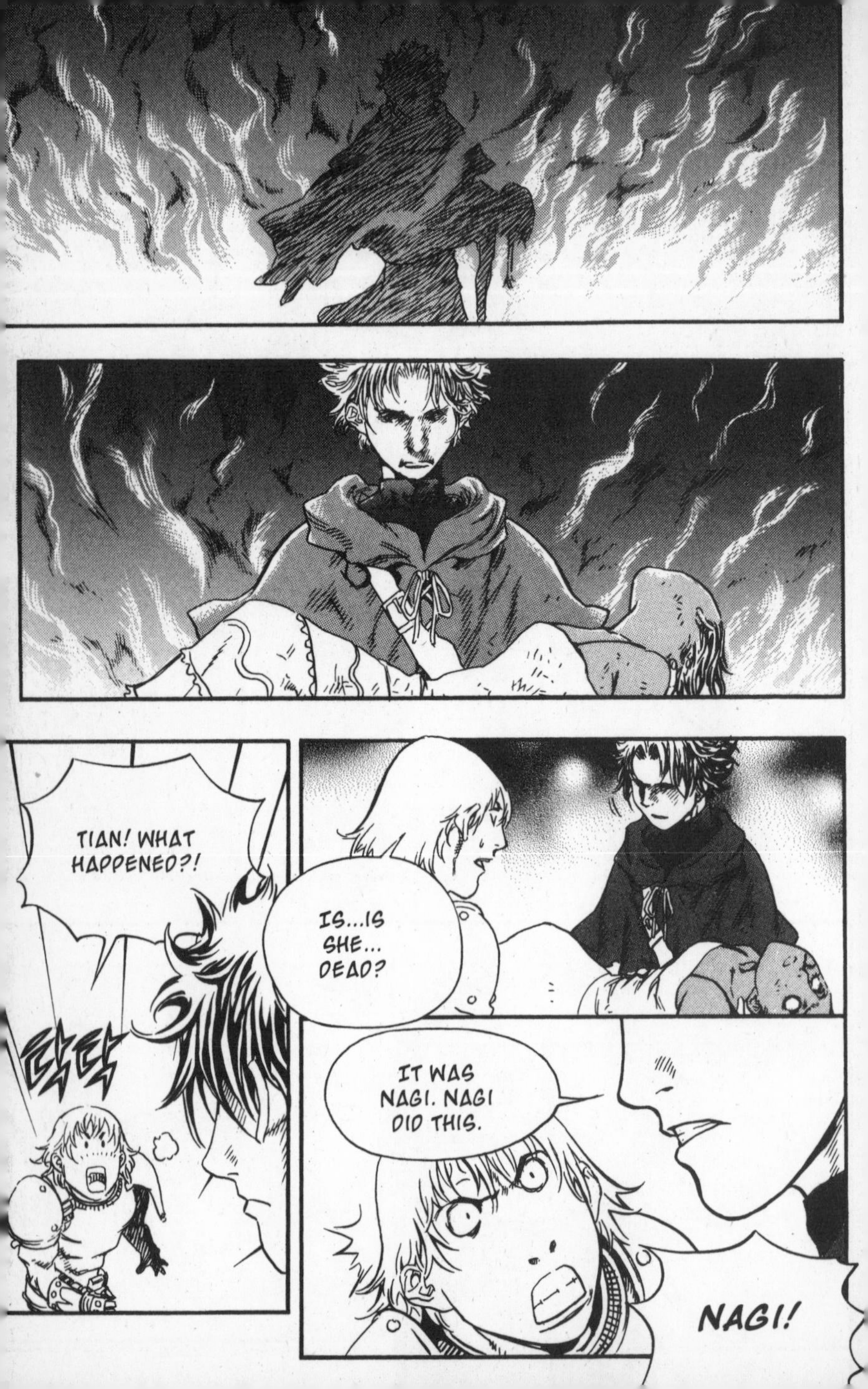
TIAN! WHAT HAPPENED?!
IS...IS SHE... DEAD?
IT WAS NAGI. NAGI DID THIS.
NAGI!

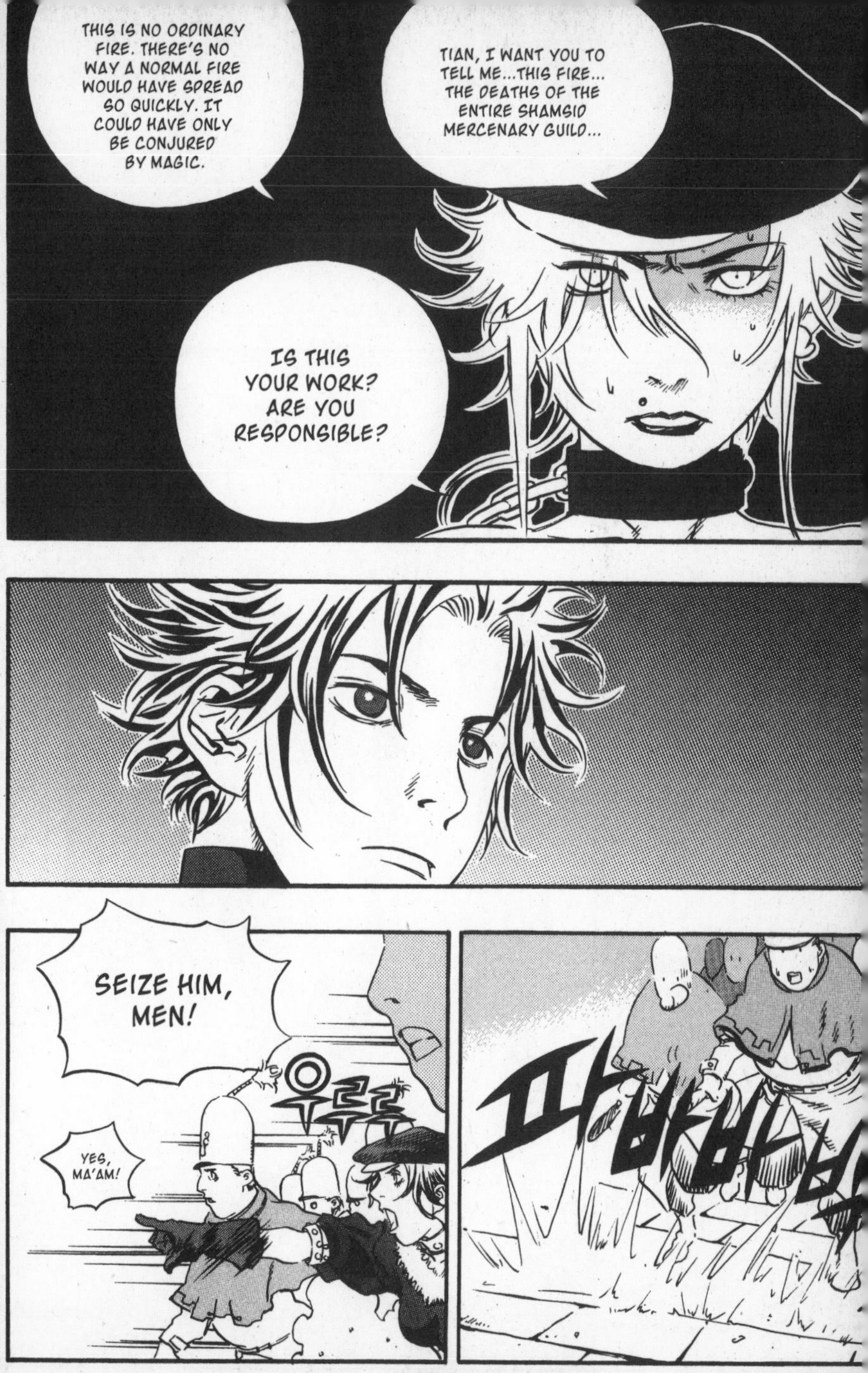
THIS IS NO ORDINARY FIRE. THERE'S NO WAY A NORMAL FIRE WOULD HAVE SPREAD SO QUICKLY. IT COULD HAVE ONLY BE CONJURED BY MAGIC.
TIAN, I WANT YOU TO TELL ME...THIS FIRE... THE DEATHS OF THE ENTIRE SHAMSID MERCENARY GUILD...
IS THIS YOUR WORK? ARE YOU RESPONSIBLE?
SEIZE HIM, MEN!
YES, MA'AM!

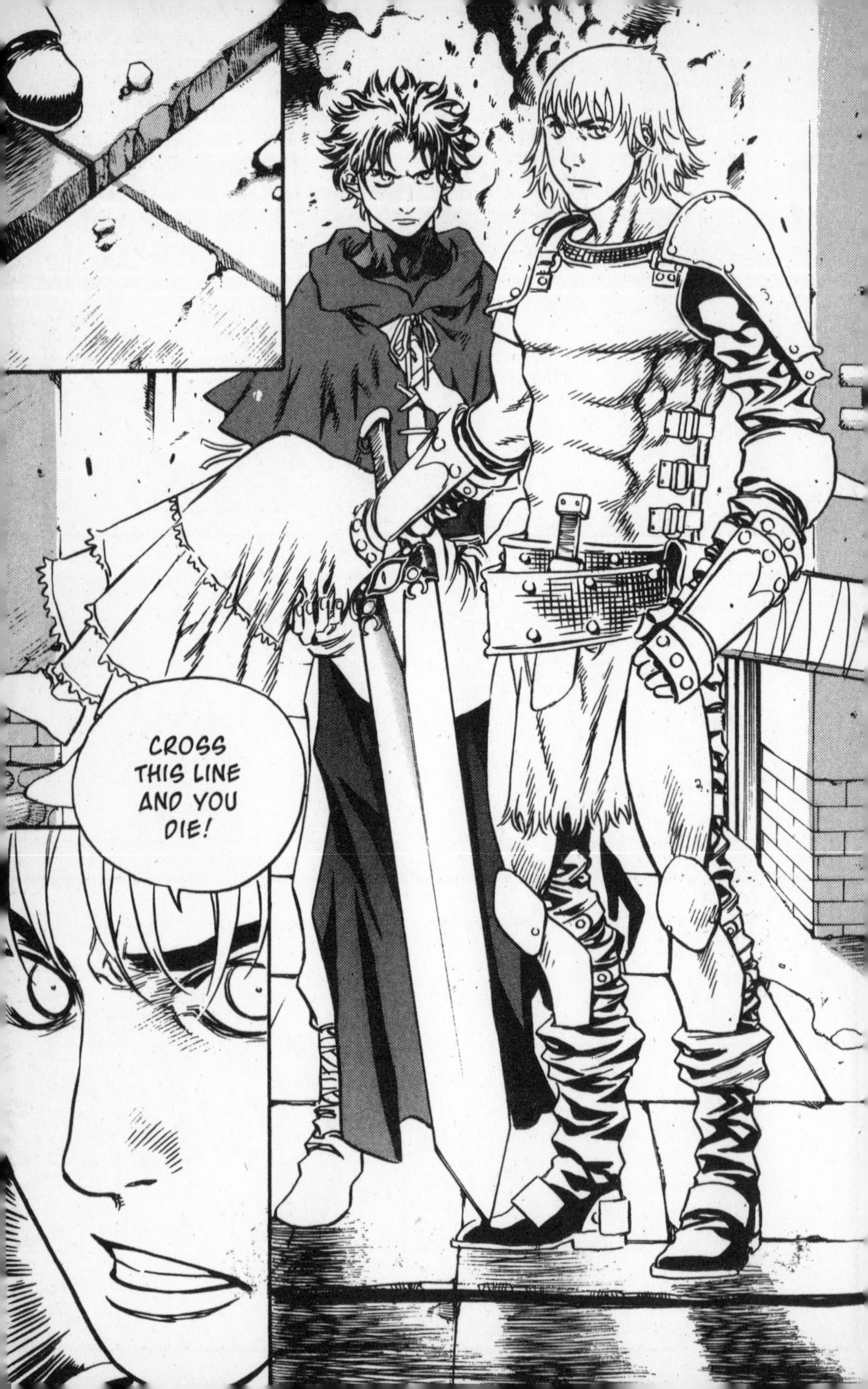
CROSS THIS LINE AND YOU DIE!

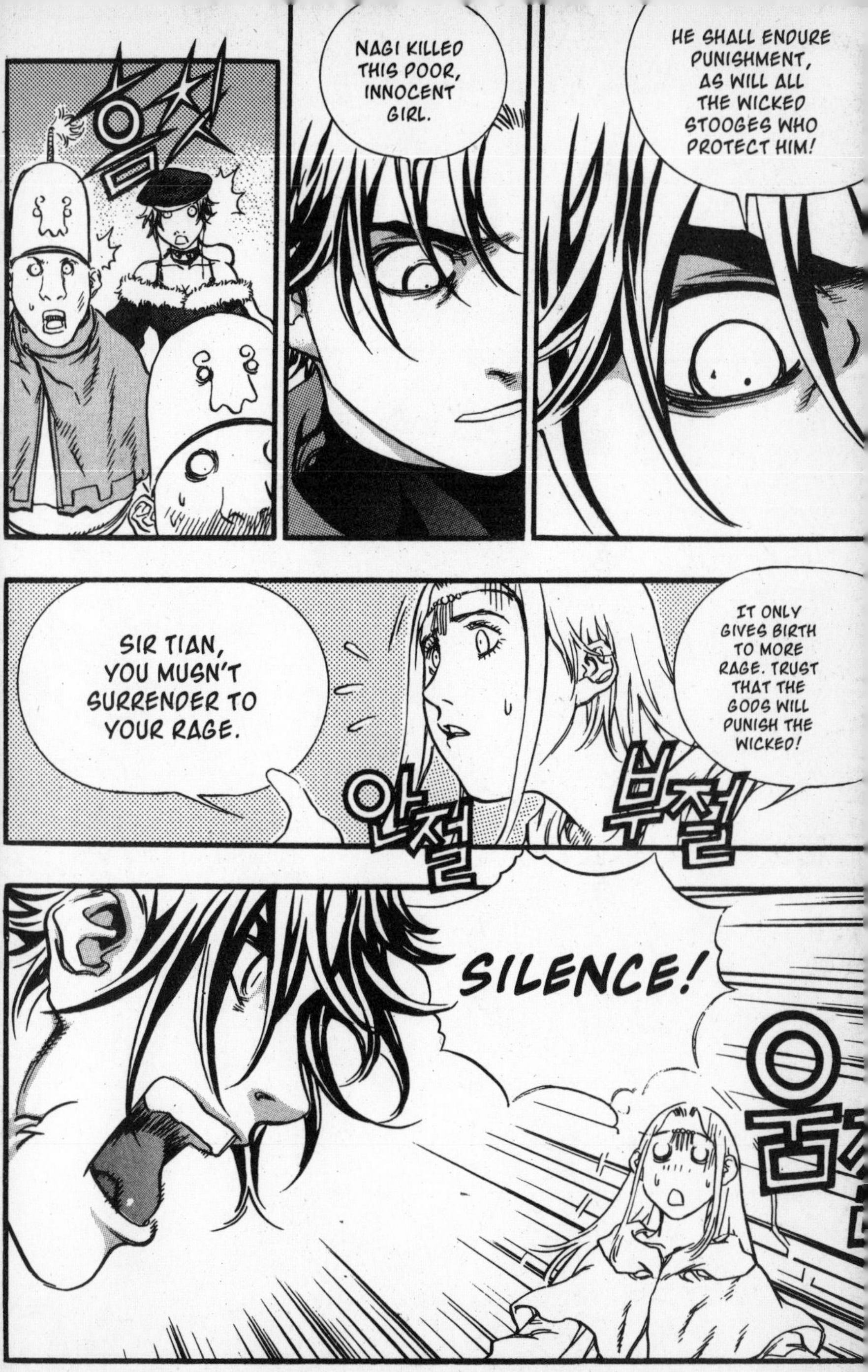
NAGI KILLED THIS POOR, INNOCENT GIRL.
HE SHALL ENDURE PUNISHMENT, AS WILL ALL THE WICKED STOOGES WHO PROTECT HIM!
SIR TIAN, YOU MUSN'T SURRENDER TO YOUR RAGE.
IT ONLY GIVES BIRTH TO MORE RAGE. TRUST THAT THE GODS WILL PUNISH THE WICKED!
안절 부절
SILENCE!

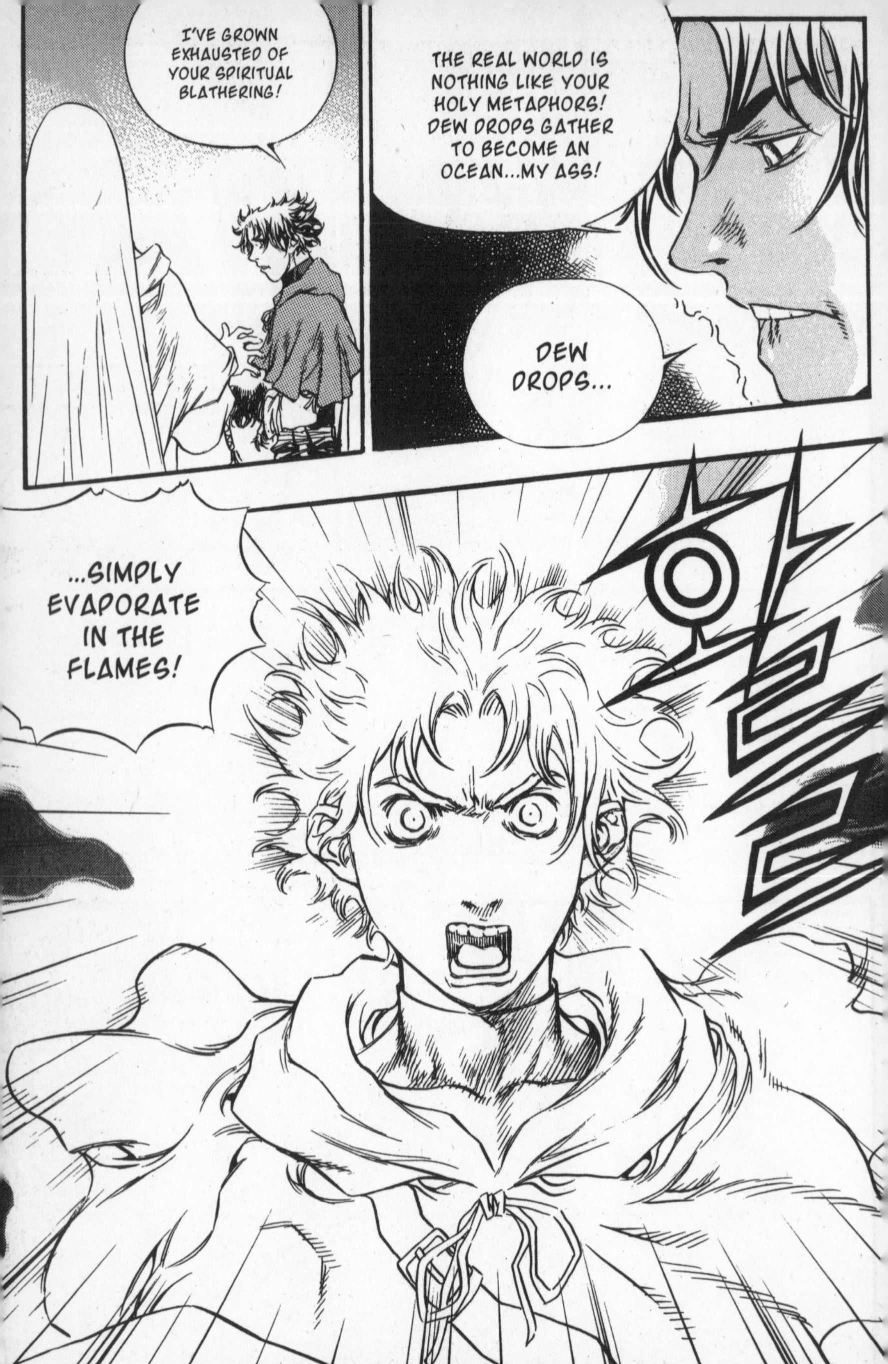
I'VE GROWN EXHAUSTED OF YOUR SPIRITUAL BLATHERING!
THE REAL WORLD IS NOTHING LIKE YOUR HOLY METAPHORS! DEW DROPS GATHER TO BECOME AN OCEAN...MY ASS!
DEW DROPS...
...SIMPLY EVAPORATE IN THE FLAMES!

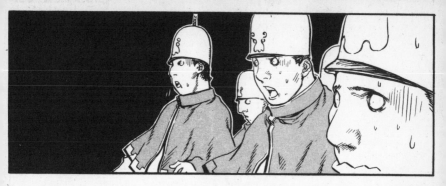

DREI, HELP ME.

COMMANDER ANNA...

I WILL DO AS YOU ORDERED AND CAPTURE THIEF NAGI...

...BUT THEN HIS LIFE IS MINE FOR THE TAKING.

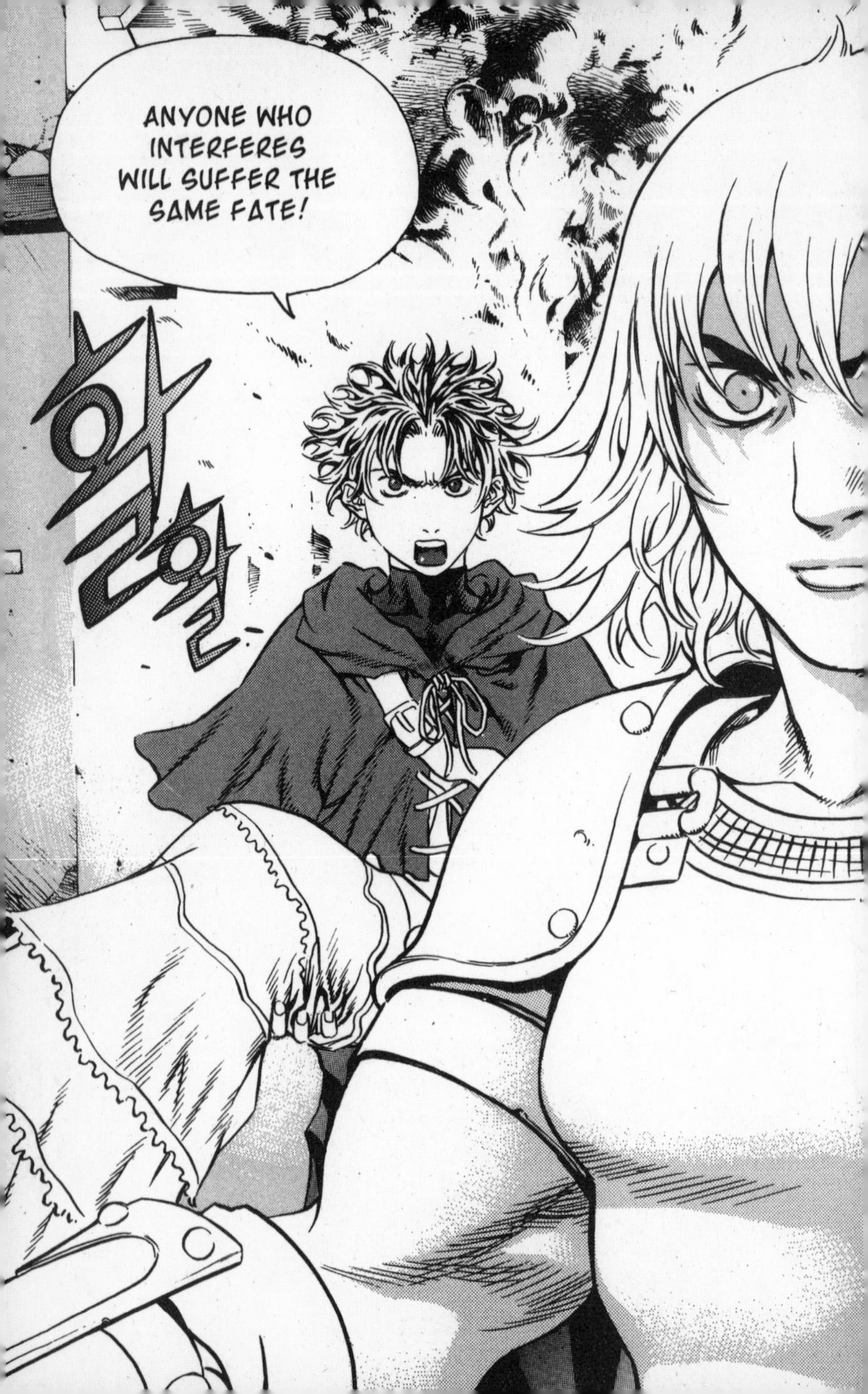
ANYONE WHO INTERFERES WILL SUFFER THE SAME FATE!

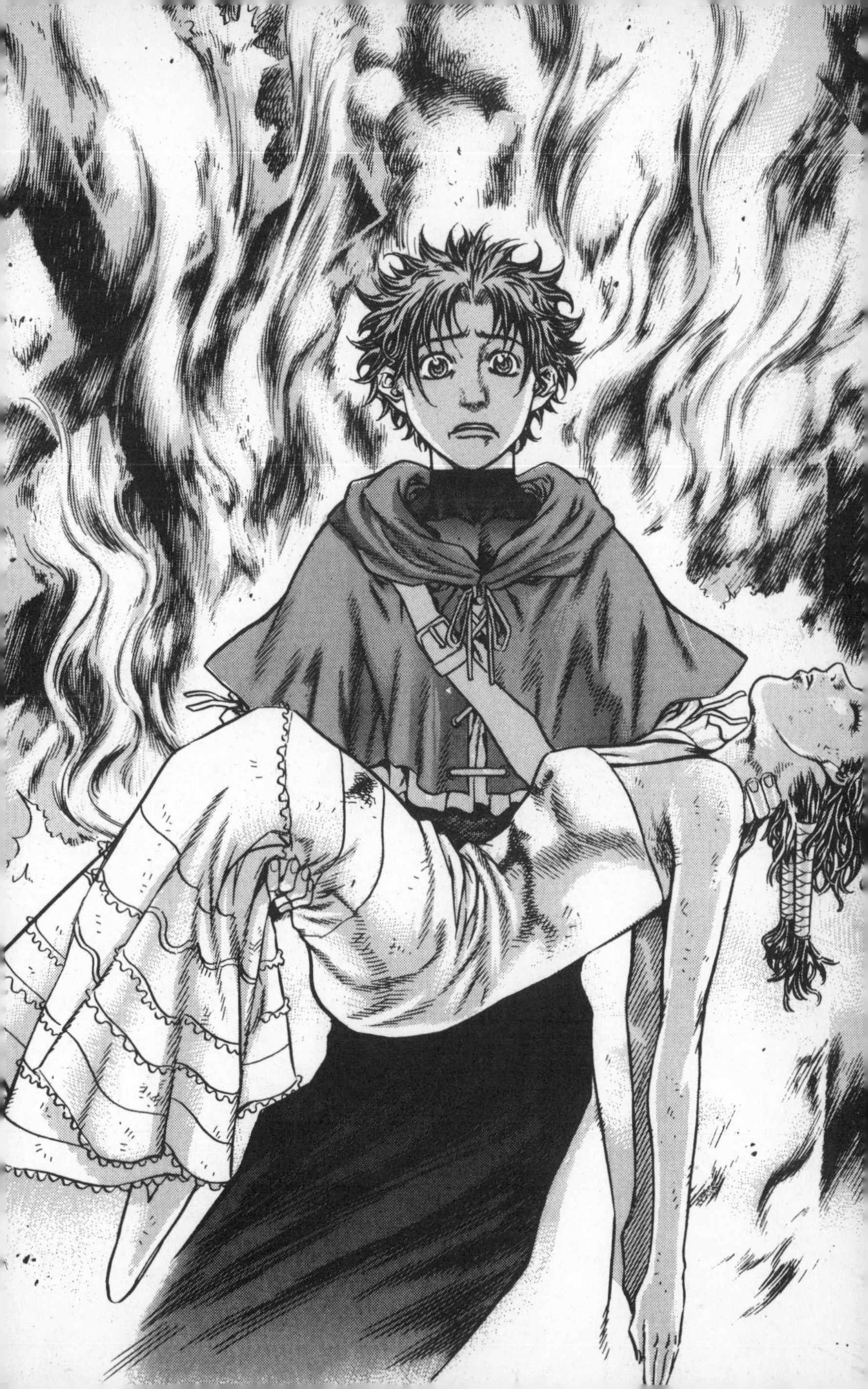

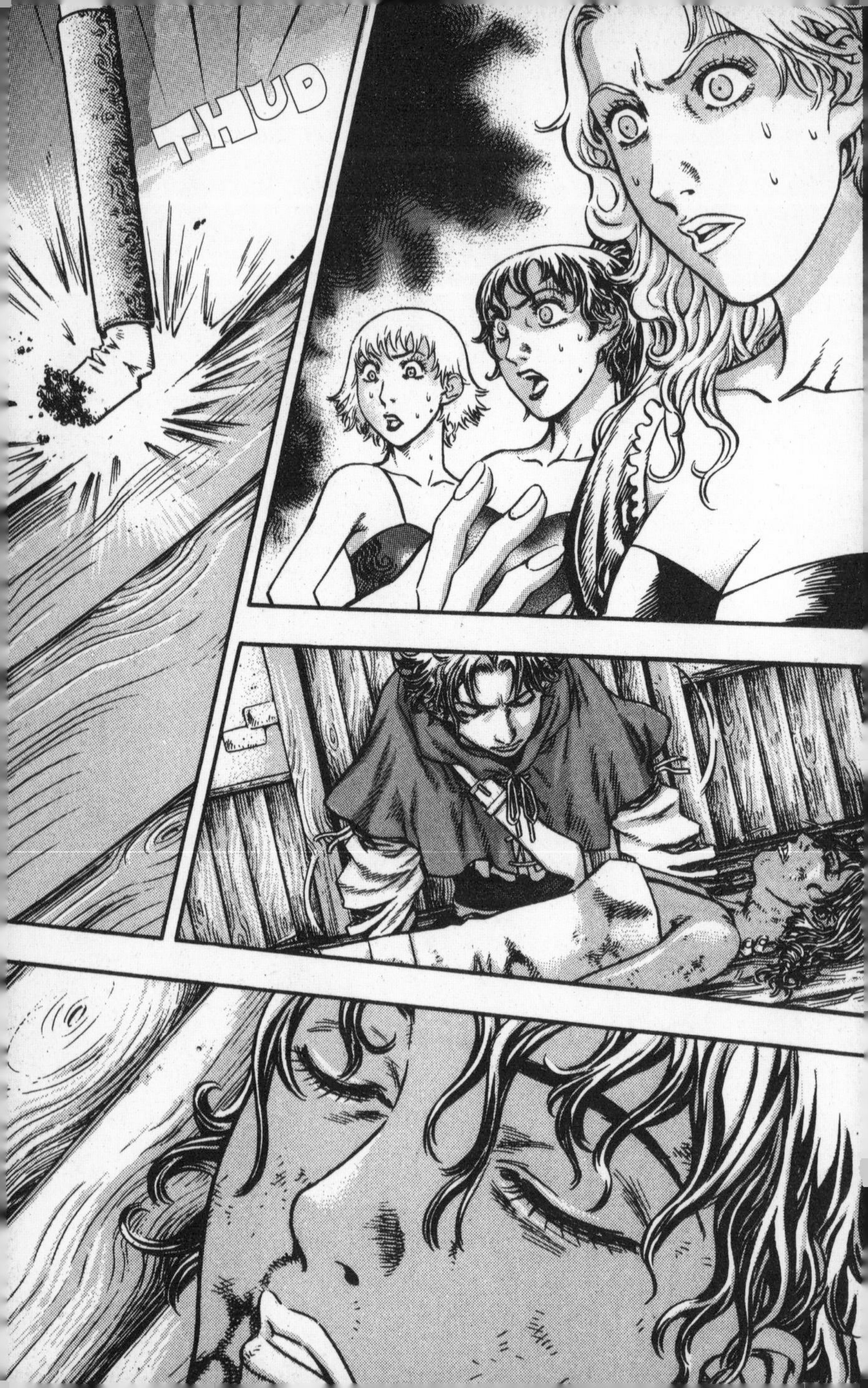
THUD

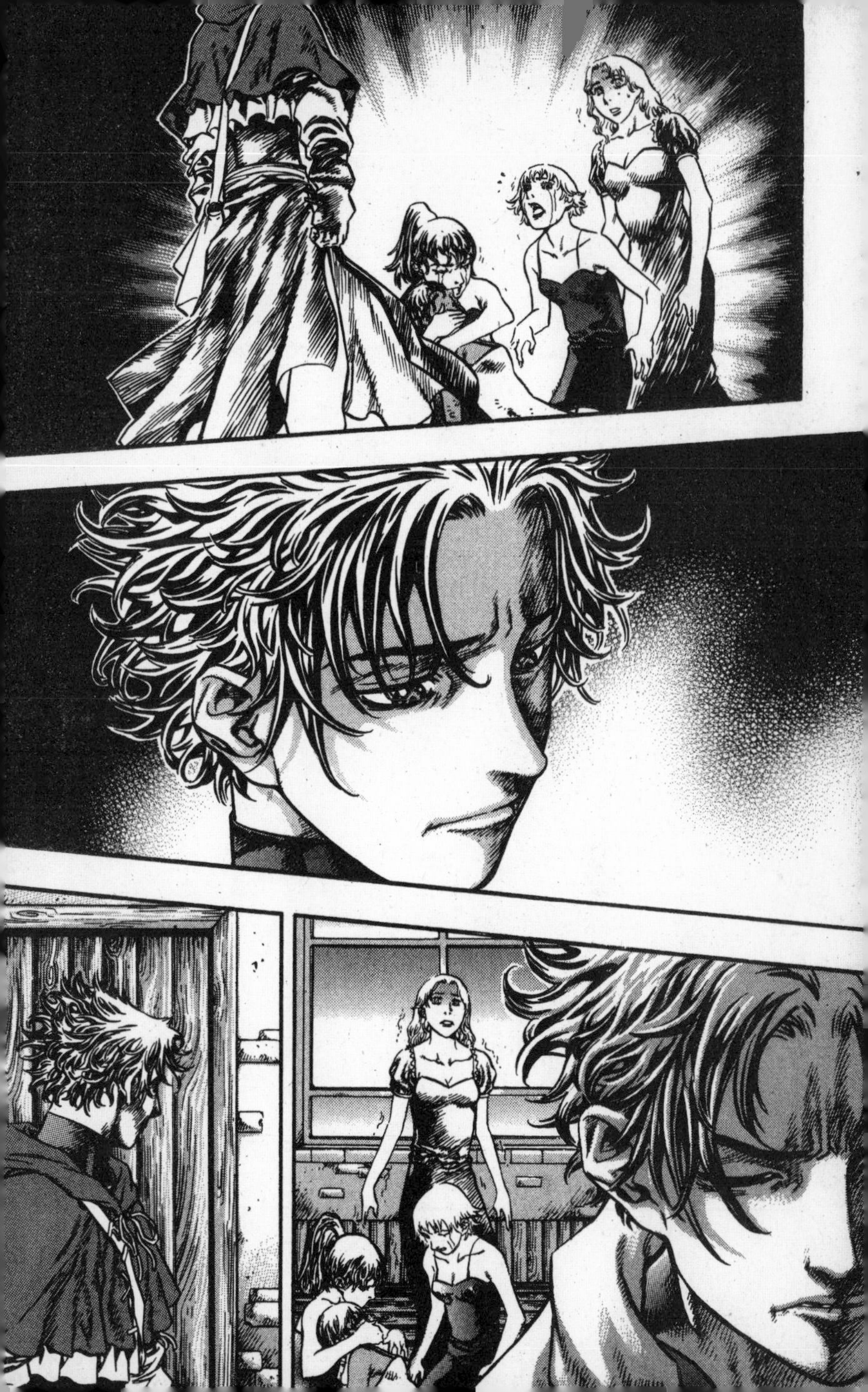

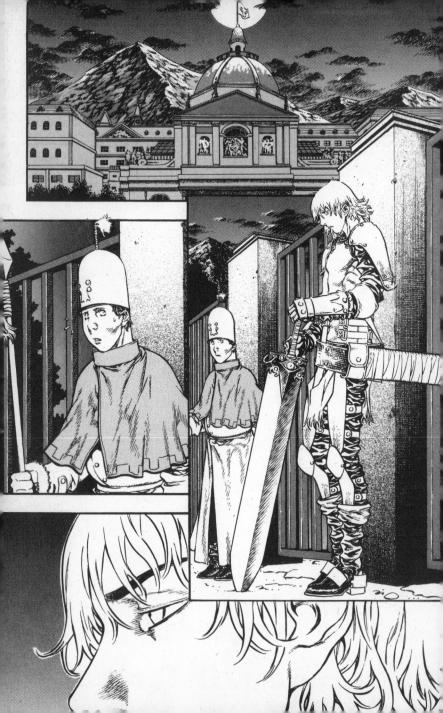

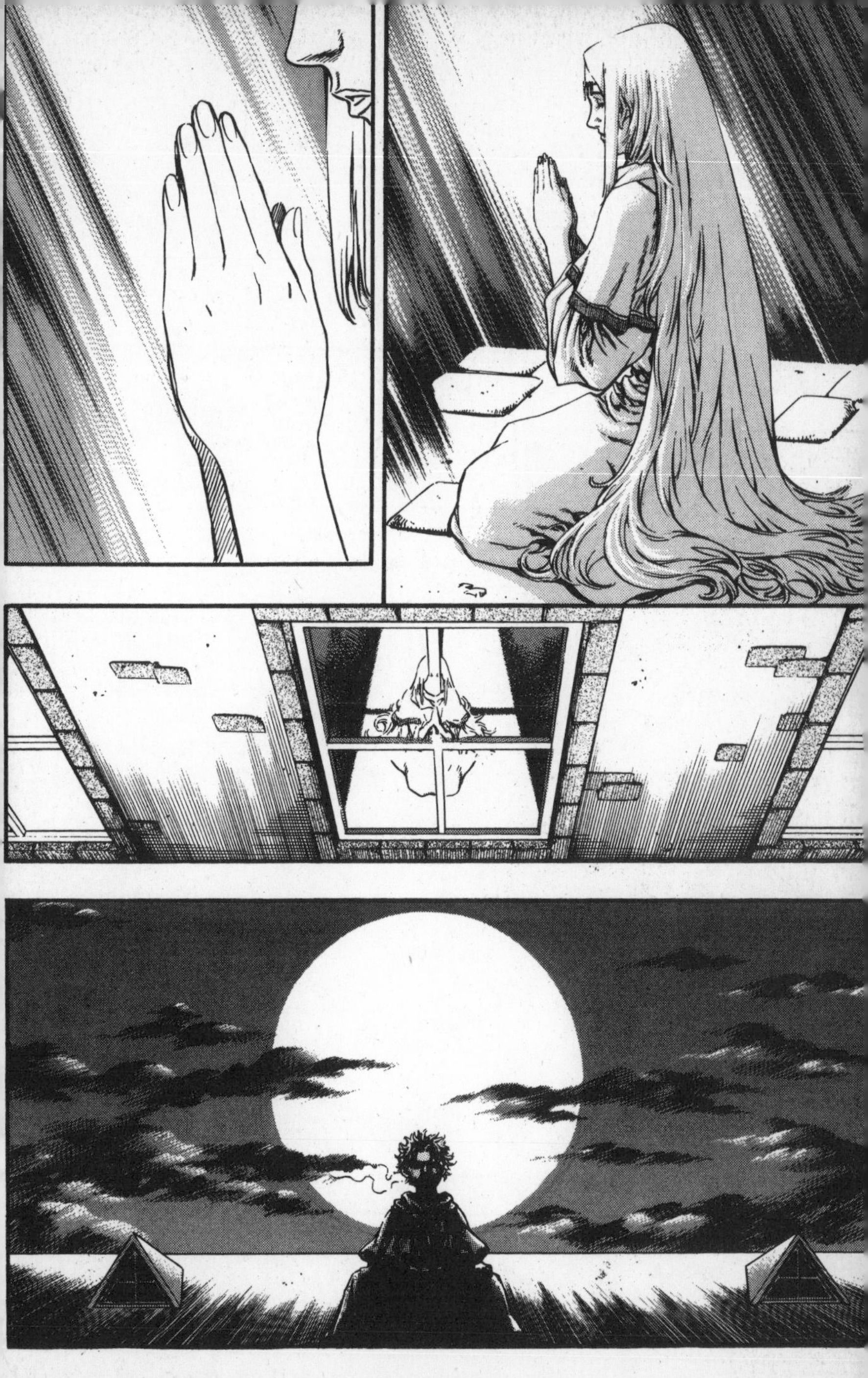

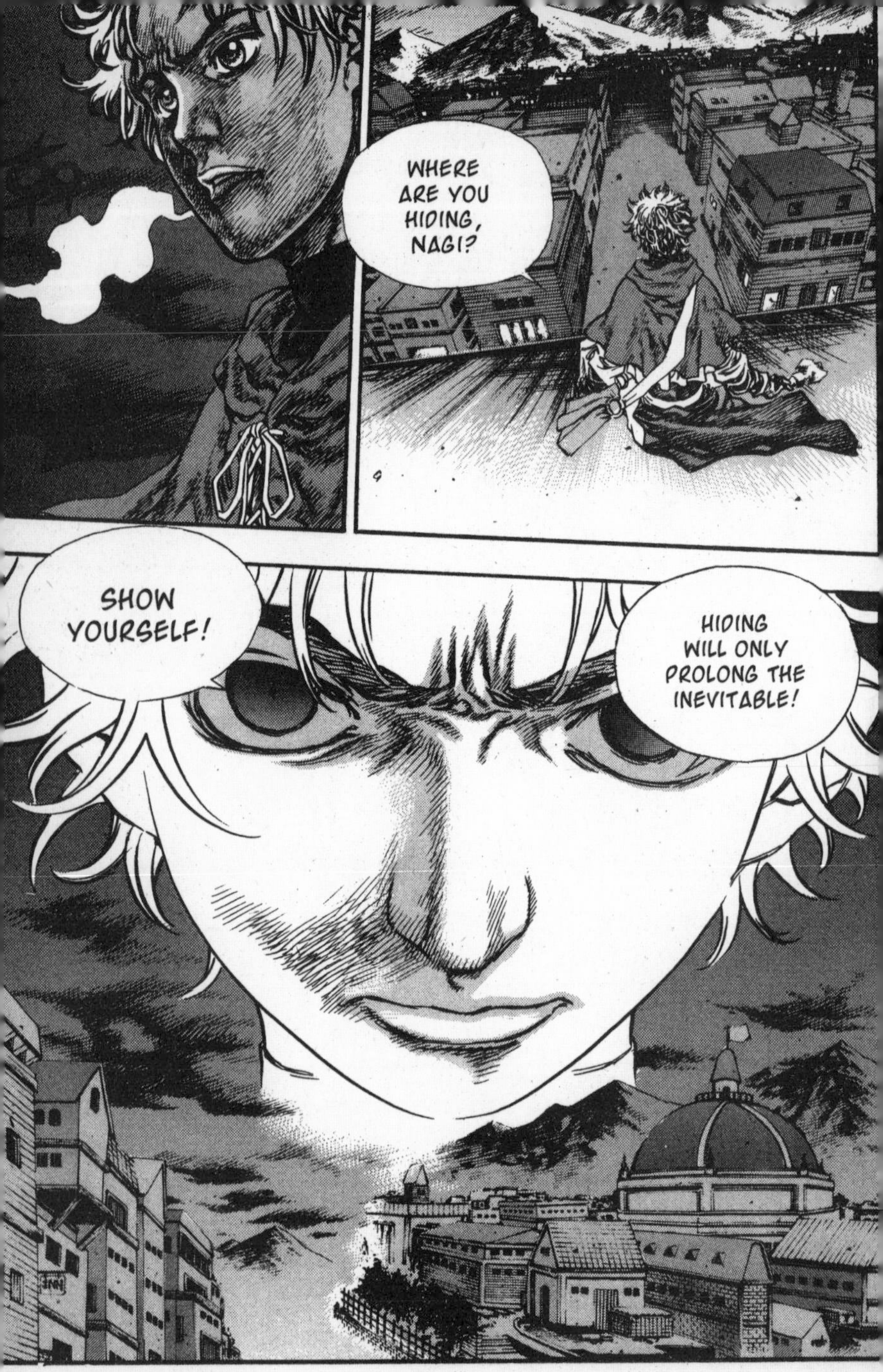
WHERE ARE YOU HIDING, NAGI?
HIDING WILL ONLY PROLONG THE INEVITABLE!
SHOW YOURSELF!
INN

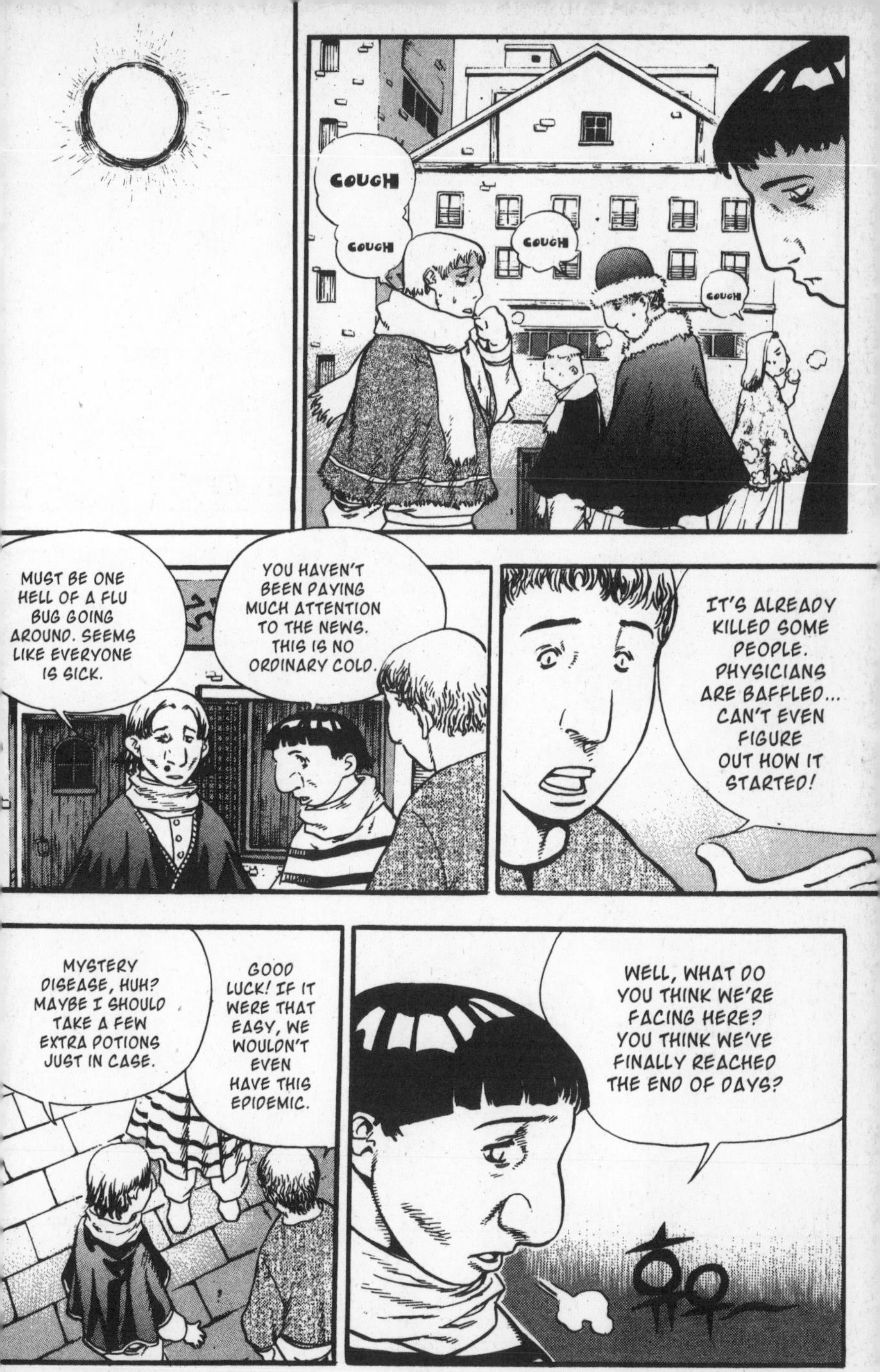
COUGH
COUGH
COUGH
COUGH
MUST BE ONE HELL OF A FLU BUG GOING AROUND. SEEMS LIKE EVERYONE IS SICK.
YOU HAVEN'T BEEN PAYING MUCH ATTENTION TO THE NEWS. THIS IS NO ORDINARY COLD.
IT'S ALREADY KILLED SOME PEOPLE. PHYSICIANS ARE BAFFLED... CAN'T EVEN FIGURE OUT HOW IT STARTED!
MYSTERY DISEASE, HUH? MAYBE I SHOULD TAKE A FEW EXTRA POTIONS JUST IN CASE.
GOOD LUCK! IF IT WERE THAT EASY, WE WOULDN'T EVEN HAVE THIS EPIDEMIC.
WELL, WHAT DO YOU THINK WE'RE FACING HERE? YOU THINK WE'VE FINALLY REACHED THE END OF DAYS?

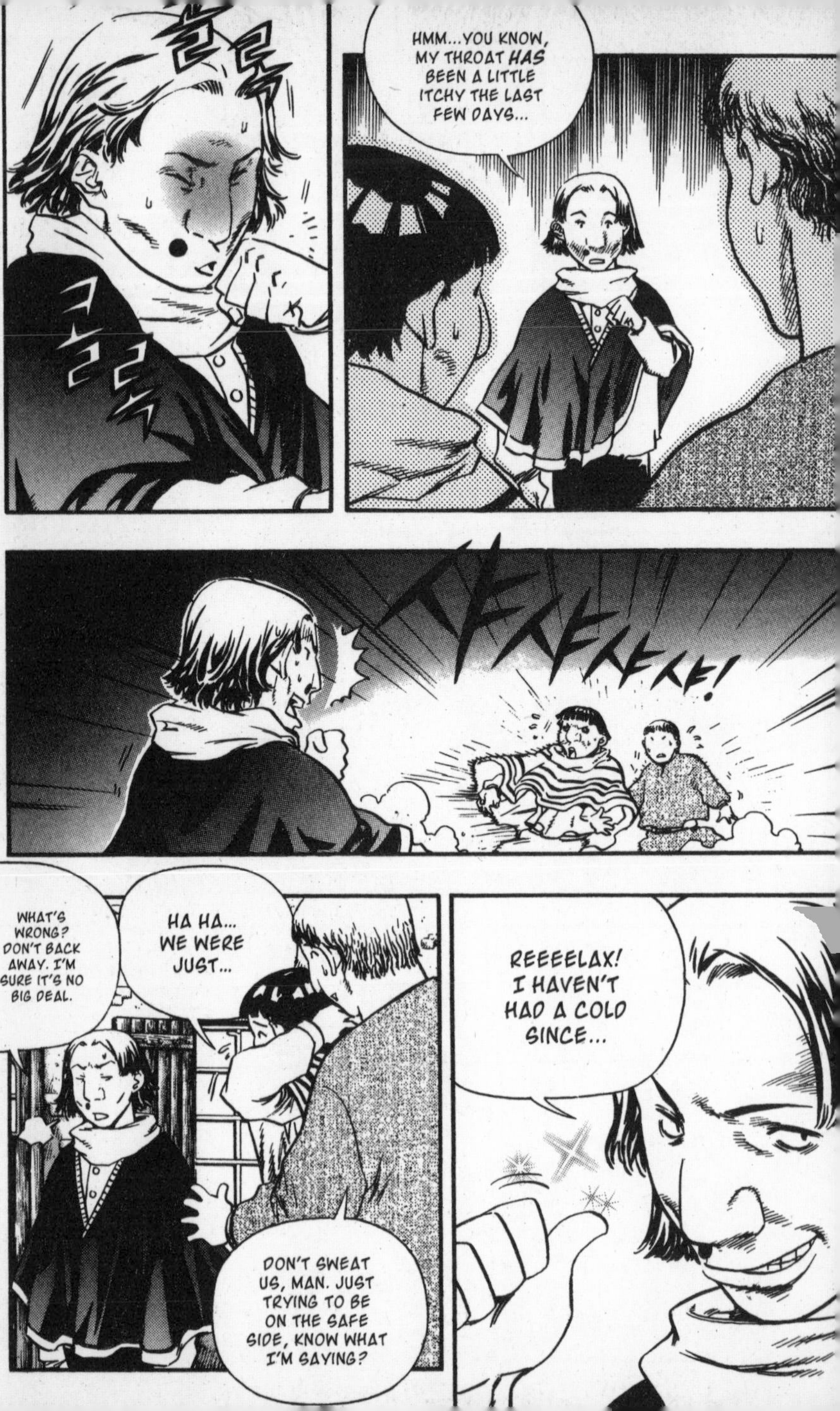
HMM...YOU KNOW, MY THROAT HAS BEEN A LITTLE ITCHY THE LAST FEW DAYS...
WHAT'S WRONG? DON'T BACK AWAY. I'M SURE IT'S NO BIG DEAL.
HA HA... WE WERE JUST...
DON'T SWEAT US, MAN. JUST TRYING TO BE ON THE SAFE SIDE, KNOW WHAT I'M SAYING?
REEEELAX! I HAVEN'T HAD A COLD SINCE...

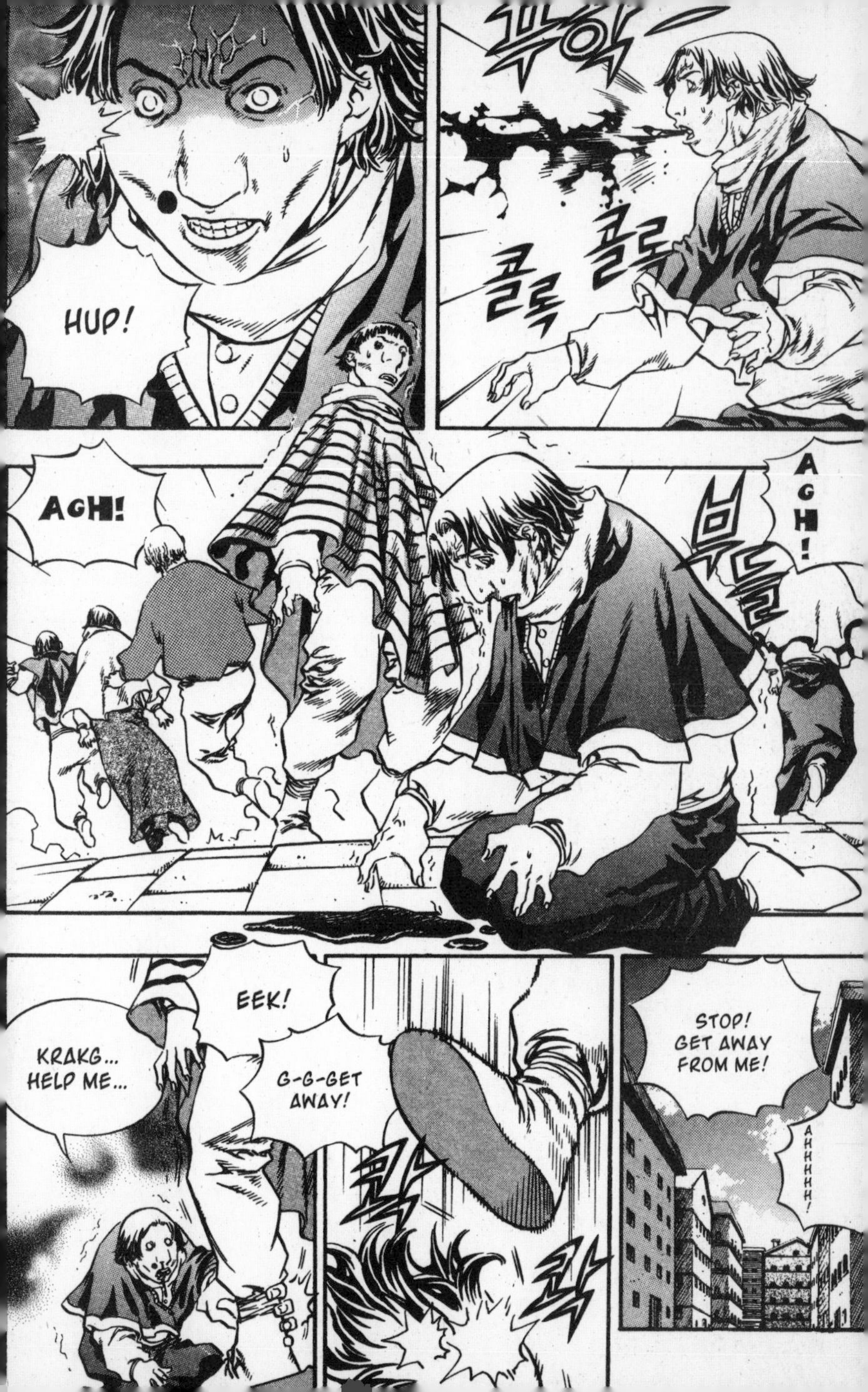

HUP!
콜록
콜록
AGH!
AGH!
부들
EEK!
KRAKG...
HELP ME...
G-G-GET
AWAY!
STOP!
GET AWAY
FROM ME!
AHHHHH!

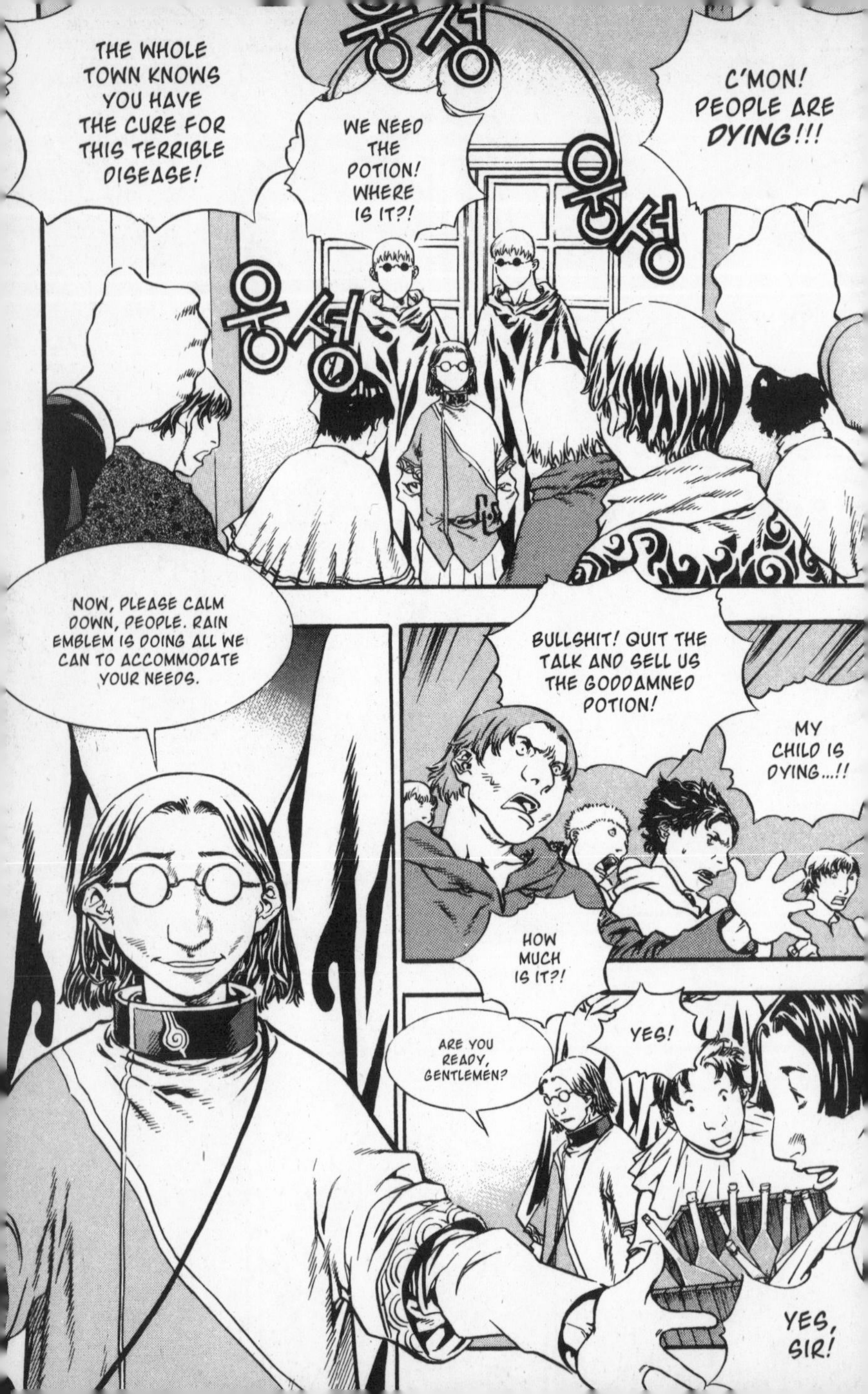

웅성
THE WHOLE TOWN KNOWS YOU HAVE THE CURE FOR THIS TERRIBLE DISEASE!
WE NEED THE POTION! WHERE IS IT?!
C'MON! PEOPLE ARE *DYING*!!!
웅성
웅성
NOW, PLEASE CALM DOWN, PEOPLE. RAIN EMBLEM IS DOING ALL WE CAN TO ACCOMMODATE YOUR NEEDS.
BULLSHIT! QUIT THE TALK AND SELL US THE GODDAMNED POTION!
MY CHILD IS DYING...!!
HOW MUCH IS IT?!
ARE YOU READY, GENTLEMEN?
YES!
YES, SIR!

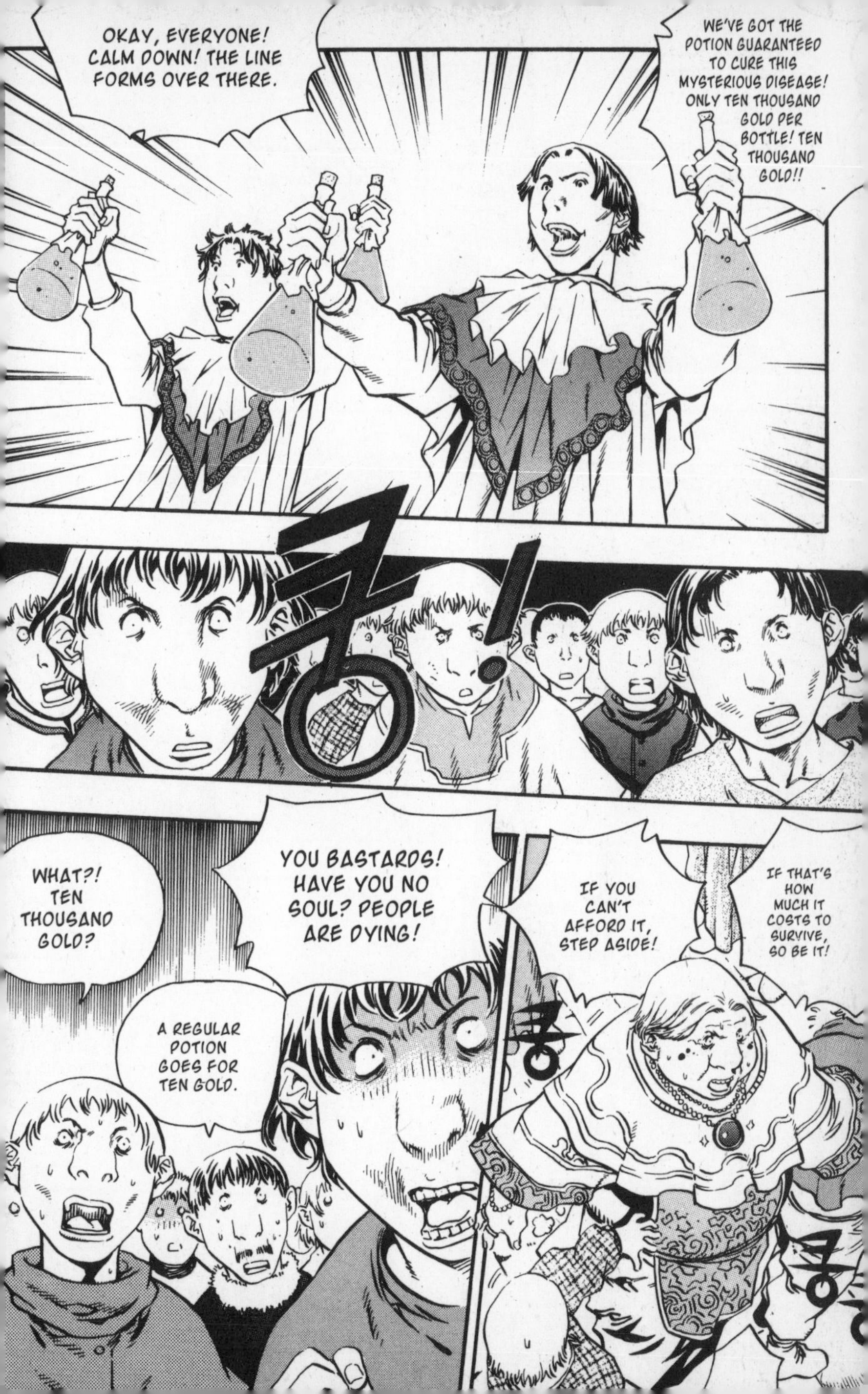

OKAY, EVERYONE! CALM DOWN! THE LINE FORMS OVER THERE.
WE'VE GOT THE POTION GUARANTEED TO CURE THIS MYSTERIOUS DISEASE! ONLY TEN THOUSAND GOLD PER BOTTLE! TEN THOUSAND GOLD!!
WHAT?! TEN THOUSAND GOLD?
A REGULAR POTION GOES FOR TEN GOLD.
YOU BASTARDS! HAVE YOU NO SOUL? PEOPLE ARE DYING!
IF YOU CAN'T AFFORD IT, STEP ASIDE!
IF THAT'S HOW MUCH IT COSTS TO SURVIVE, SO BE IT!

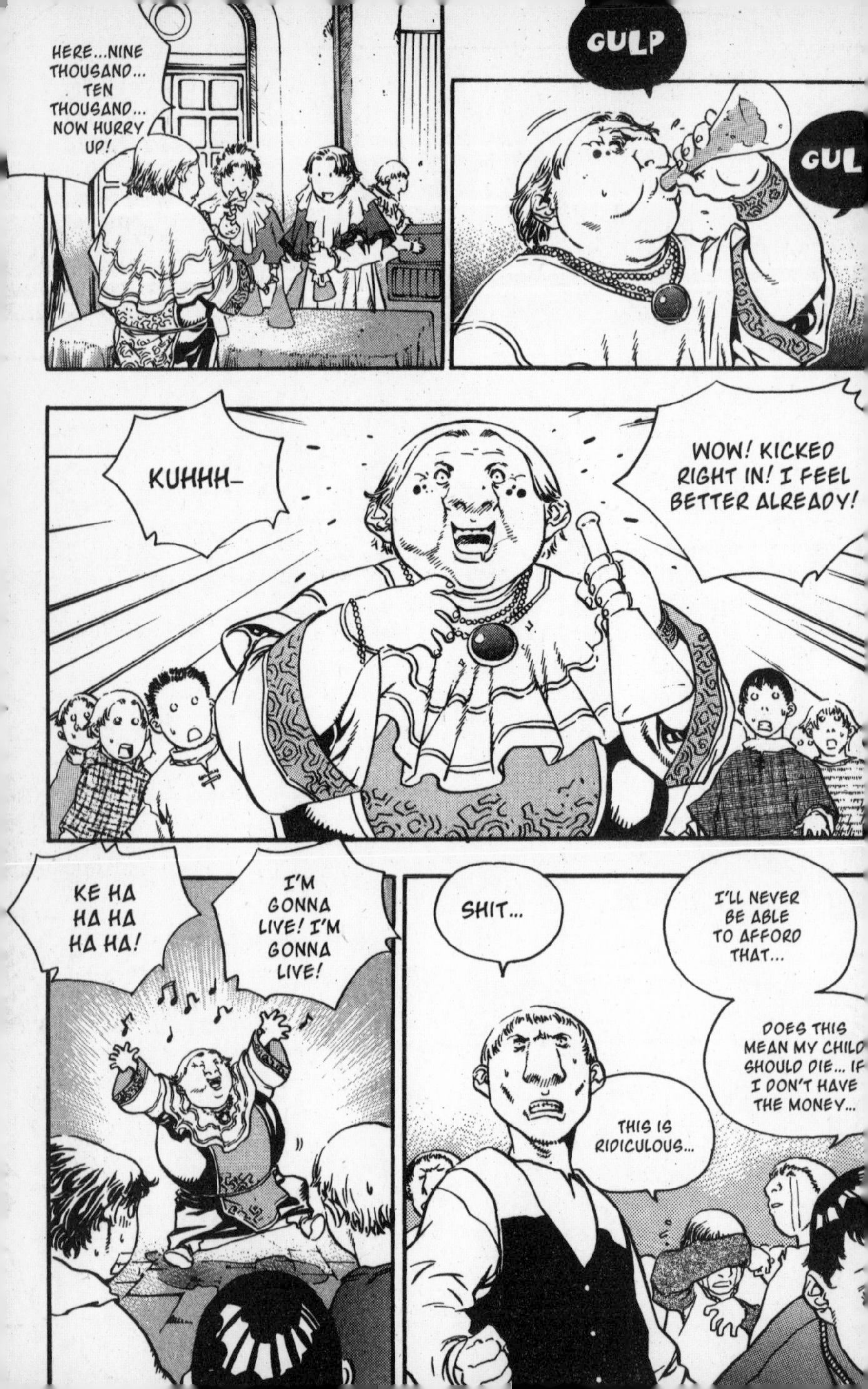
HERE...NINE THOUSAND... TEN THOUSAND... NOW HURRY UP!
GULP
GUL
KUHHH-
WOW! KICKED RIGHT IN! I FEEL BETTER ALREADY!
KE HA HA HA HA HA!
I'M GONNA LIVE! I'M GONNA LIVE!
SHIT...
I'LL NEVER BE ABLE TO AFFORD THAT...
DOES THIS MEAN MY CHILD SHOULD DIE... IF I DON'T HAVE THE MONEY...
THIS IS RIDICULOUS...

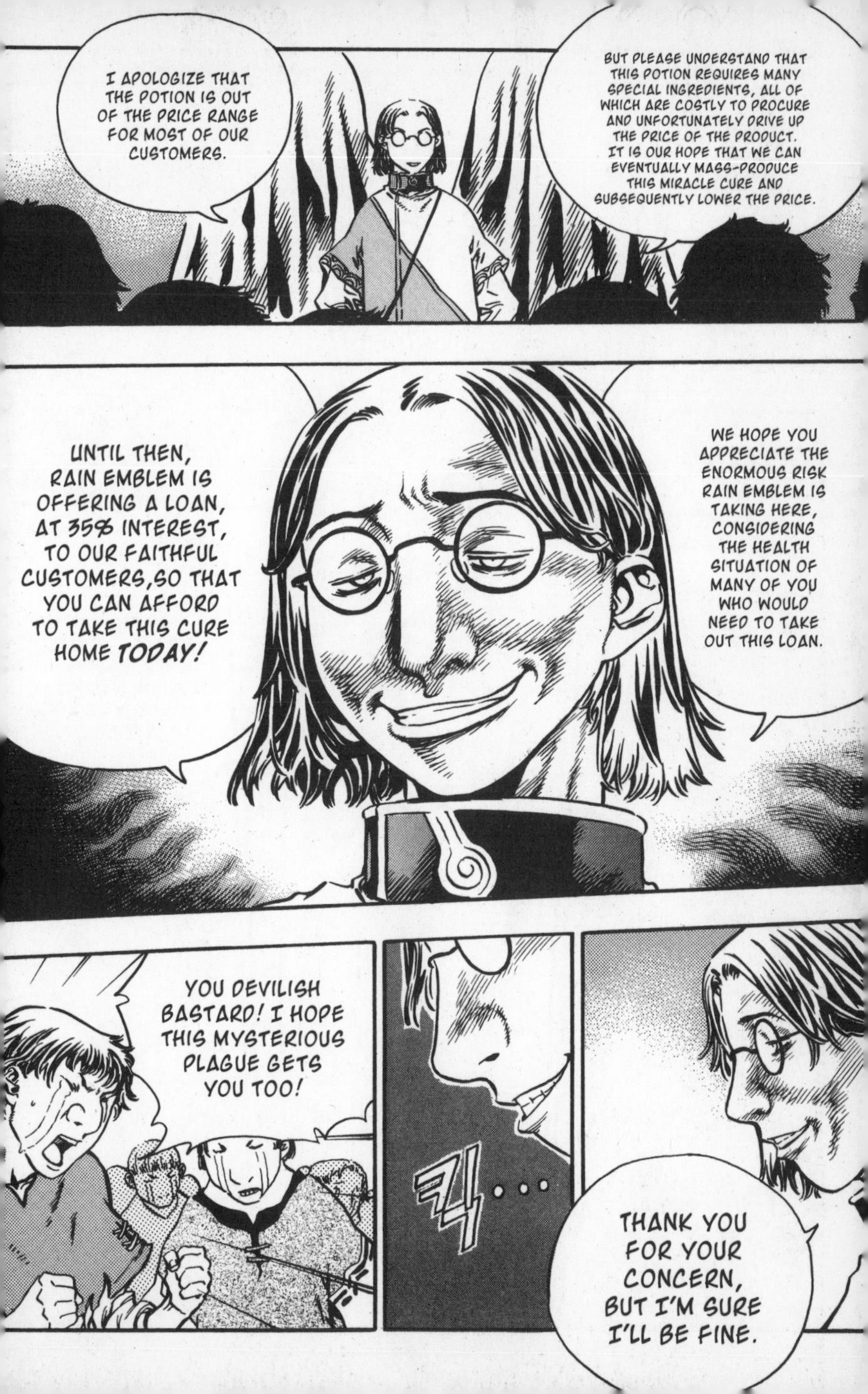
I APOLOGIZE THAT THE POTION IS OUT OF THE PRICE RANGE FOR MOST OF OUR CUSTOMERS.
BUT PLEASE UNDERSTAND THAT THIS POTION REQUIRES MANY SPECIAL INGREDIENTS, ALL OF WHICH ARE COSTLY TO PROCURE AND UNFORTUNATELY DRIVE UP THE PRICE OF THE PRODUCT. IT IS OUR HOPE THAT WE CAN EVENTUALLY MASS-PRODUCE THIS MIRACLE CURE AND SUBSEQUENTLY LOWER THE PRICE.
UNTIL THEN, RAIN EMBLEM IS OFFERING A LOAN, AT 35% INTEREST, TO OUR FAITHFUL CUSTOMERS, SO THAT YOU CAN AFFORD TO TAKE THIS CURE HOME *TODAY!*
WE HOPE YOU APPRECIATE THE ENORMOUS RISK RAIN EMBLEM IS TAKING HERE, CONSIDERING THE HEALTH SITUATION OF MANY OF YOU WHO WOULD NEED TO TAKE OUT THIS LOAN.
YOU DEVILISH BASTARD! I HOPE THIS MYSTERIOUS PLAGUE GETS YOU TOO!
...
THANK YOU FOR YOUR CONCERN, BUT I'M SURE I'LL BE FINE.

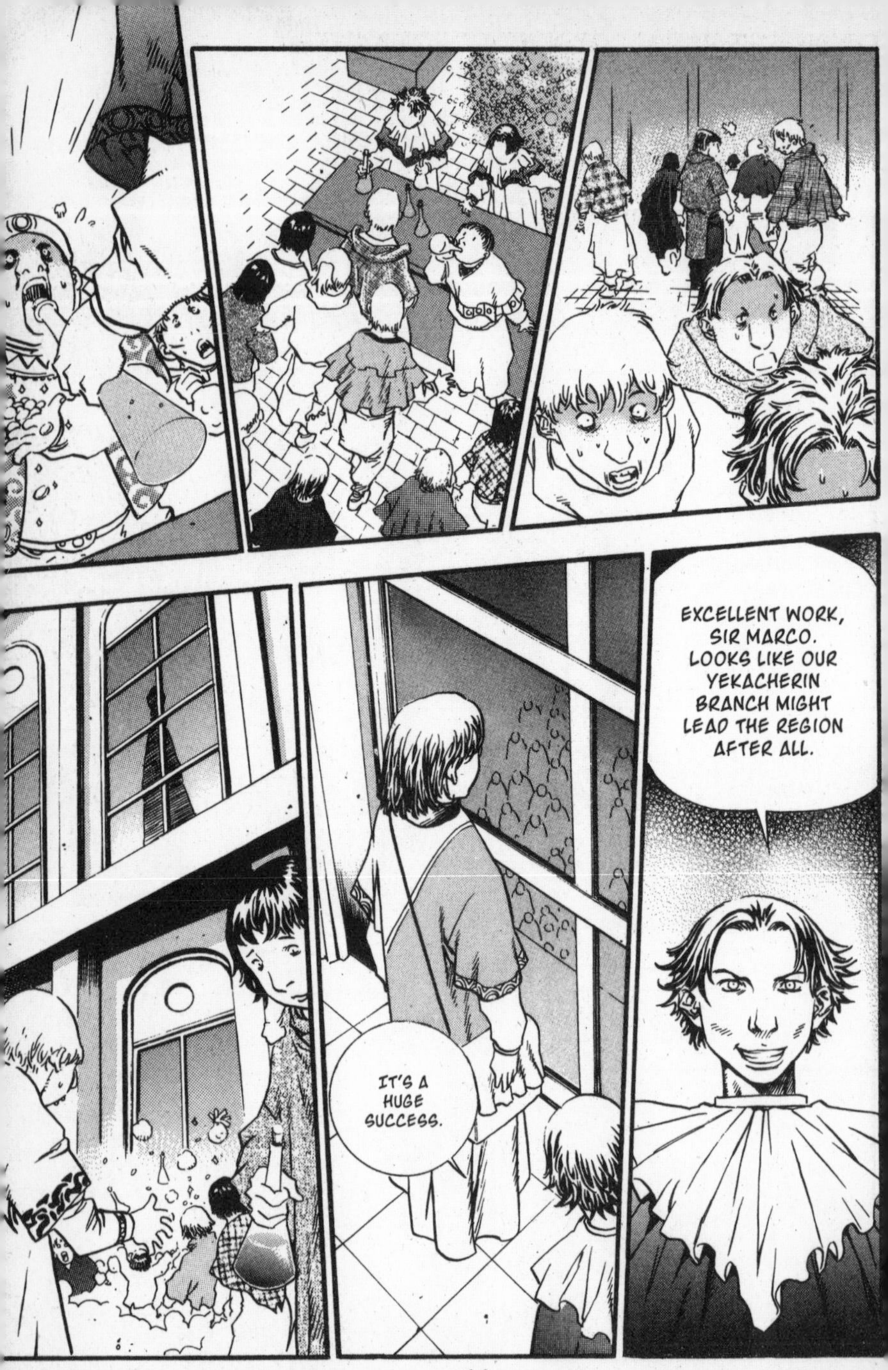
EXCELLENT WORK, SIR MARCO. LOOKS LIKE OUR YEKACHERIN BRANCH MIGHT LEAD THE REGION AFTER ALL.
IT'S A HUGE SUCCESS.

THE DISEASE IS SPREADING MORE QUICKLY THAN EVEN I IMAGINED. PERHAPS THE TOXIN LEVEL WAS TOO HIGH.

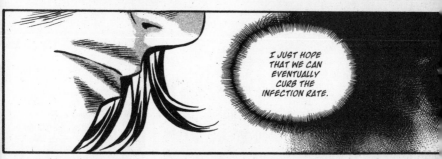

I JUST HOPE THAT WE CAN EVENTUALLY CURB THE INFECTION RATE.

HOLY LADY! PLEASE SAVE US!

PLEASE EXTEND YOUR HAND OF SALVATION!

HOLY LADY!

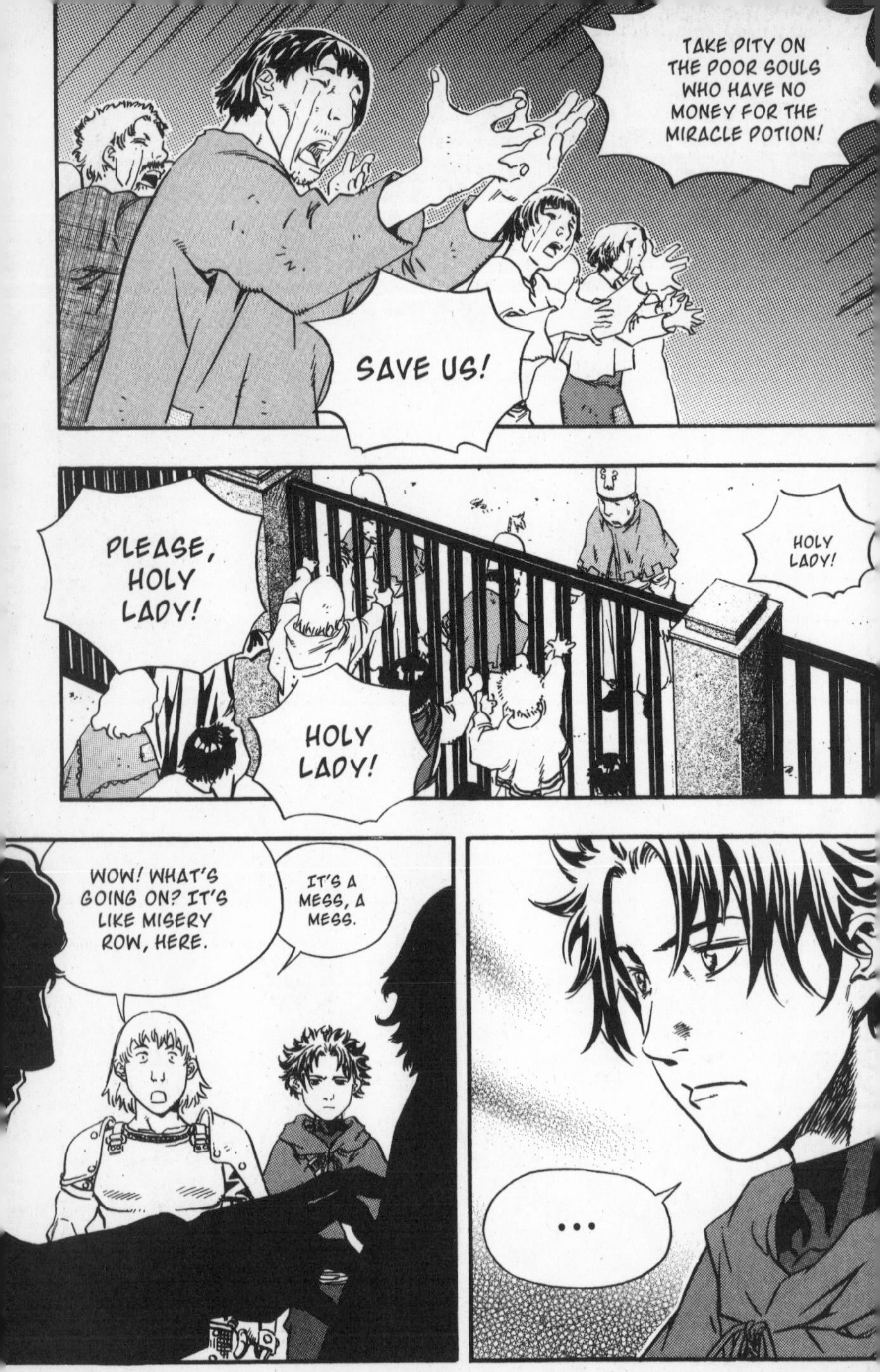
TAKE PITY ON THE POOR SOULS WHO HAVE NO MONEY FOR THE MIRACLE POTION!
SAVE US!
PLEASE, HOLY LADY!
HOLY LADY!
HOLY LADY!
WOW! WHAT'S GOING ON? IT'S LIKE MISERY ROW, HERE.
IT'S A MESS, A MESS.
...

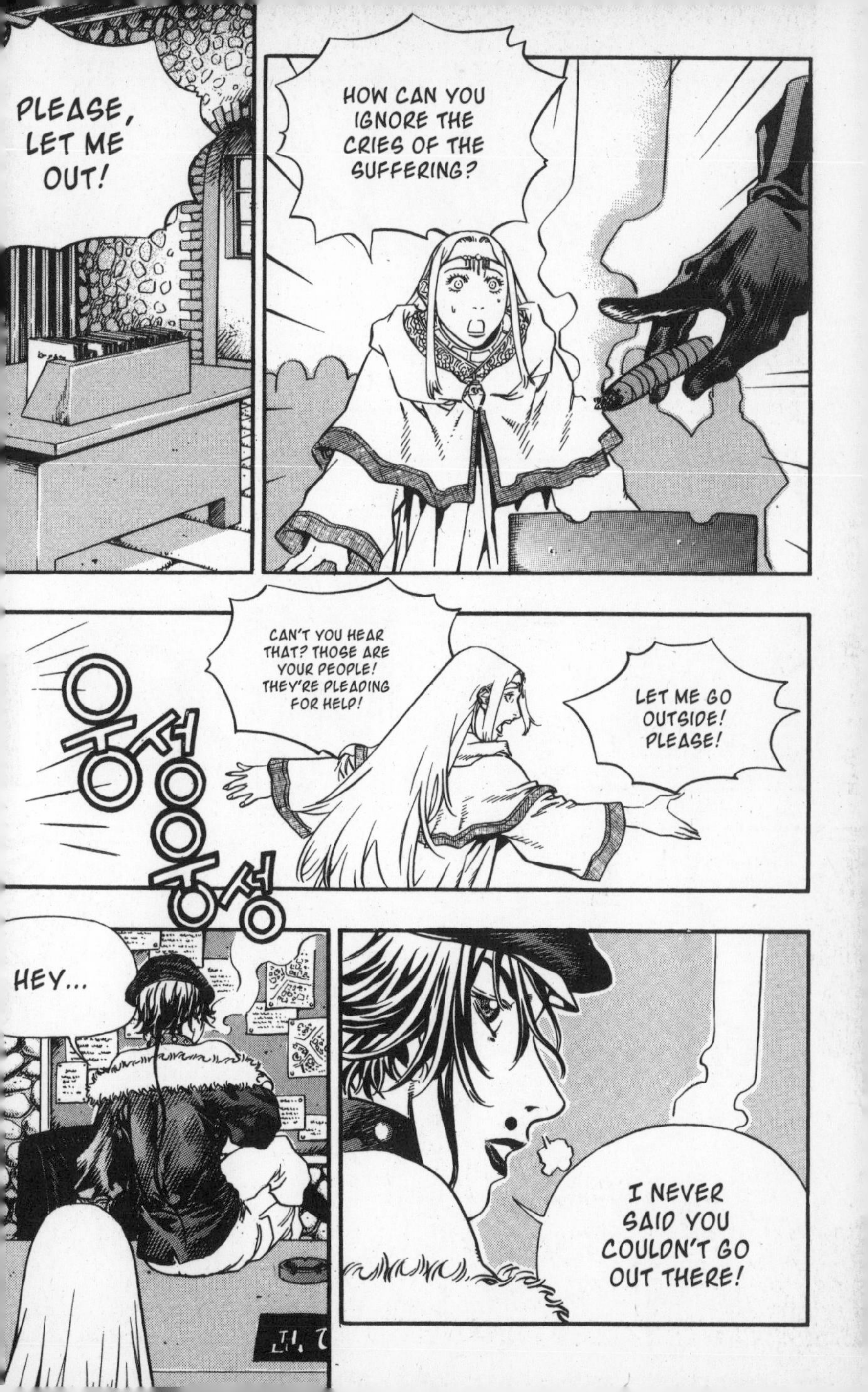
PLEASE, LET ME OUT!
HOW CAN YOU IGNORE THE CRIES OF THE SUFFERING?
CAN'T YOU HEAR THAT? THOSE ARE YOUR PEOPLE! THEY'RE PLEADING FOR HELP!
LET ME GO OUTSIDE! PLEASE!
웅성웅성
HEY...
I NEVER SAID YOU COULDN'T GO OUT THERE!

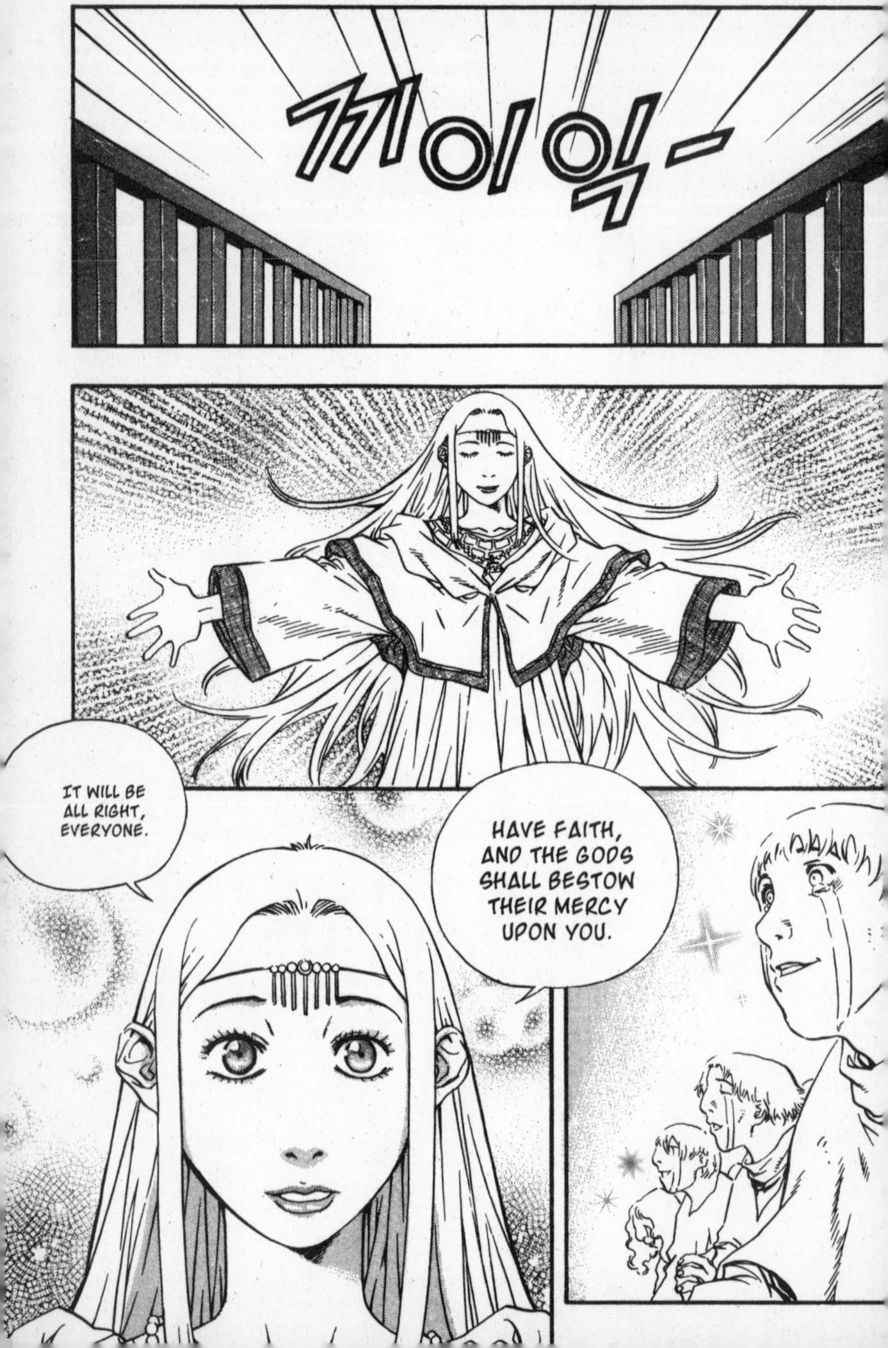
IT WILL BE ALL RIGHT, EVERYONE.
HAVE FAITH, AND THE GODS SHALL BESTOW THEIR MERCY UPON YOU.

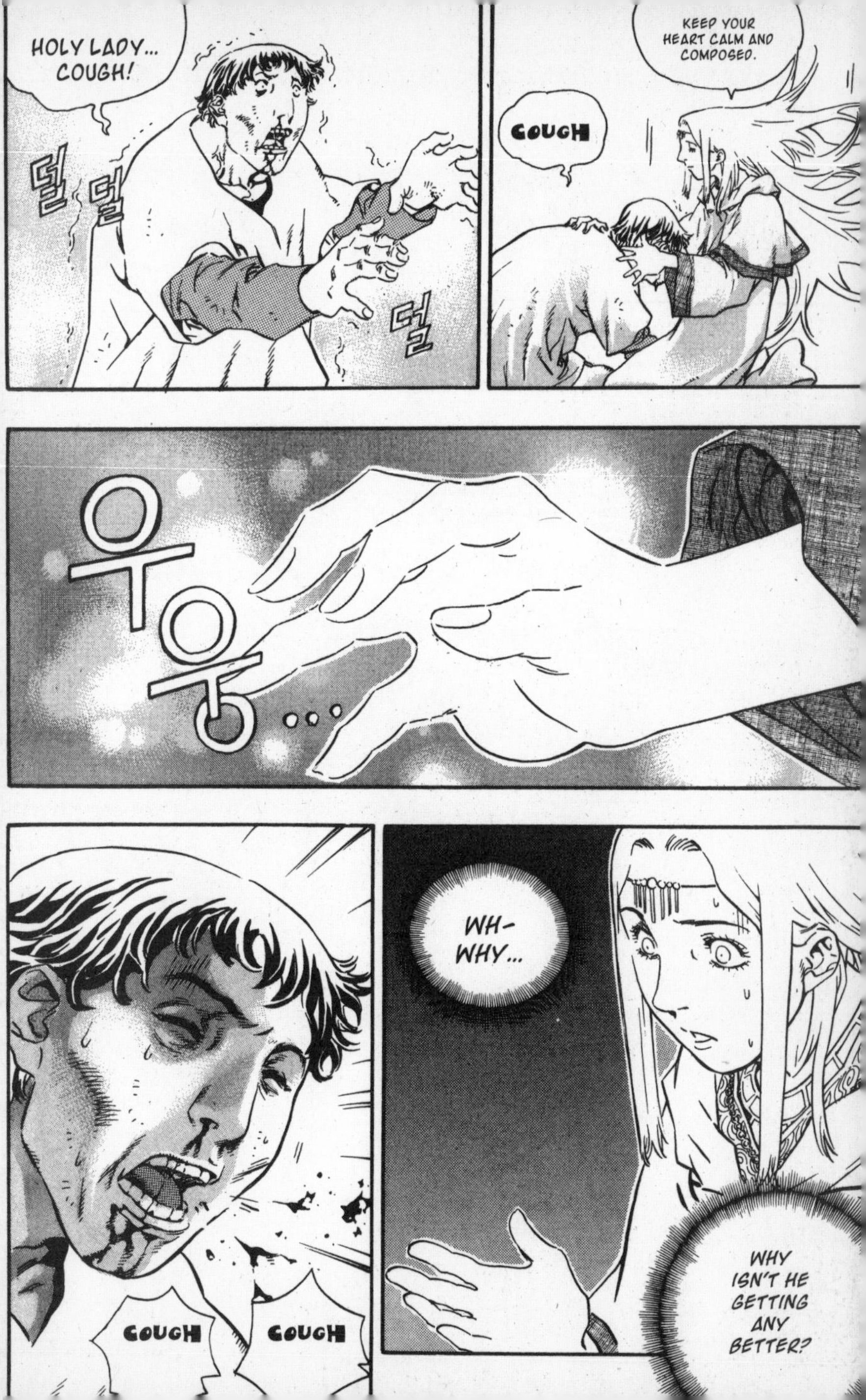
HOLY LADY... COUGH!
덜 덜
덜
KEEP YOUR HEART CALM AND COMPOSED.
COUGH
우웅...
COUGH
COUGH
WH- WHY...
WHY ISN'T HE GETTING ANY BETTER?

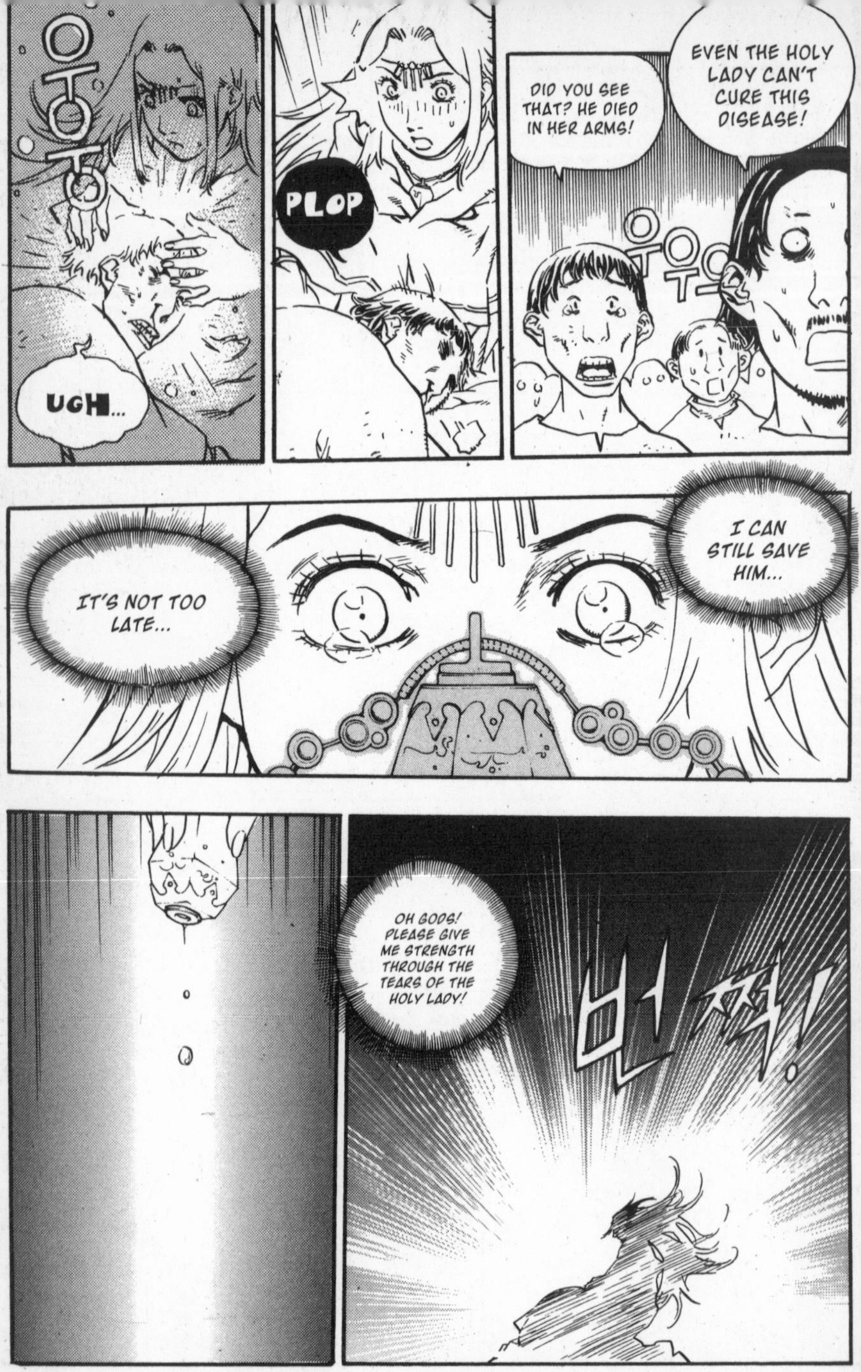
UGH...
PLOP
DID YOU SEE THAT? HE DIED IN HER ARMS!
EVEN THE HOLY LADY CAN'T CURE THIS DISEASE!
IT'S NOT TOO LATE...
I CAN STILL SAVE HIM...
OH GODS! PLEASE GIVE ME STRENGTH THROUGH THE TEARS OF THE HOLY LADY!

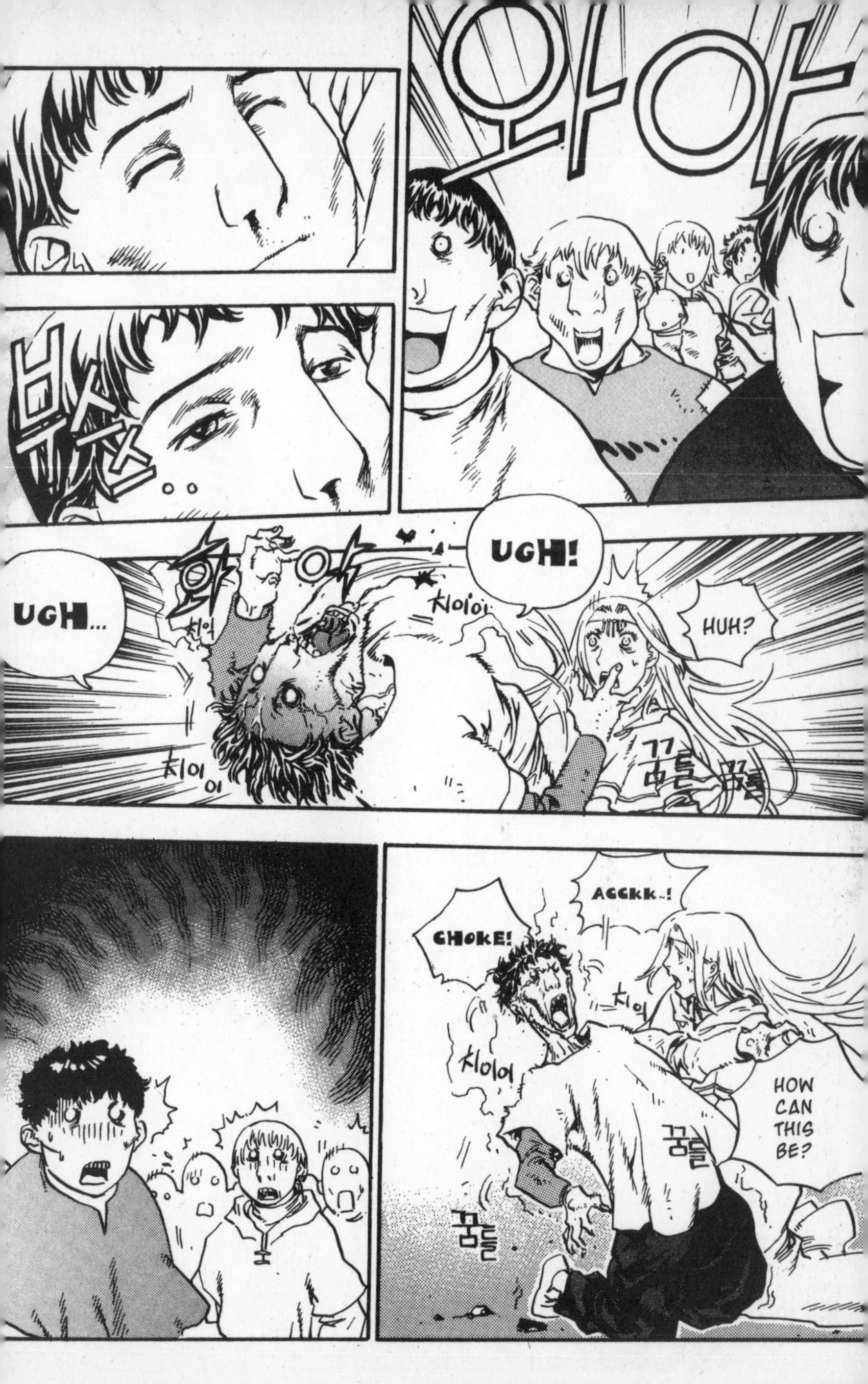

와아
UGH...
치익
치이이
UGH!
치이이
HUH?
ACCKK~!
CHOKE!
치익
치이이
꿈틀
HOW CAN THIS BE?
꿈틀

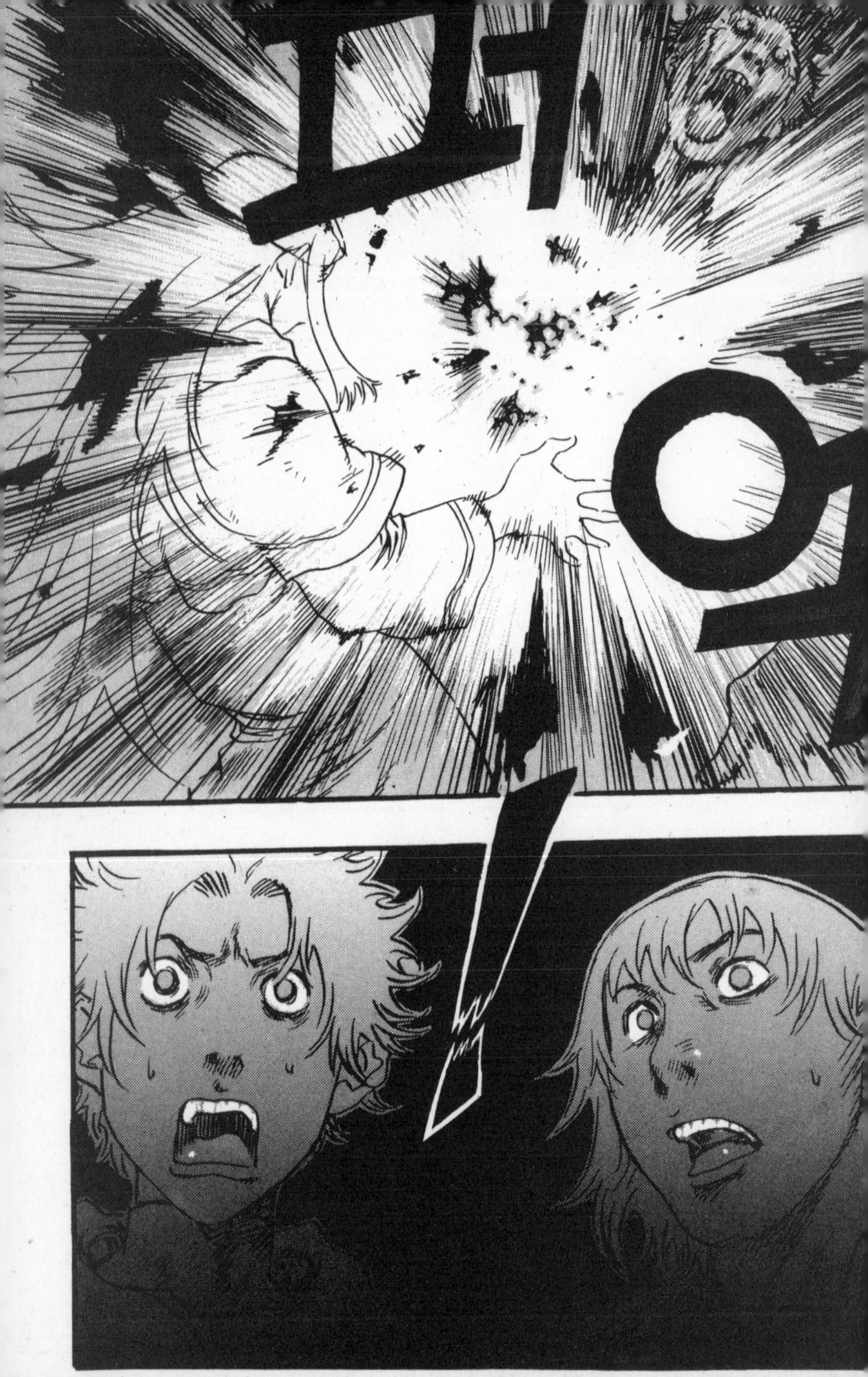

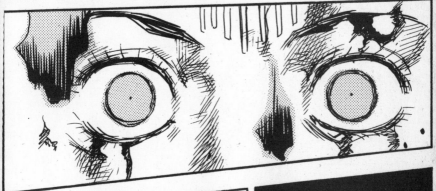

HOLY...
LADY...

AH... AH....
AH...

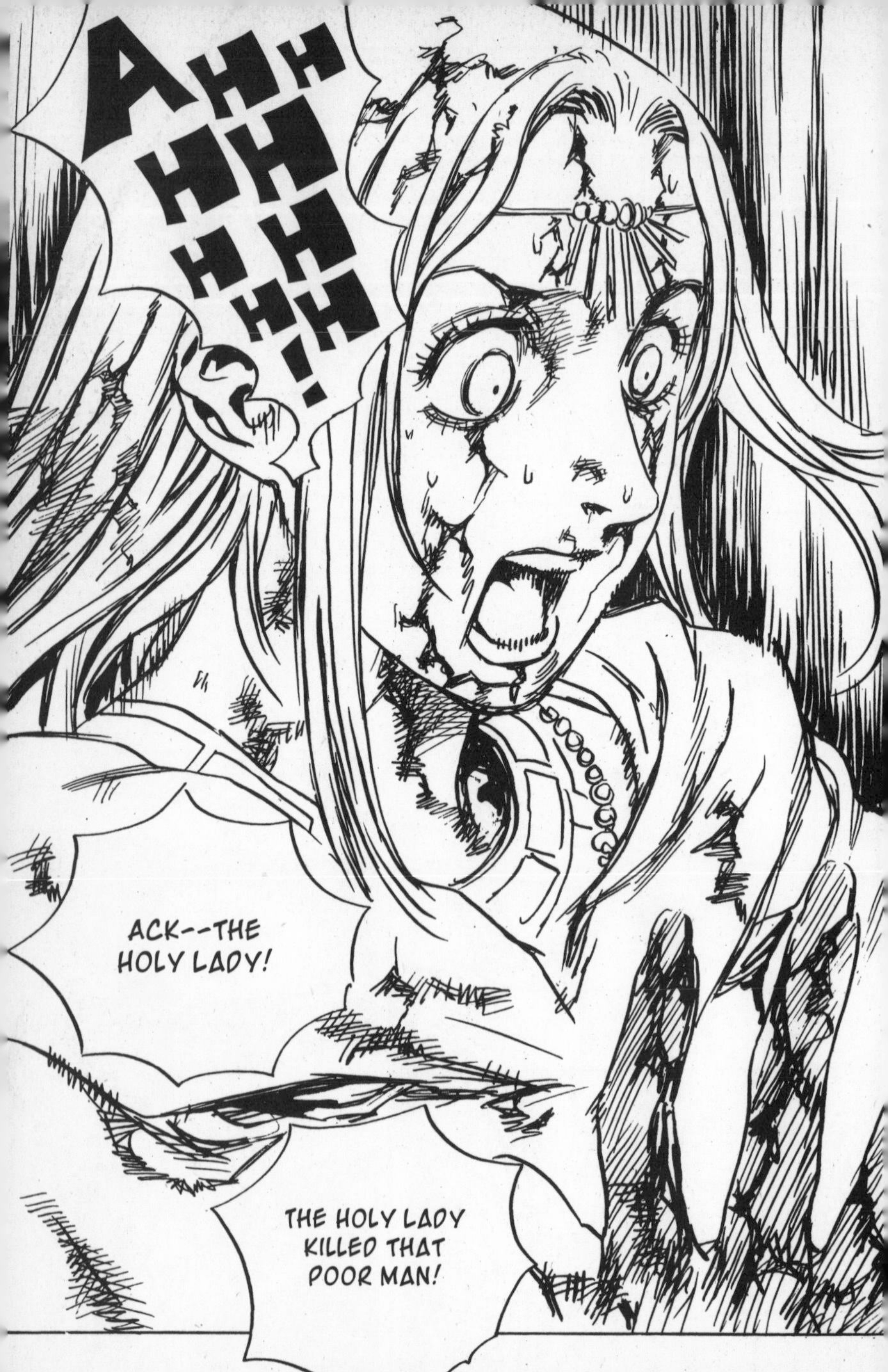
AHHHHHHHHHHH!!
ACK--THE HOLY LADY!
THE HOLY LADY KILLED THAT POOR MAN!

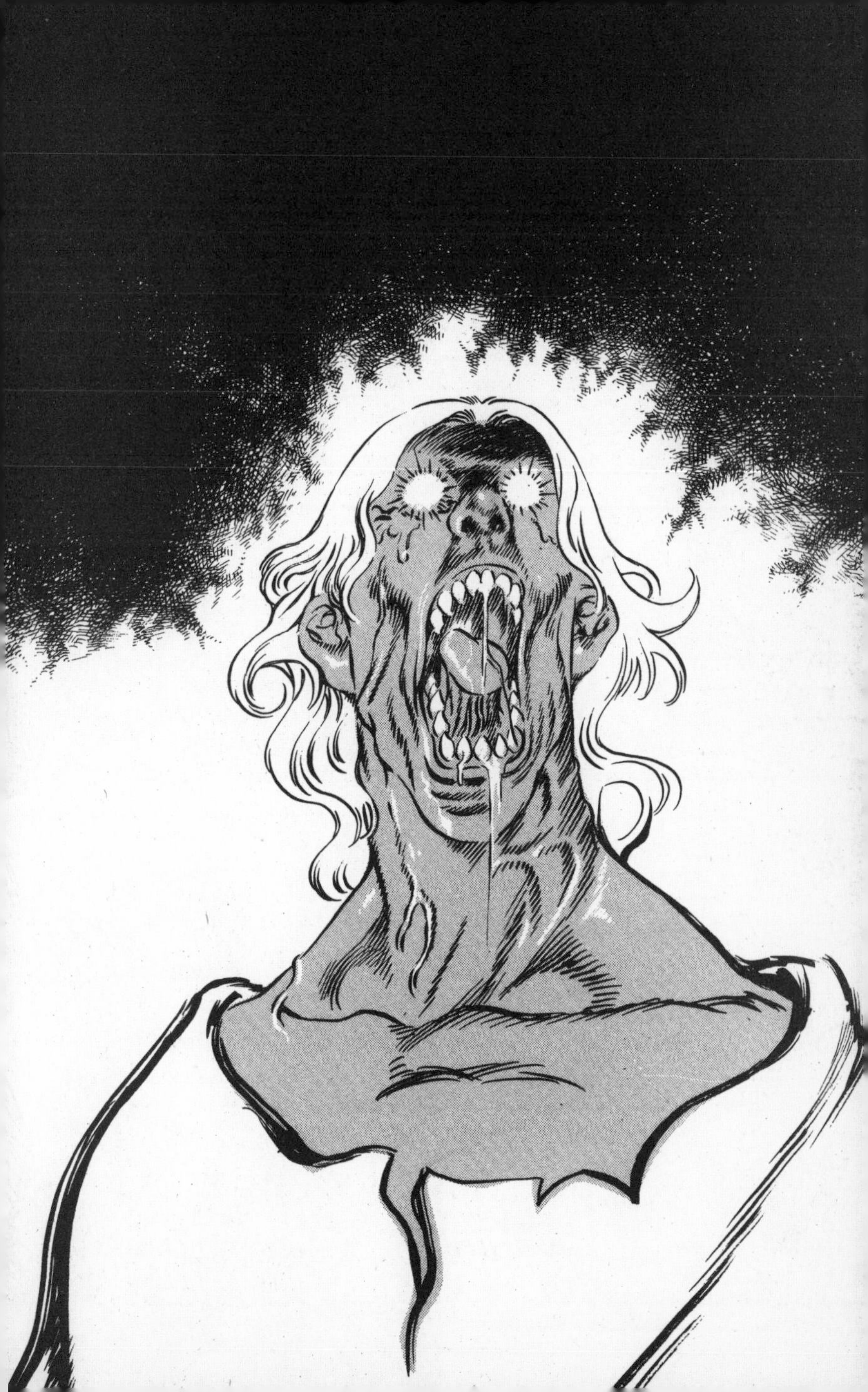

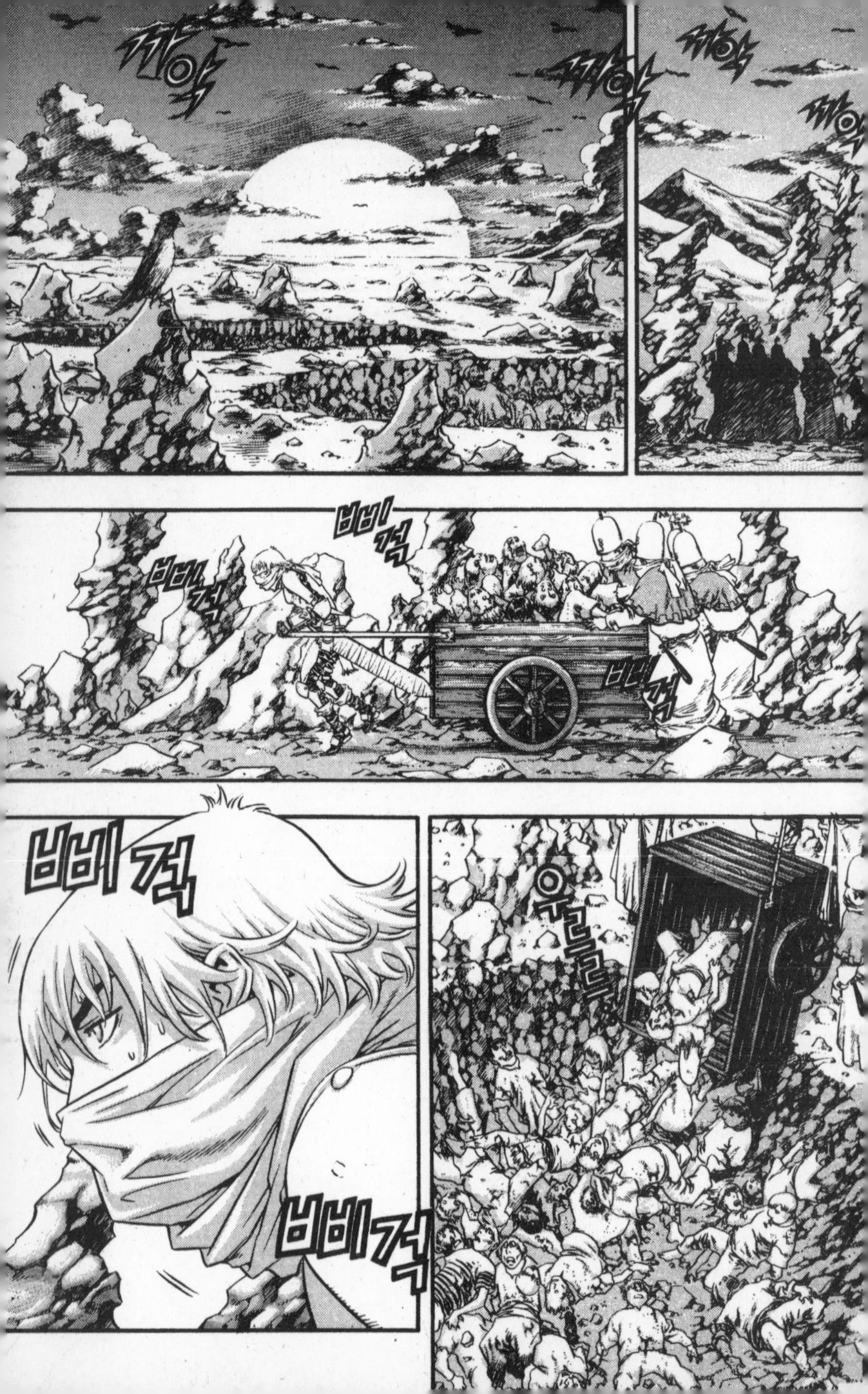

까악
까악
까악
까악
삐걱
삐걱
삐걱
삐걱
삐걱
우르르

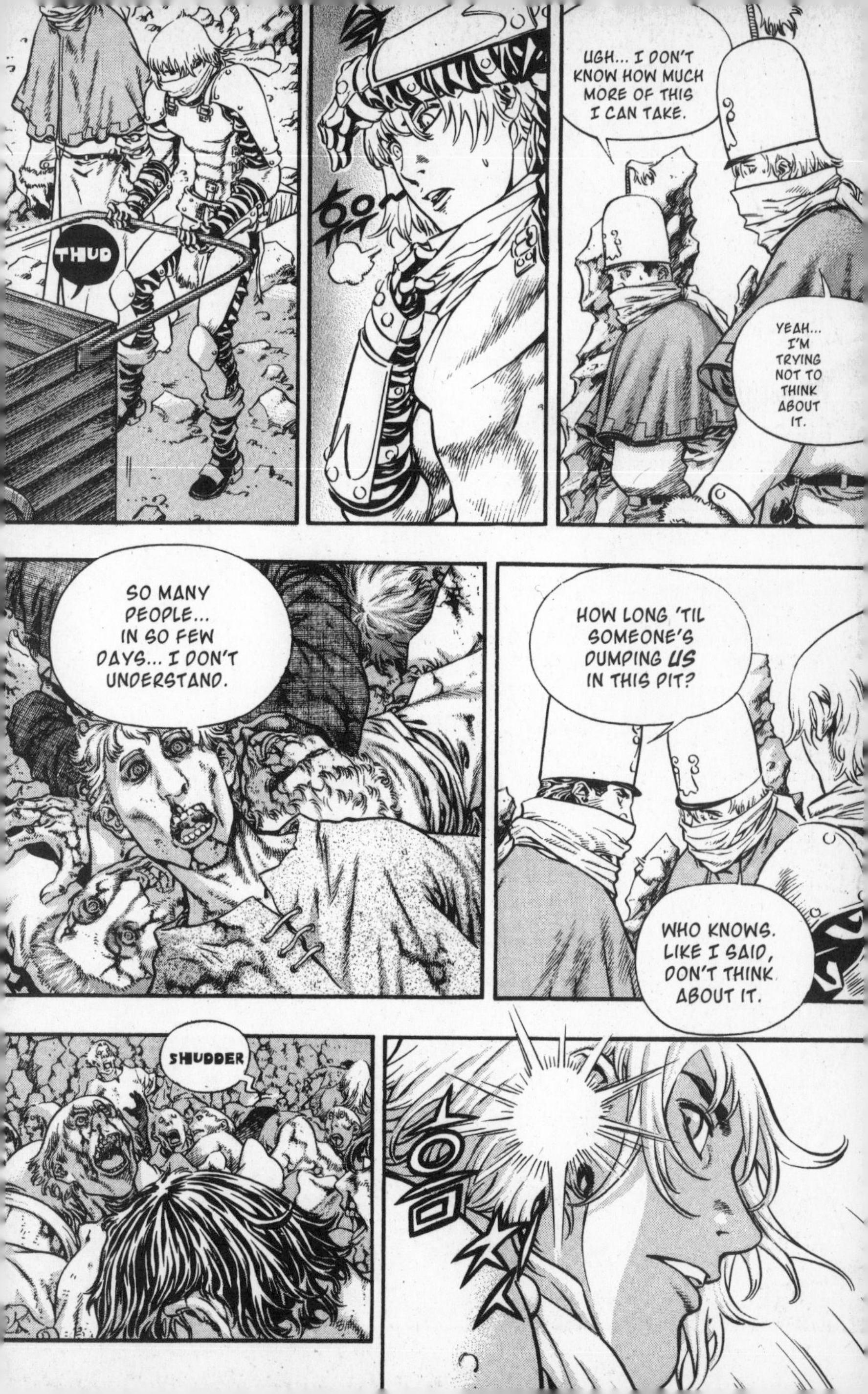
THUD
UGH... I DON'T KNOW HOW MUCH MORE OF THIS I CAN TAKE.
YEAH... I'M TRYING NOT TO THINK ABOUT IT.
SO MANY PEOPLE... IN SO FEW DAYS... I DON'T UNDERSTAND.
HOW LONG 'TIL SOMEONE'S DUMPING US IN THIS PIT?
WHO KNOWS. LIKE I SAID, DON'T THINK ABOUT IT.
SHUDDER

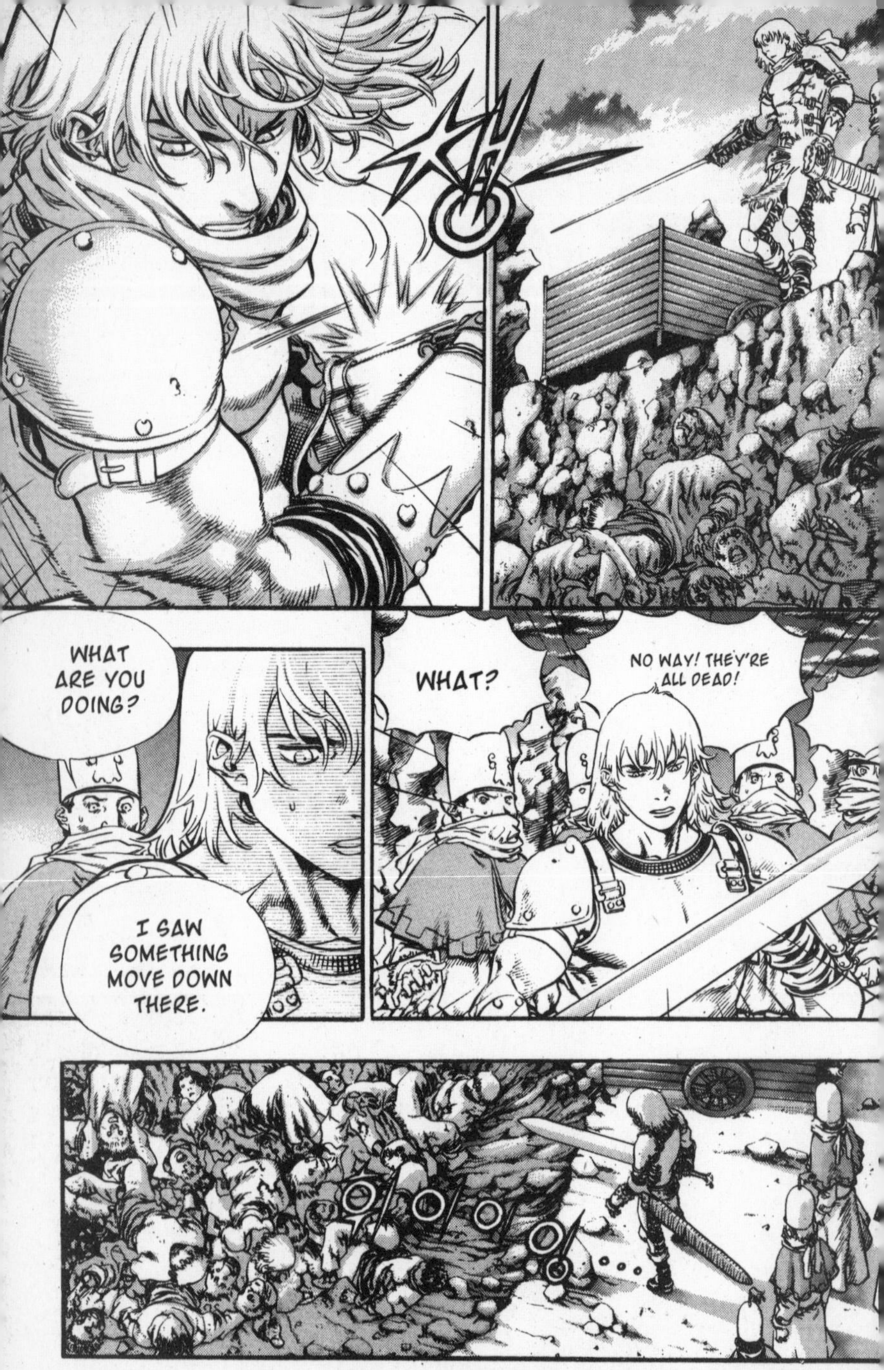
WHAT ARE YOU DOING?
I SAW SOMETHING MOVE DOWN THERE.
WHAT?
NO WAY! THEY'RE ALL DEAD!
...

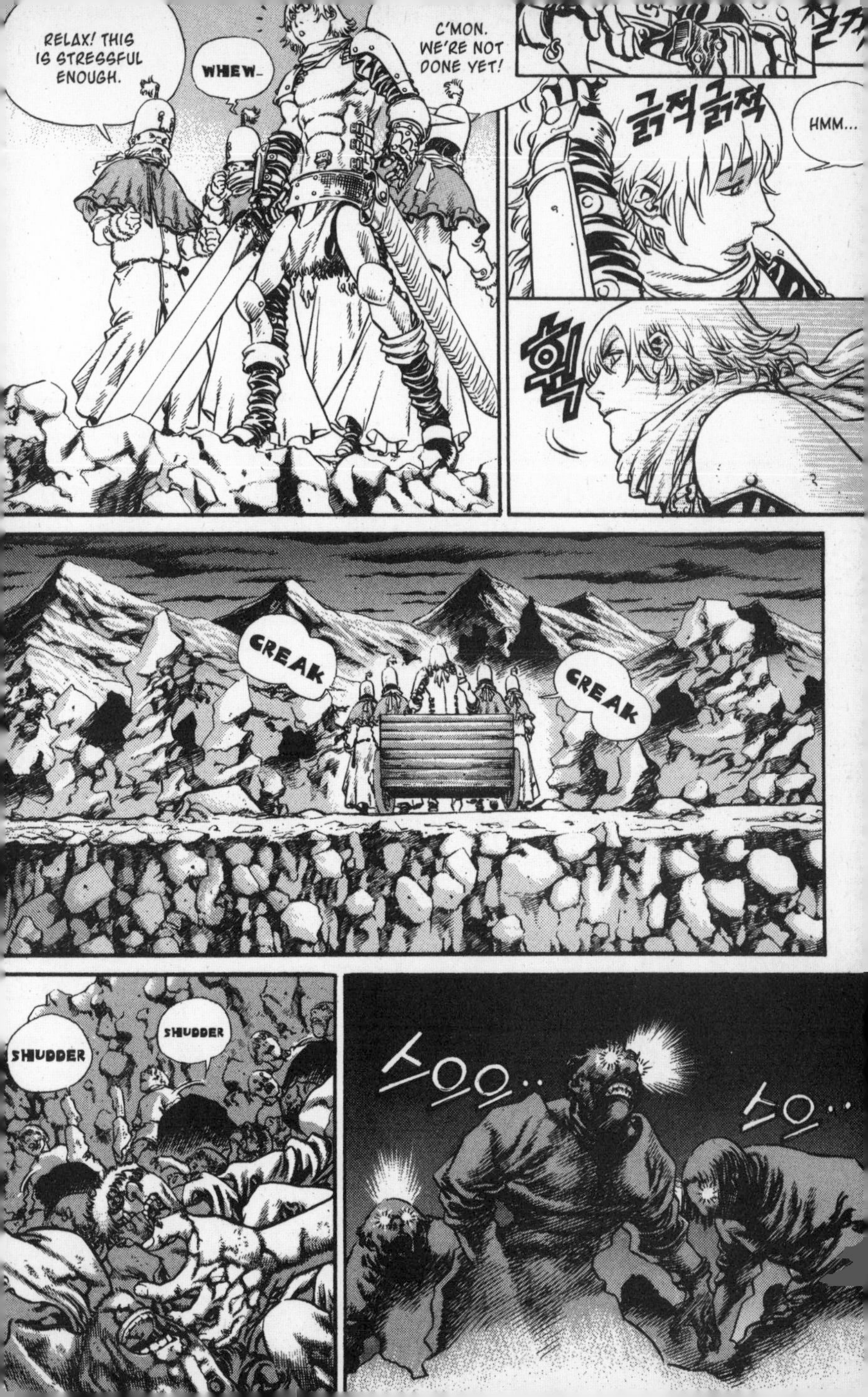
RELAX! THIS IS STRESSFUL ENOUGH.
WHEW_
C'MON. WE'RE NOT DONE YET!
긁적긁적
HMM...
휙
CREAK
CREAK
SHUDDER
SHUDDER
스으으..
스으..

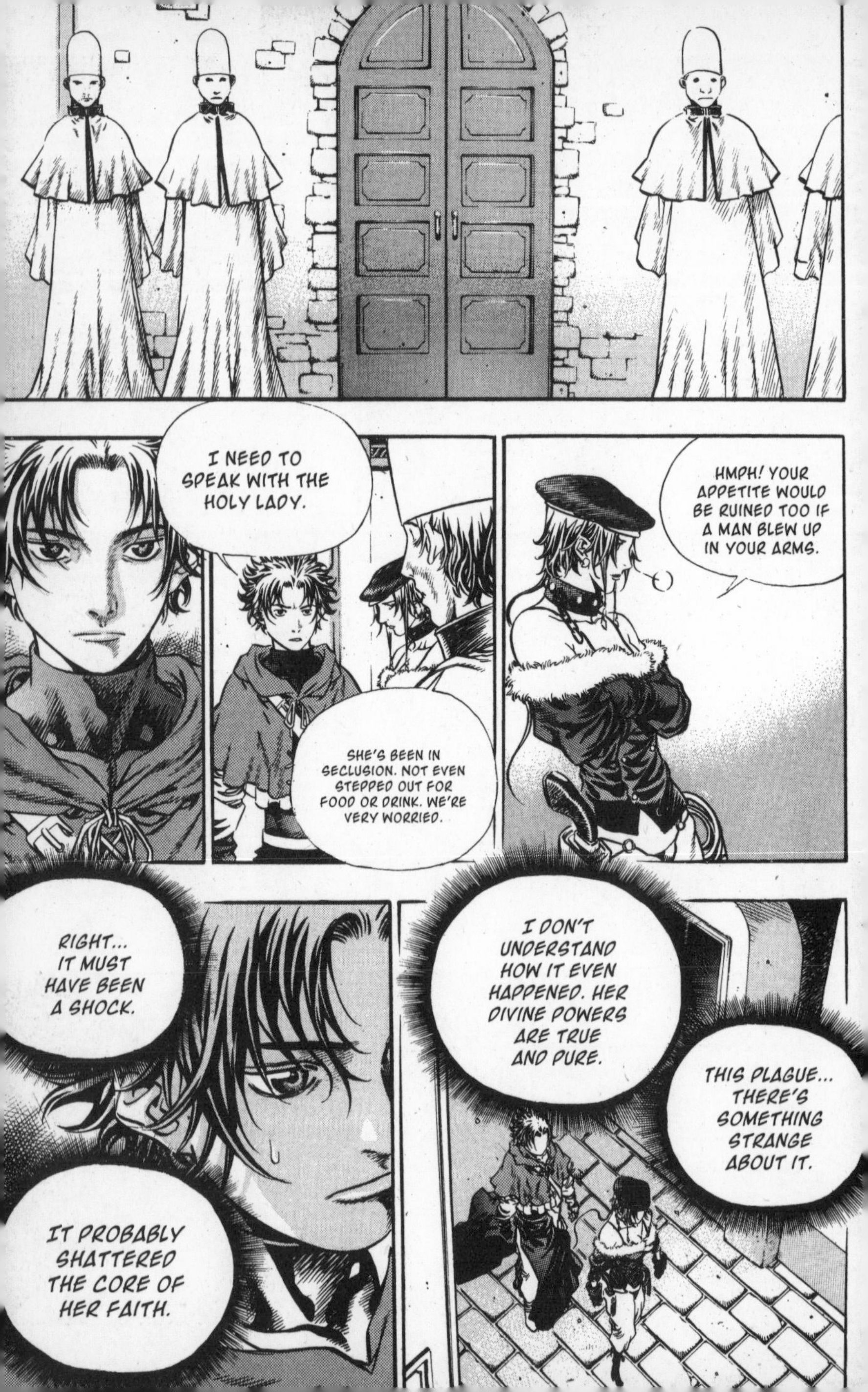
I NEED TO SPEAK WITH THE HOLY LADY.
SHE'S BEEN IN SECLUSION. NOT EVEN STEPPED OUT FOR FOOD OR DRINK. WE'RE VERY WORRIED.
HMPH! YOUR APPETITE WOULD BE RUINED TOO IF A MAN BLEW UP IN YOUR ARMS.
RIGHT... IT MUST HAVE BEEN A SHOCK.
IT PROBABLY SHATTERED THE CORE OF HER FAITH.
I DON'T UNDERSTAND HOW IT EVEN HAPPENED. HER DIVINE POWERS ARE TRUE AND PURE.
THIS PLAGUE... THERE'S SOMETHING STRANGE ABOUT IT.

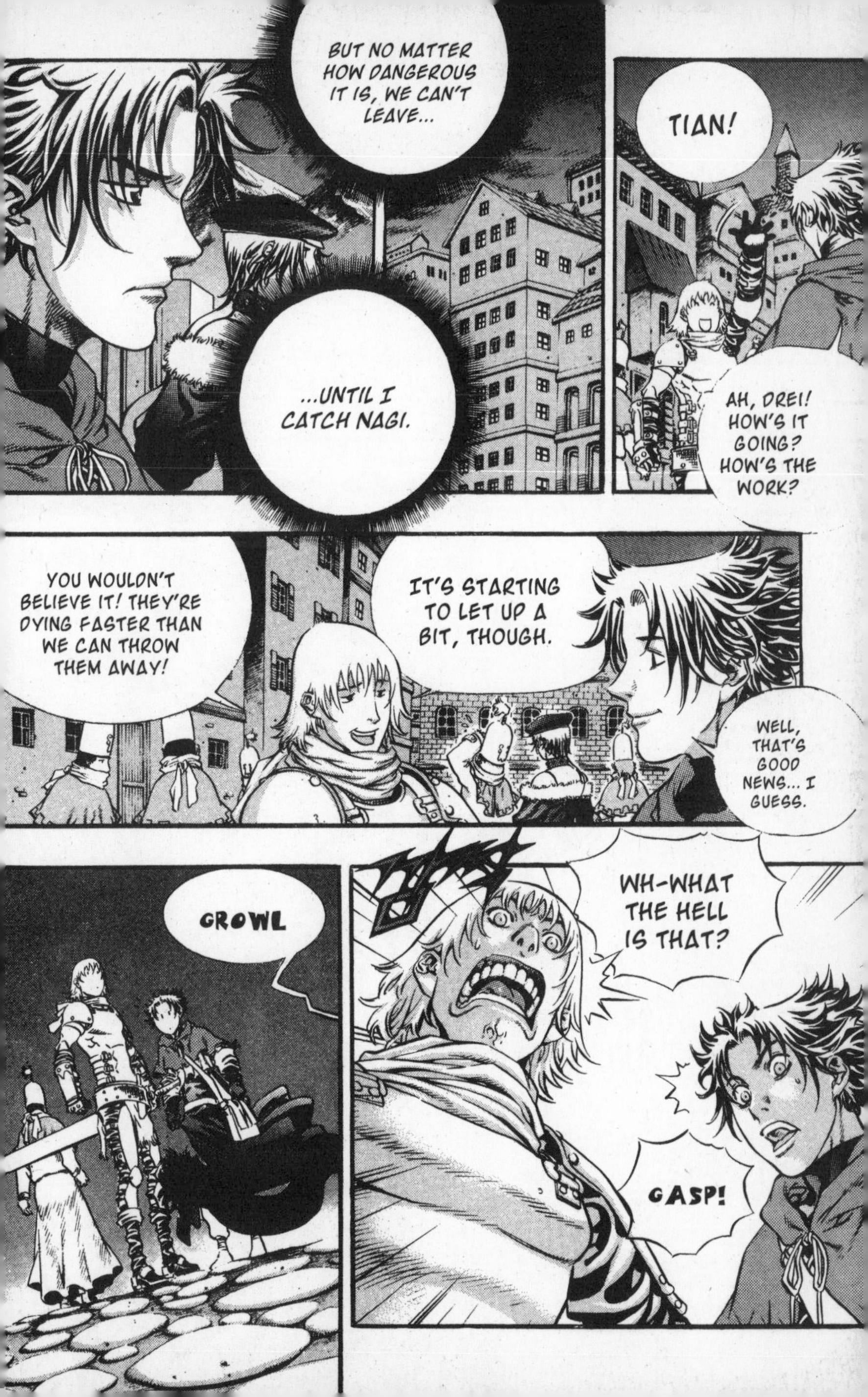
BUT NO MATTER HOW DANGEROUS IT IS, WE CAN'T LEAVE...
...UNTIL I CATCH NAGI.
TIAN!
AH, DREI! HOW'S IT GOING? HOW'S THE WORK?
YOU WOULDN'T BELIEVE IT! THEY'RE DYING FASTER THAN WE CAN THROW THEM AWAY!
IT'S STARTING TO LET UP A BIT, THOUGH.
WELL, THAT'S GOOD NEWS... I GUESS.
GROWL
WH-WHAT THE HELL IS THAT?
GASP!

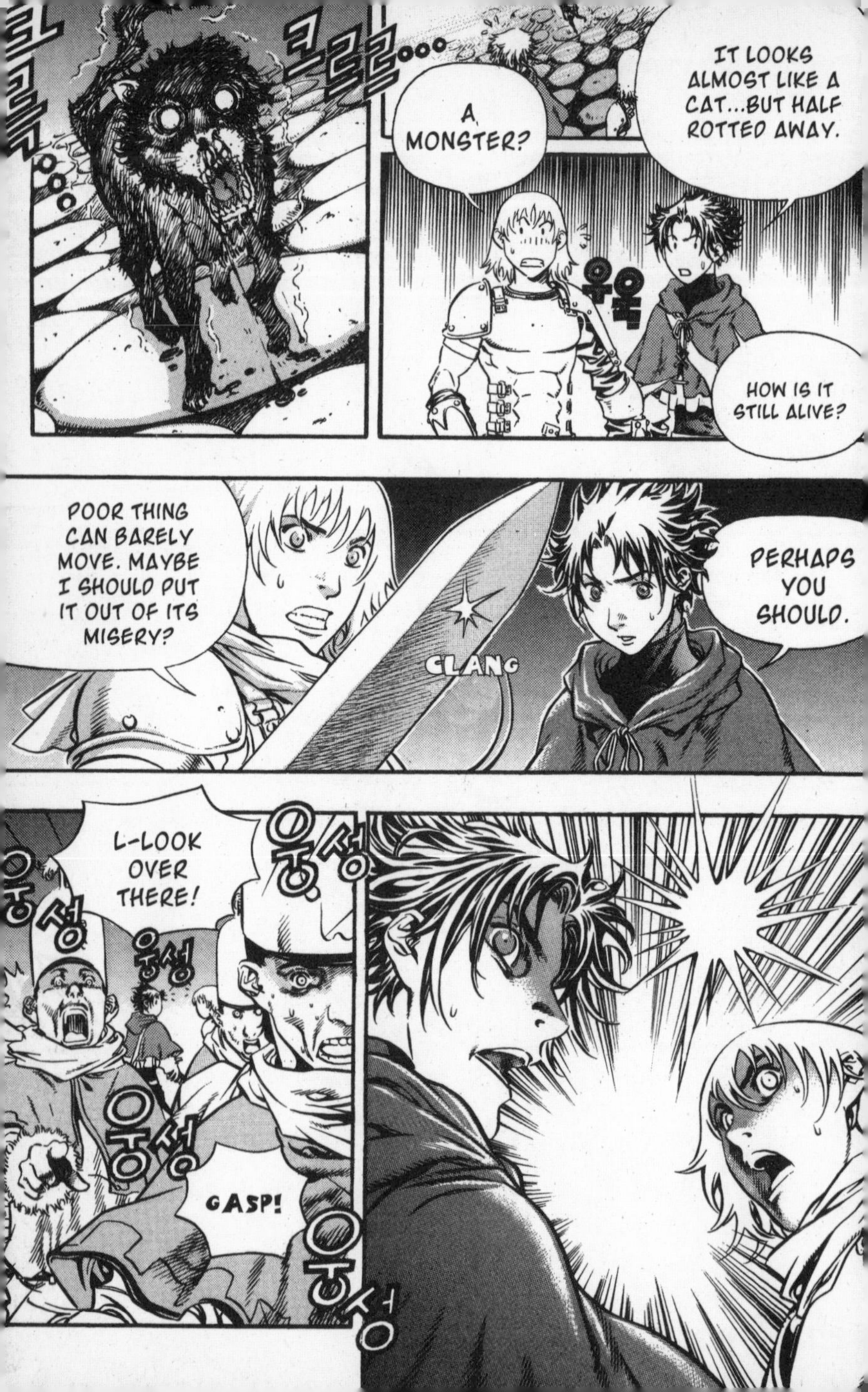
A MONSTER?
IT LOOKS ALMOST LIKE A CAT...BUT HALF ROTTED AWAY.
웅웅
HOW IS IT STILL ALIVE?
POOR THING CAN BARELY MOVE. MAYBE I SHOULD PUT IT OUT OF ITS MISERY?
CLANG
PERHAPS YOU SHOULD.
L-LOOK OVER THERE!
웅성
웅성
GASP!

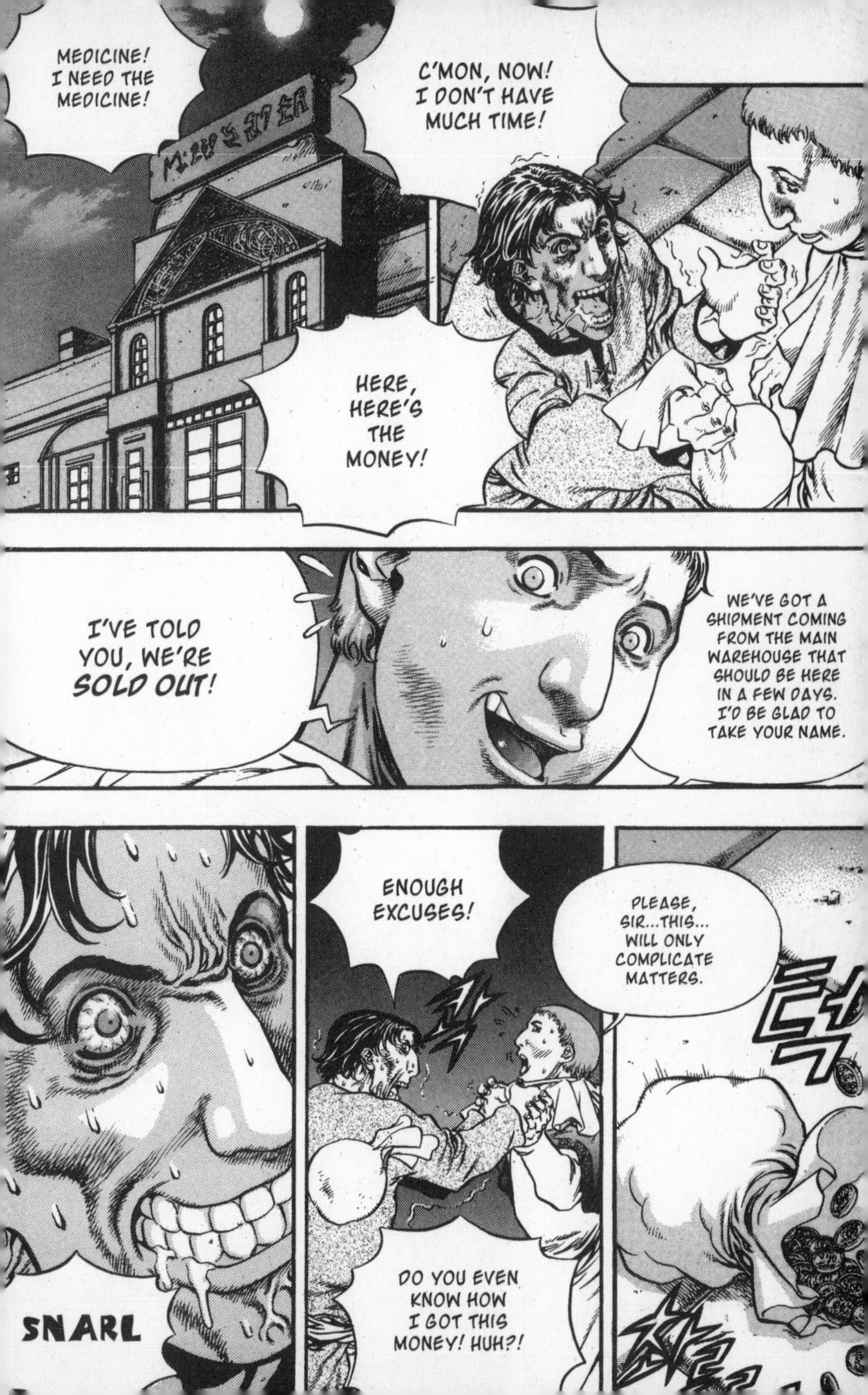
MEDICINE! I NEED THE MEDICINE!
C'MON, NOW! I DON'T HAVE MUCH TIME!
HERE, HERE'S THE MONEY!
I'VE TOLD YOU, WE'RE SOLD OUT!
WE'VE GOT A SHIPMENT COMING FROM THE MAIN WAREHOUSE THAT SHOULD BE HERE IN A FEW DAYS. I'D BE GLAD TO TAKE YOUR NAME.
SNARL
ENOUGH EXCUSES!
DO YOU EVEN KNOW HOW I GOT THIS MONEY! HUH?!
PLEASE, SIR...THIS... WILL ONLY COMPLICATE MATTERS.

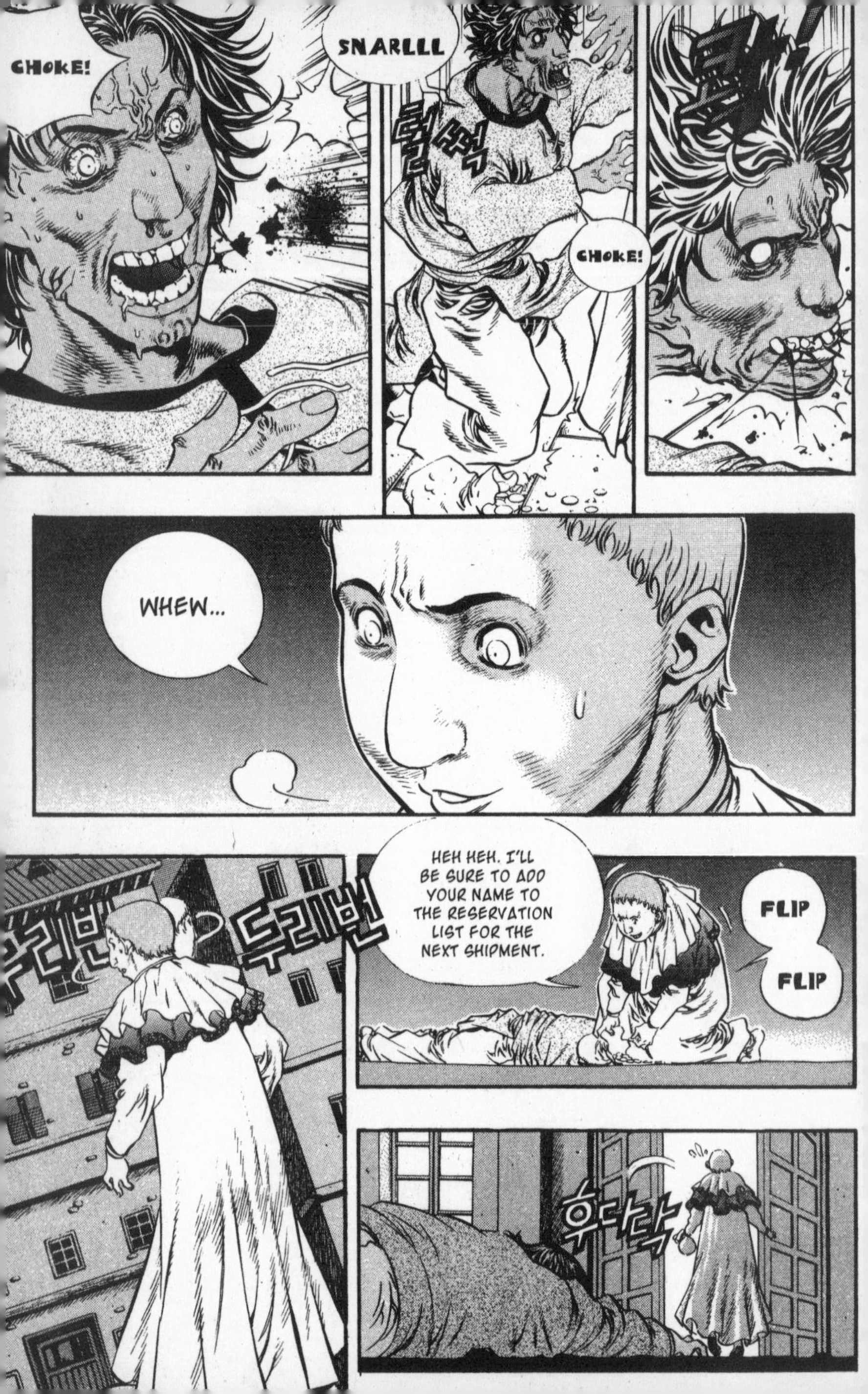
CHOKE!
SNARLLL
CHOKE!
WHEW...
두리번
두리번
HEH HEH. I'LL BE SURE TO ADD YOUR NAME TO THE RESERVATION LIST FOR THE NEXT SHIPMENT.
FLIP
FLIP
후다닥

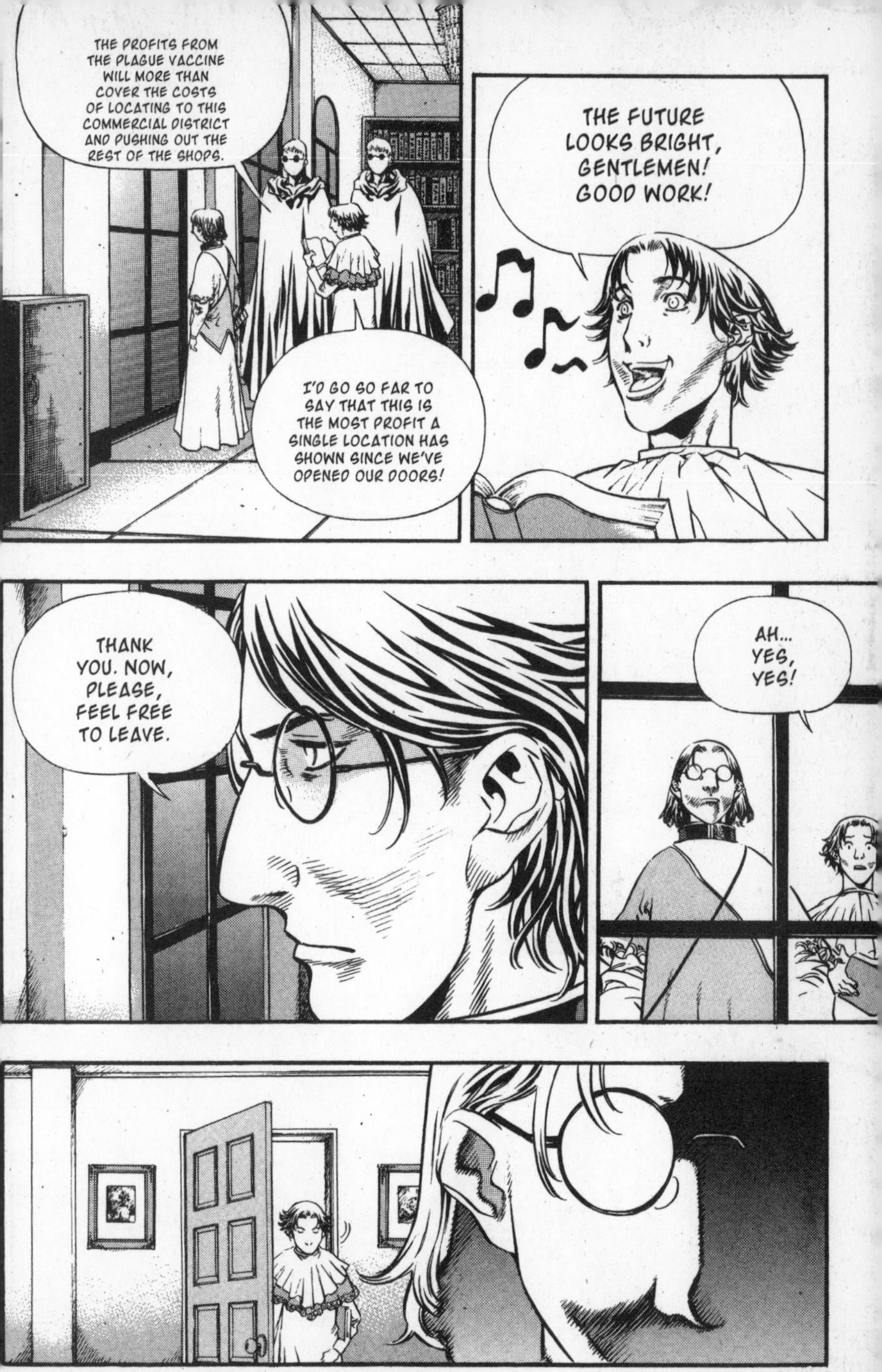
THE PROFITS FROM THE PLAGUE VACCINE WILL MORE THAN COVER THE COSTS OF LOCATING TO THIS COMMERCIAL DISTRICT AND PUSHING OUT THE REST OF THE SHOPS.
I'D GO SO FAR TO SAY THAT THIS IS THE MOST PROFIT A SINGLE LOCATION HAS SHOWN SINCE WE'VE OPENED OUR DOORS!
THE FUTURE LOOKS BRIGHT, GENTLEMEN! GOOD WORK!
THANK YOU. NOW, PLEASE, FEEL FREE TO LEAVE.
AH... YES, YES!

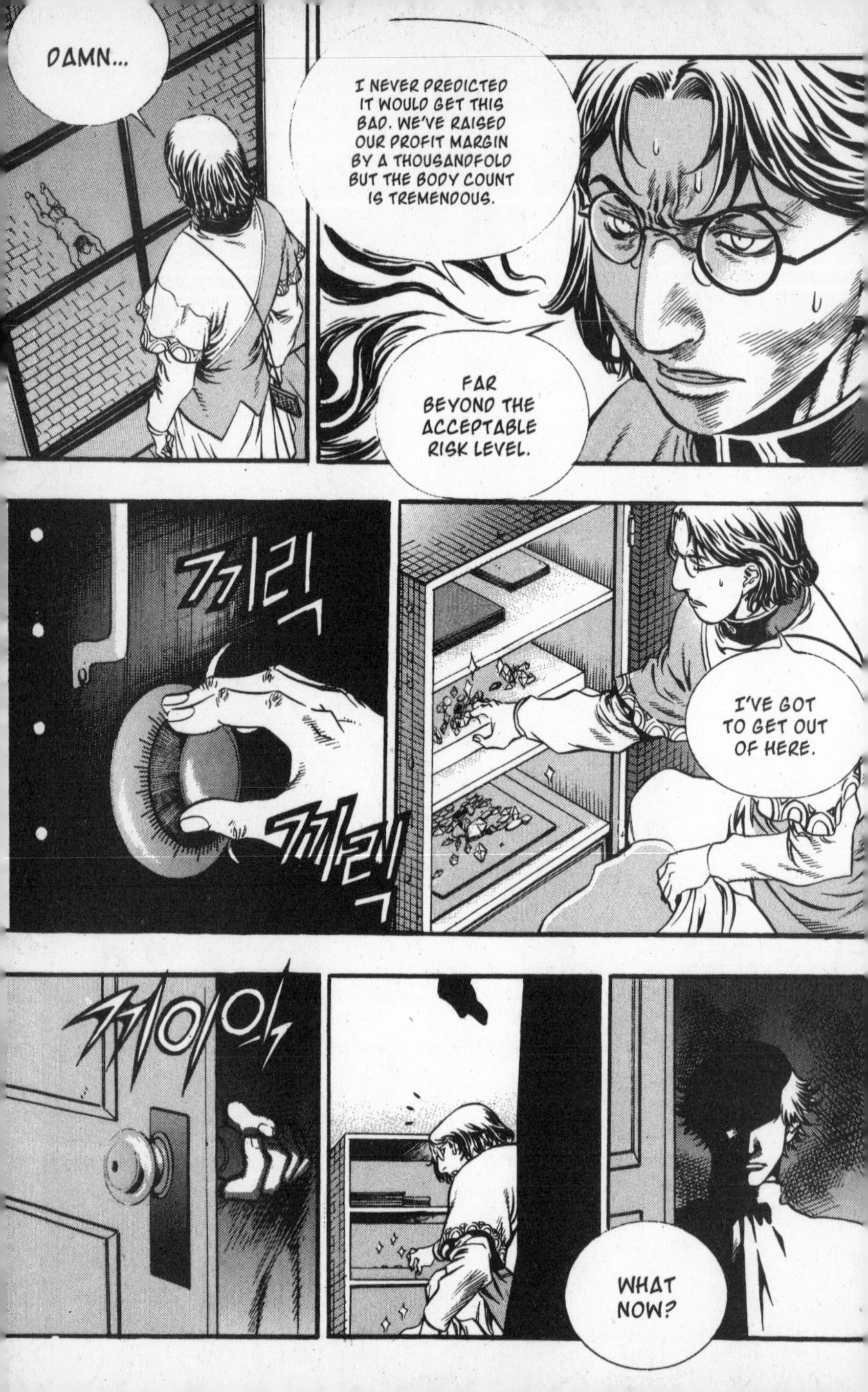
DAMN...
I NEVER PREDICTED IT WOULD GET THIS BAD. WE'VE RAISED OUR PROFIT MARGIN BY A THOUSANDFOLD BUT THE BODY COUNT IS TREMENDOUS.
FAR BEYOND THE ACCEPTABLE RISK LEVEL.
I'VE GOT TO GET OUT OF HERE.
WHAT NOW?

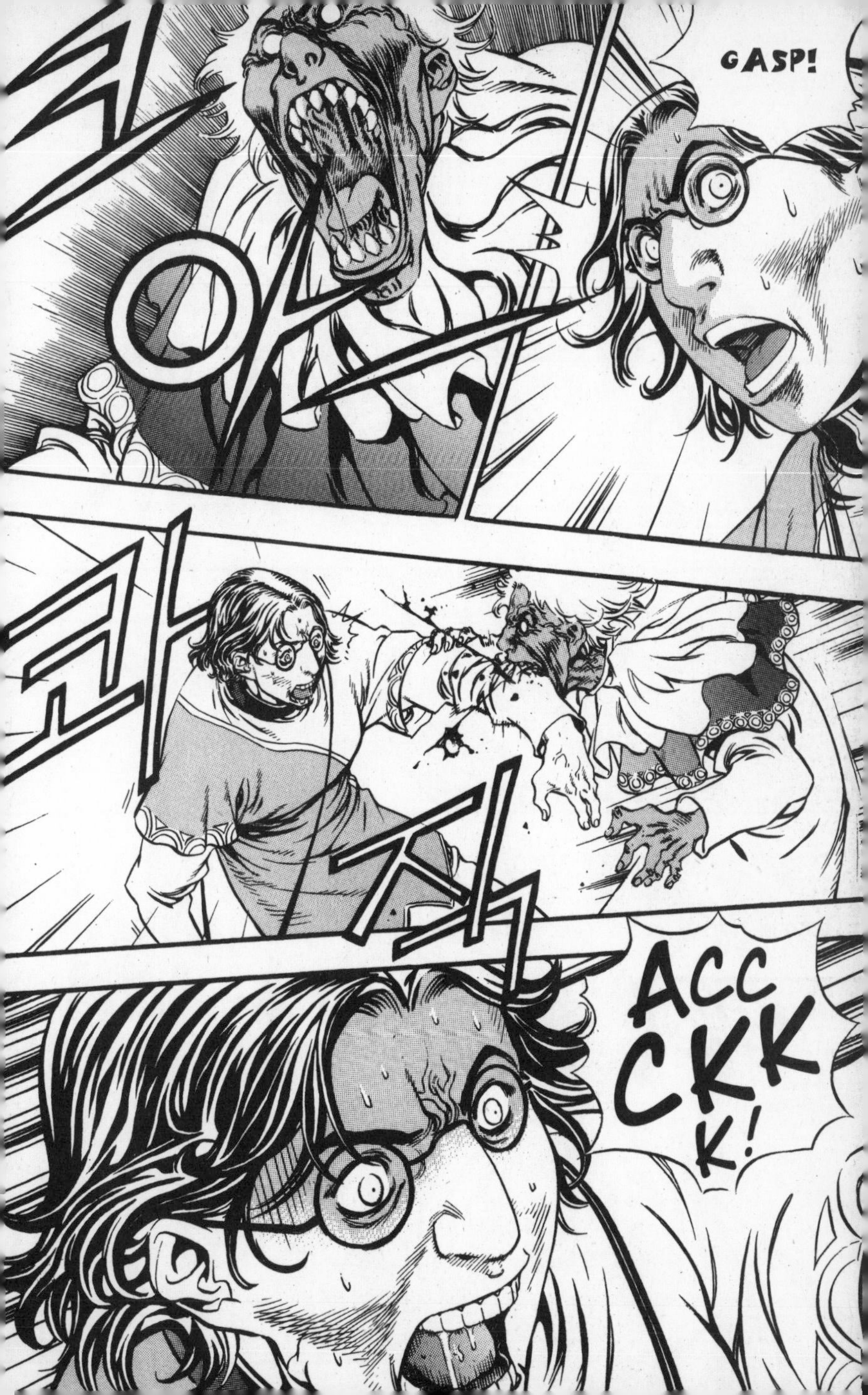
GASP!
ACC CKK K!

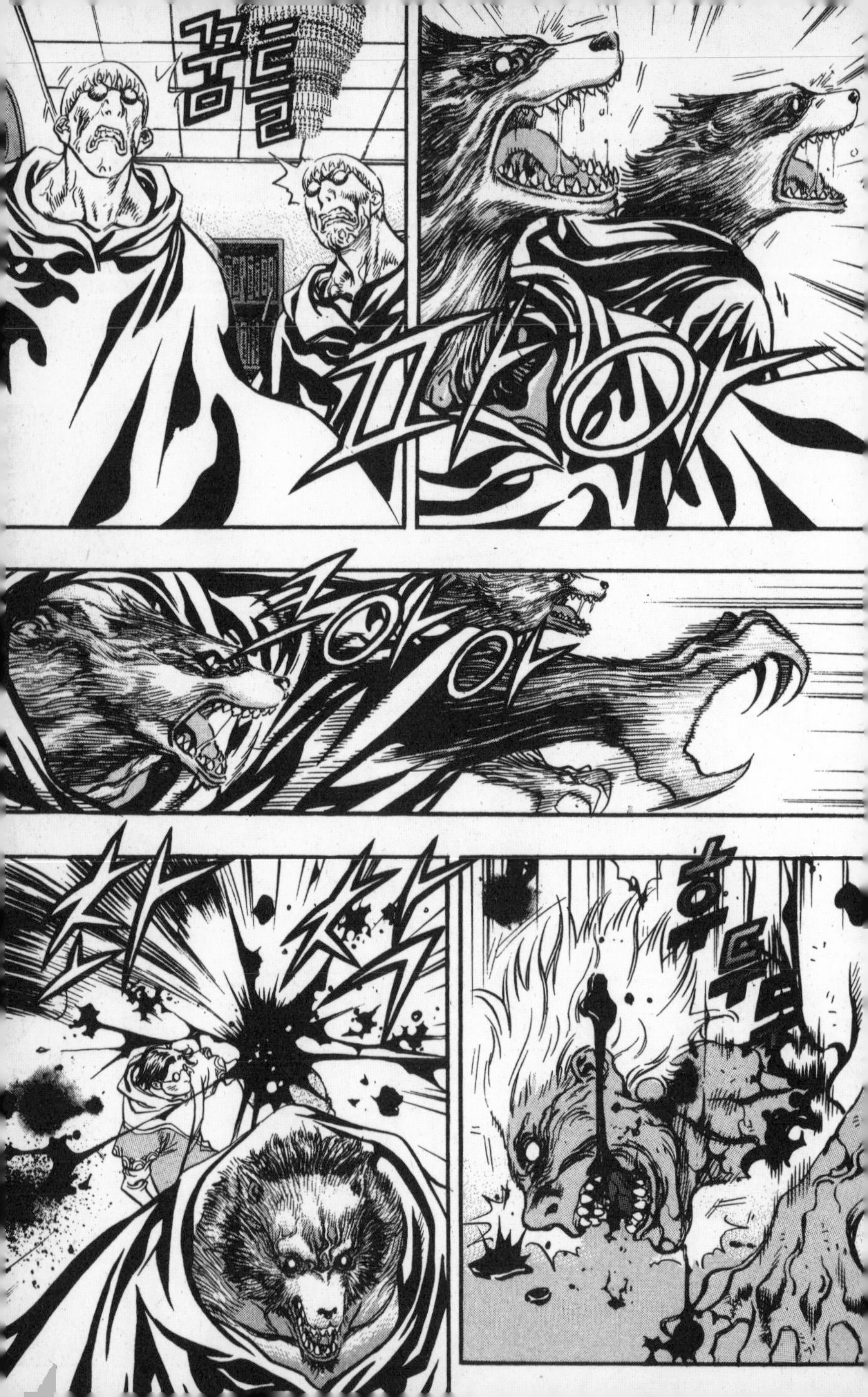
꿈틀
파앗

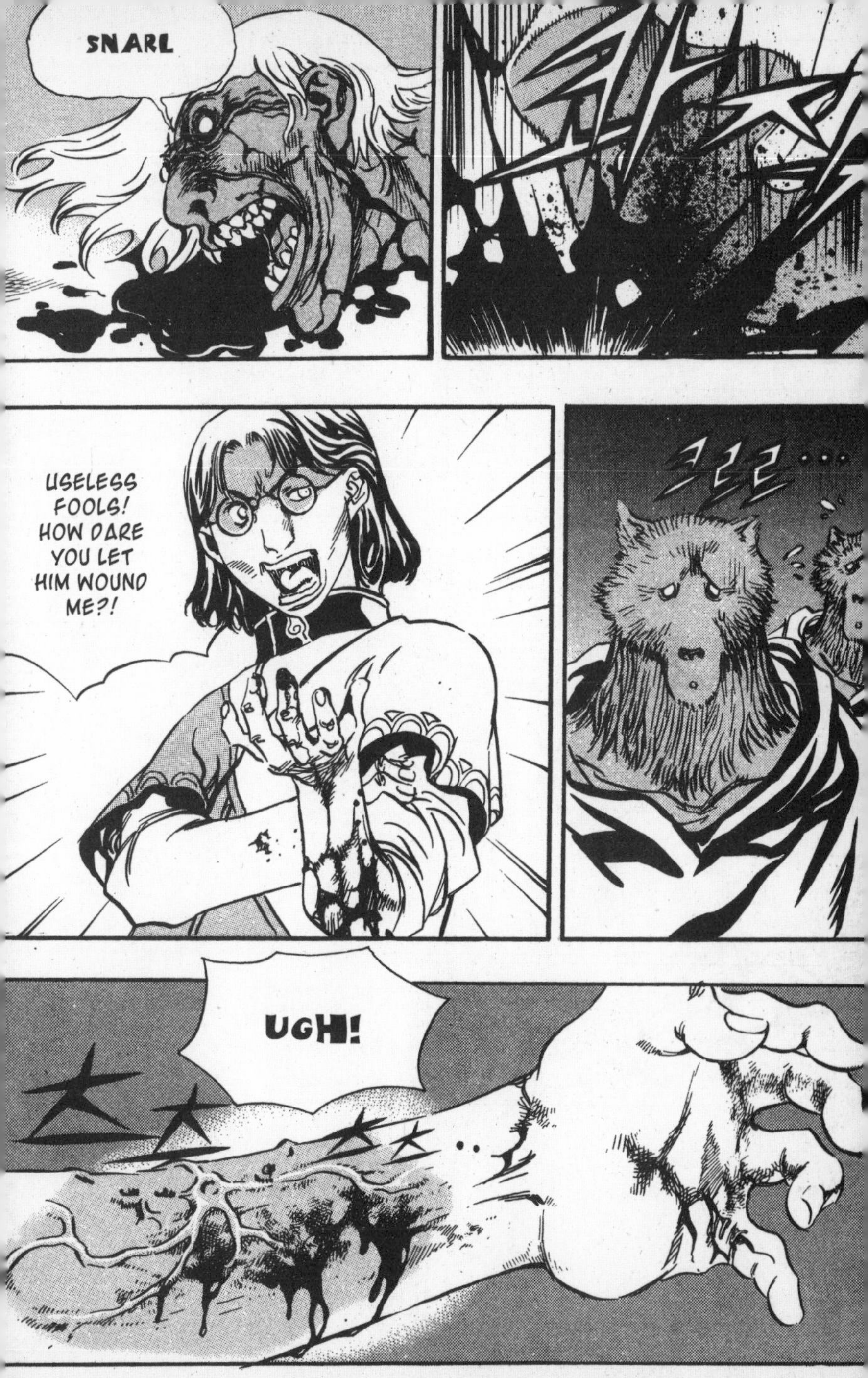

SNARL
USELESS FOOLS! HOW DARE YOU LET HIM WOUND ME?!
UGH!

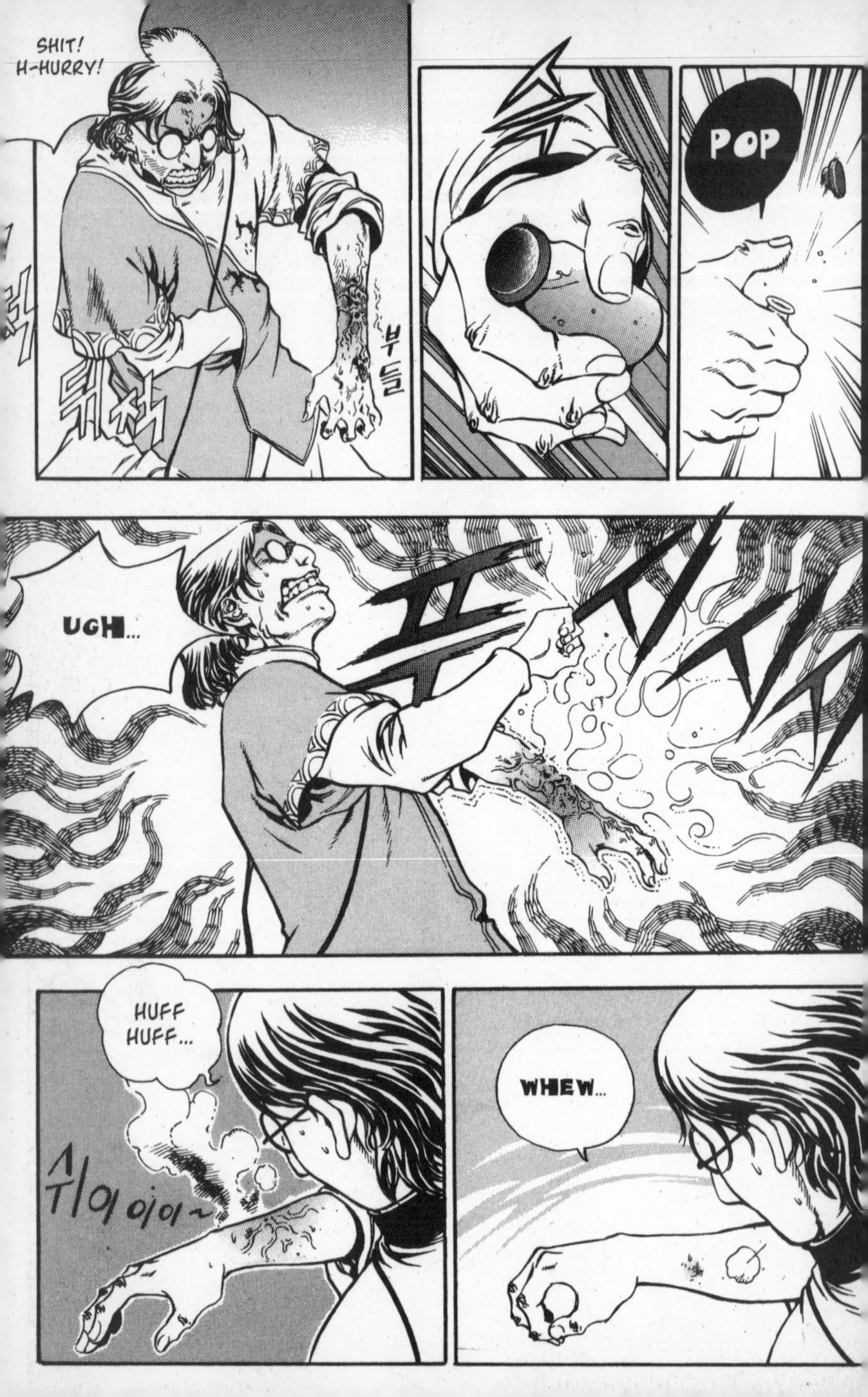
SHIT!
H-HURRY!
부들
POP
UGH...
HUFF
HUFF...
WHEW...

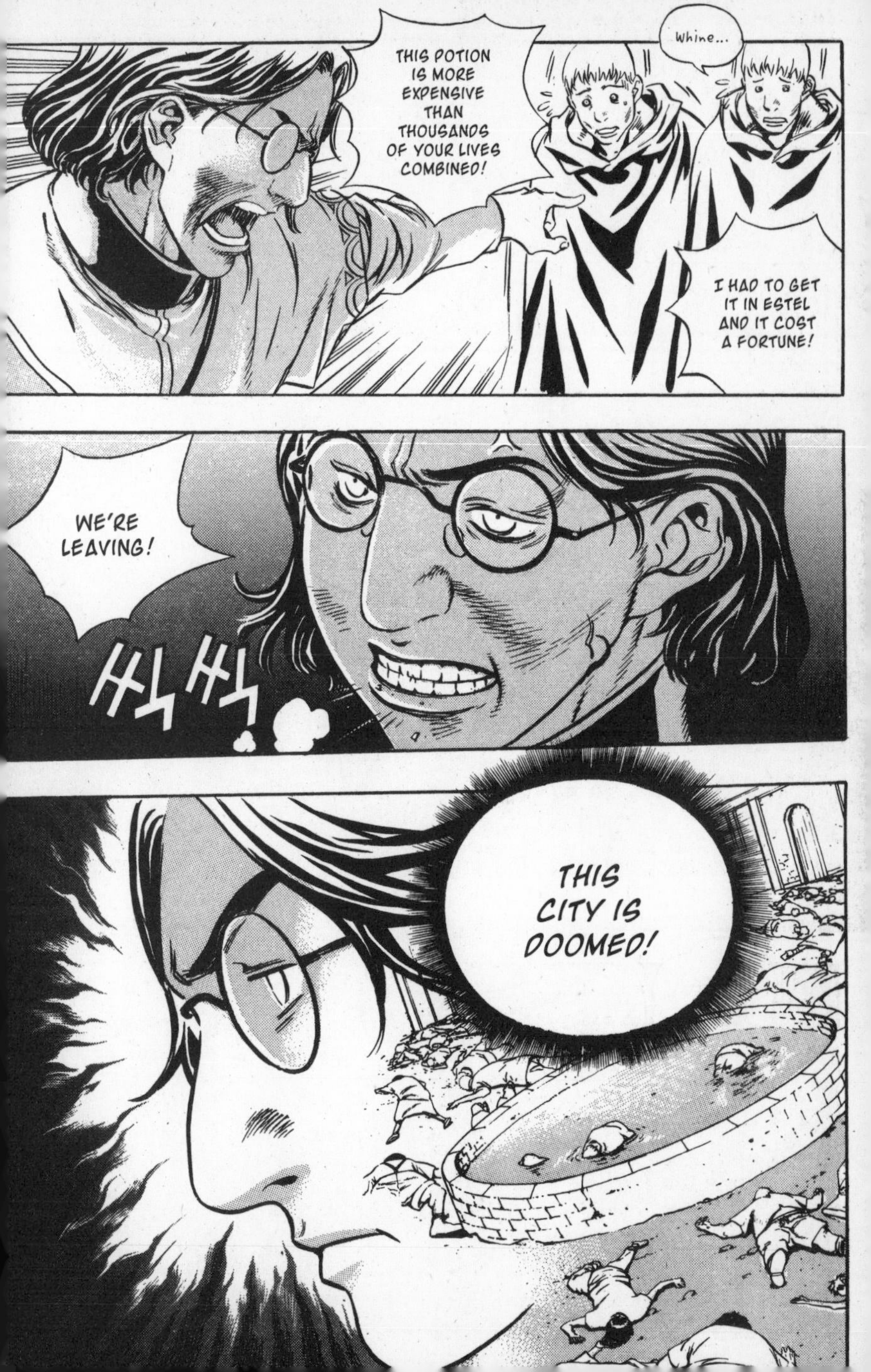
THIS POTION IS MORE EXPENSIVE THAN THOUSANDS OF YOUR LIVES COMBINED!
Whine...
I HAD TO GET IT IN ESTEL AND IT COST A FORTUNE!
WE'RE LEAVING!
THIS CITY IS DOOMED!

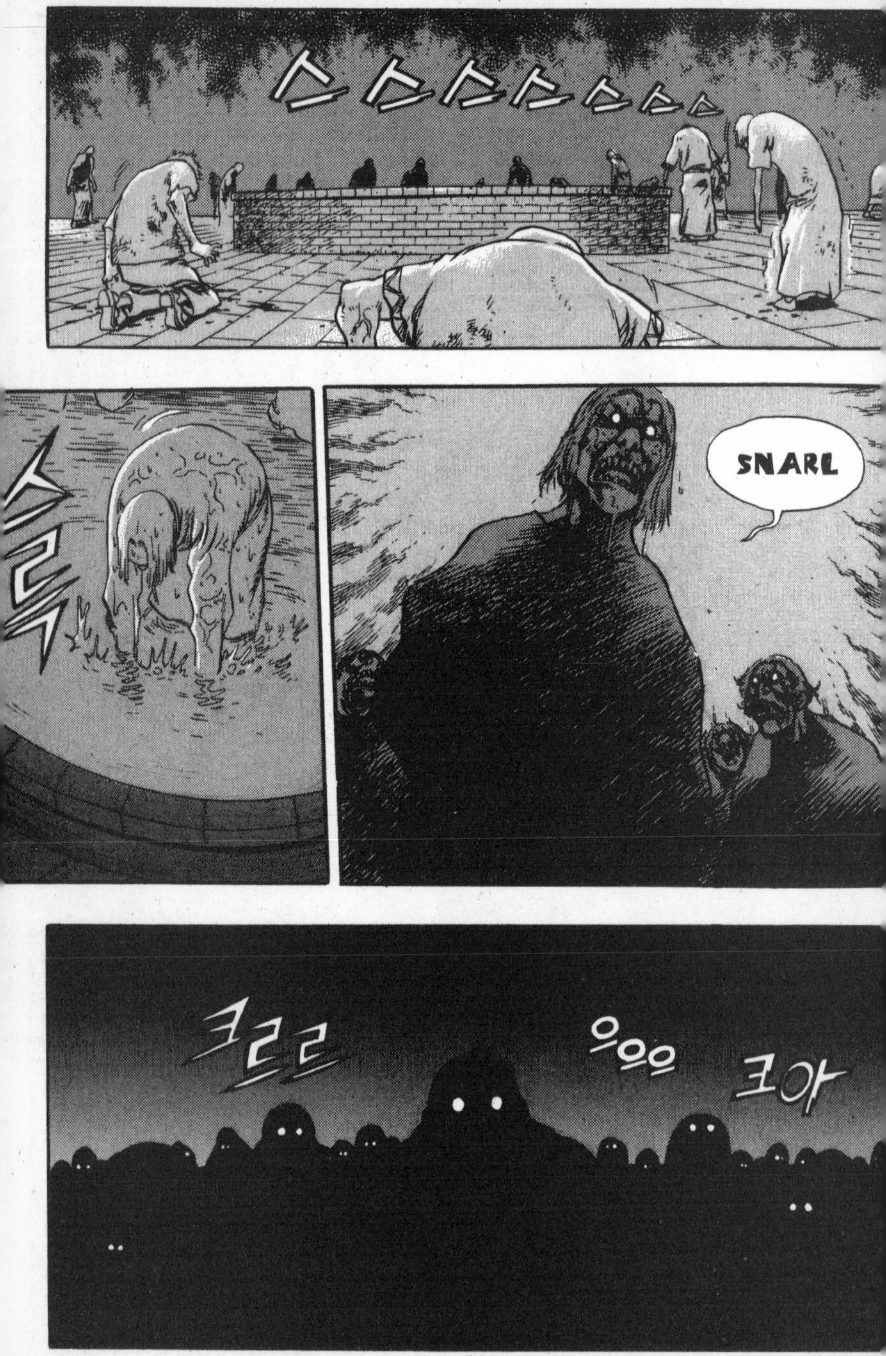
SNARL
크르르
으으으
크아

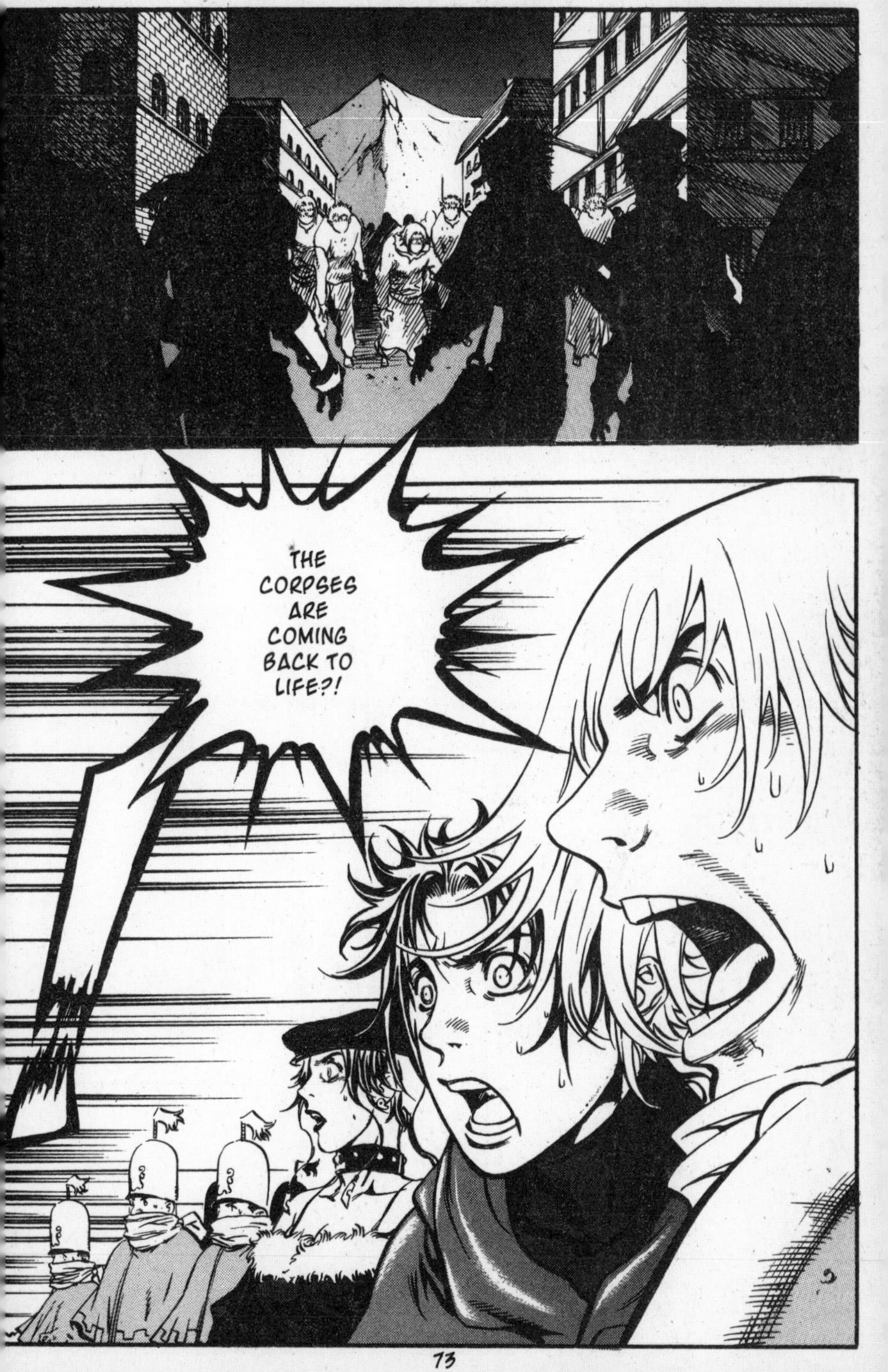
THE CORPSES ARE COMING BACK TO LIFE?!

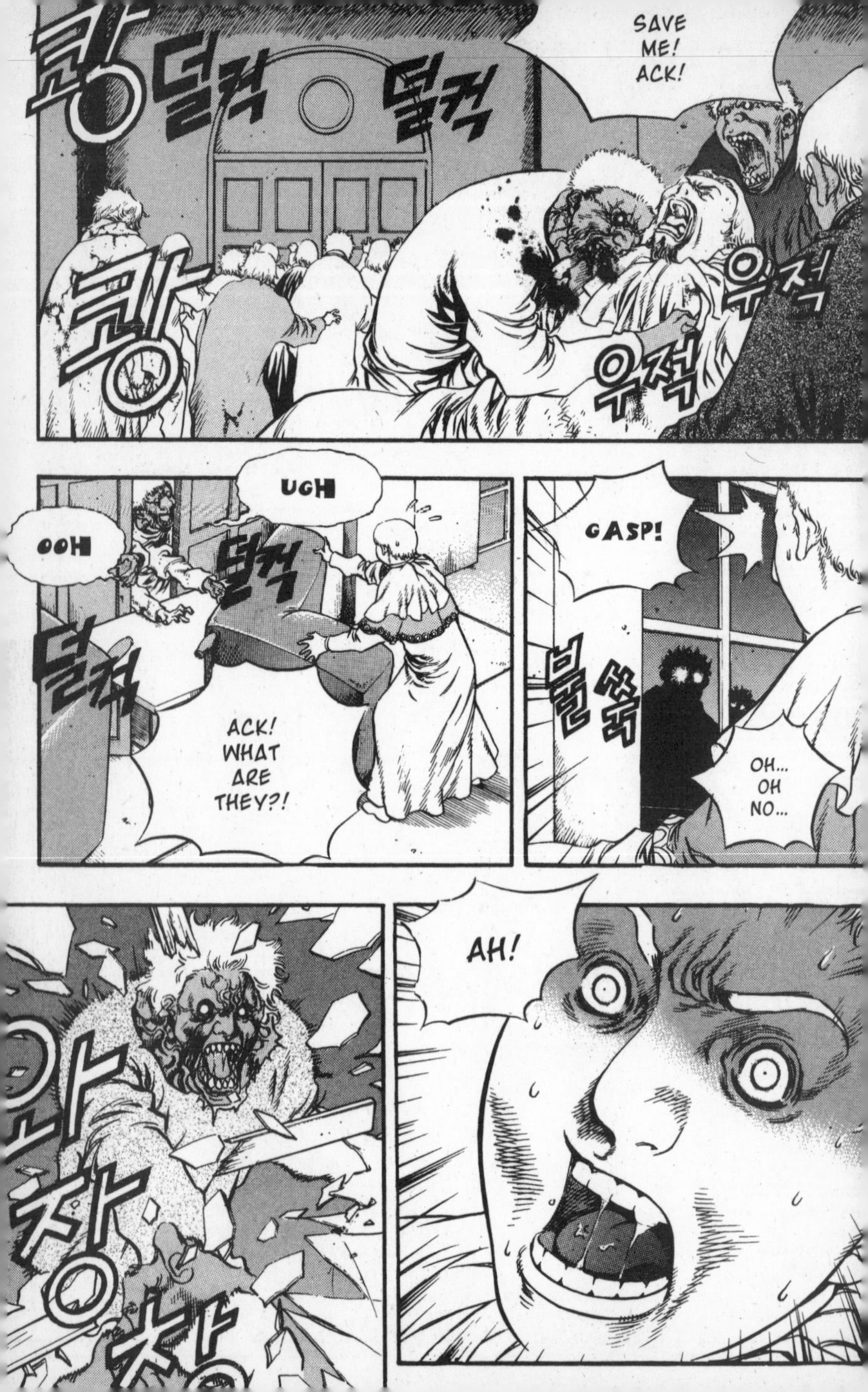
쿵
덜컥 덜컥
SAVE ME! ACK!
쾅
우적 우적
UGH
OOH
덜컥 덜컥
ACK! WHAT ARE THEY?!
GASP!
불쑥
OH... OH NO...
AH!

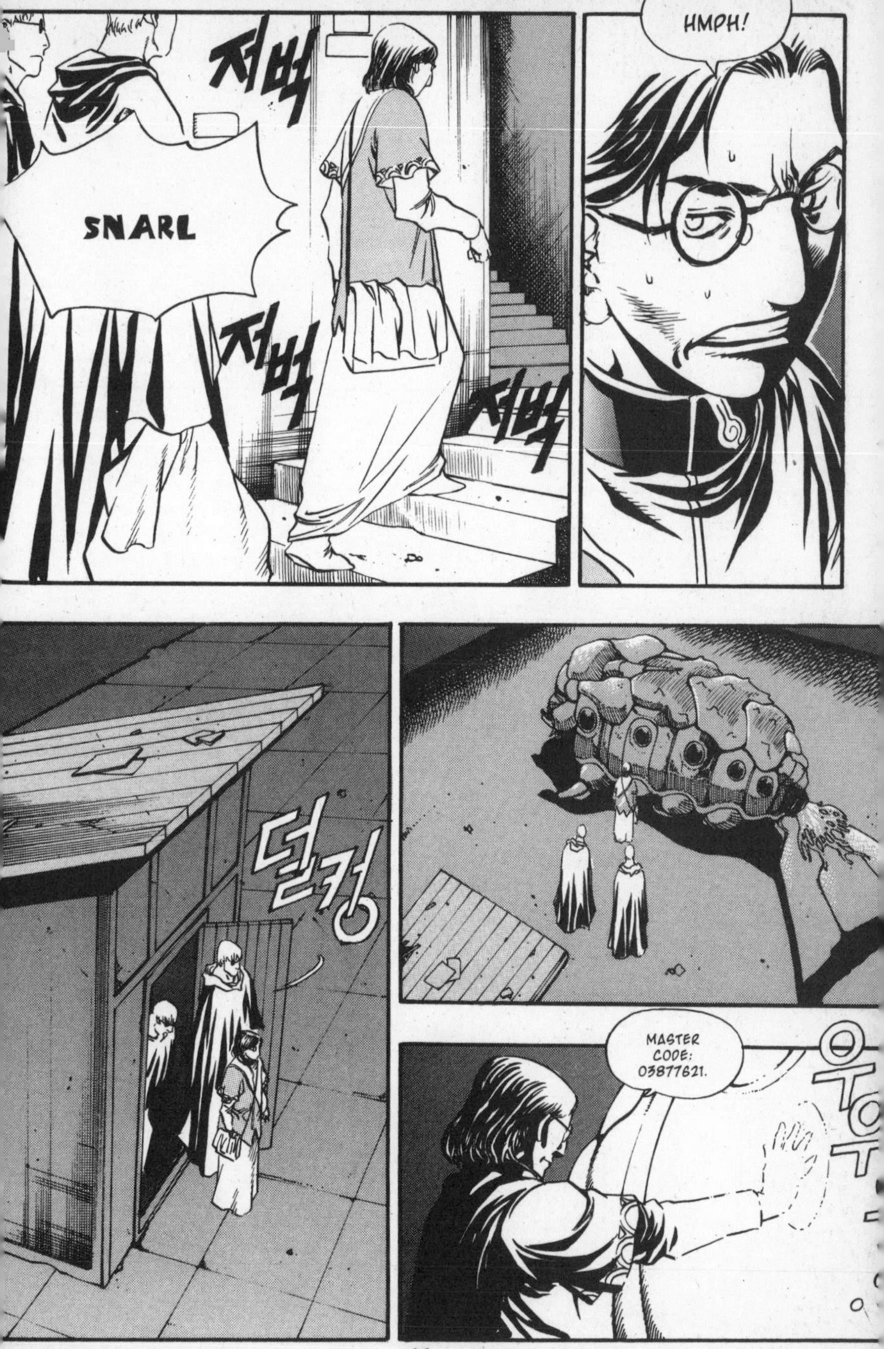
저벅
SNARL
저벅
저벅
HMPH!
덜컹
MASTER CODE: 03877621.

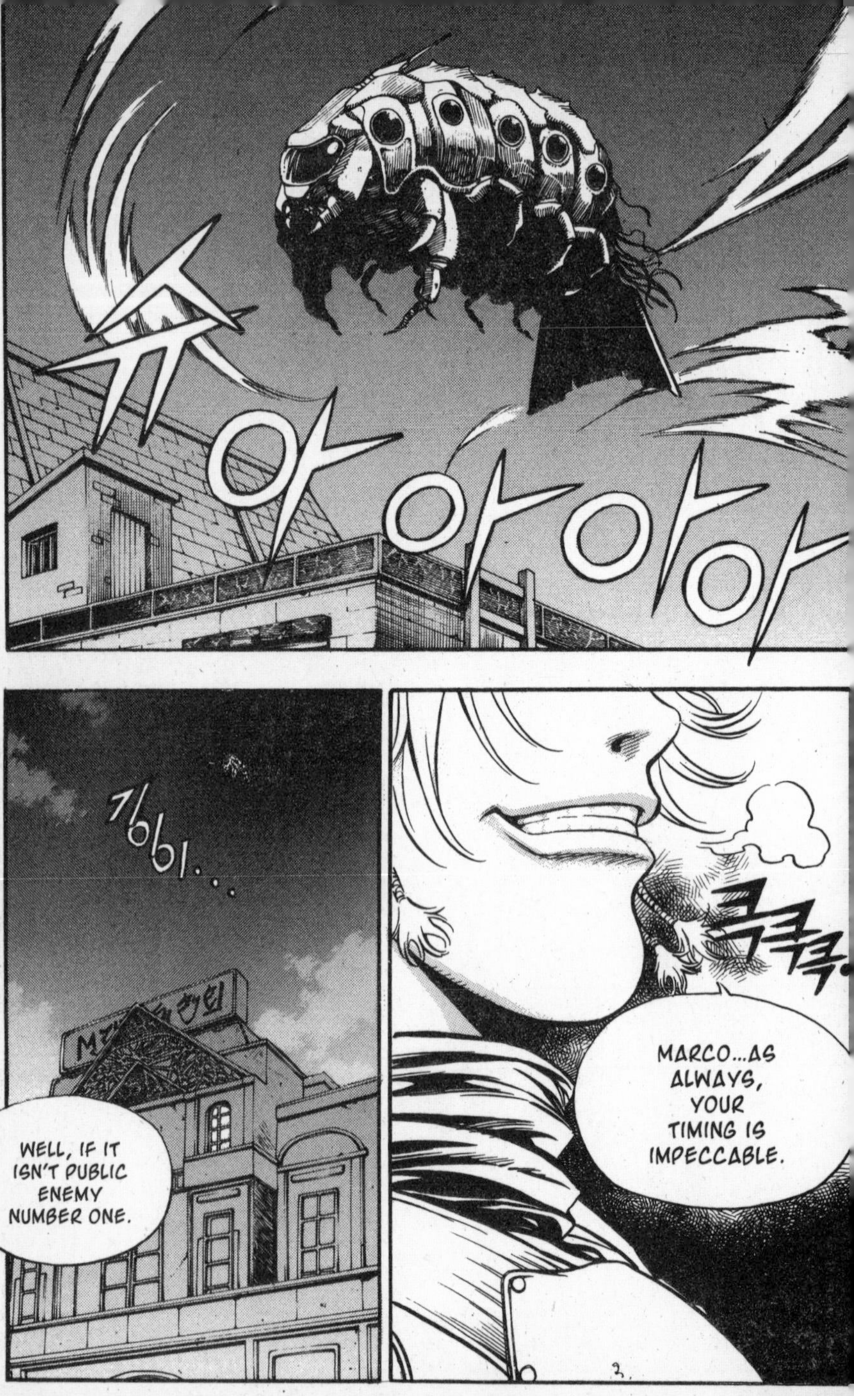
WELL, IF IT ISN'T PUBLIC ENEMY NUMBER ONE.
MARCO...AS ALWAYS, YOUR TIMING IS IMPECCABLE.

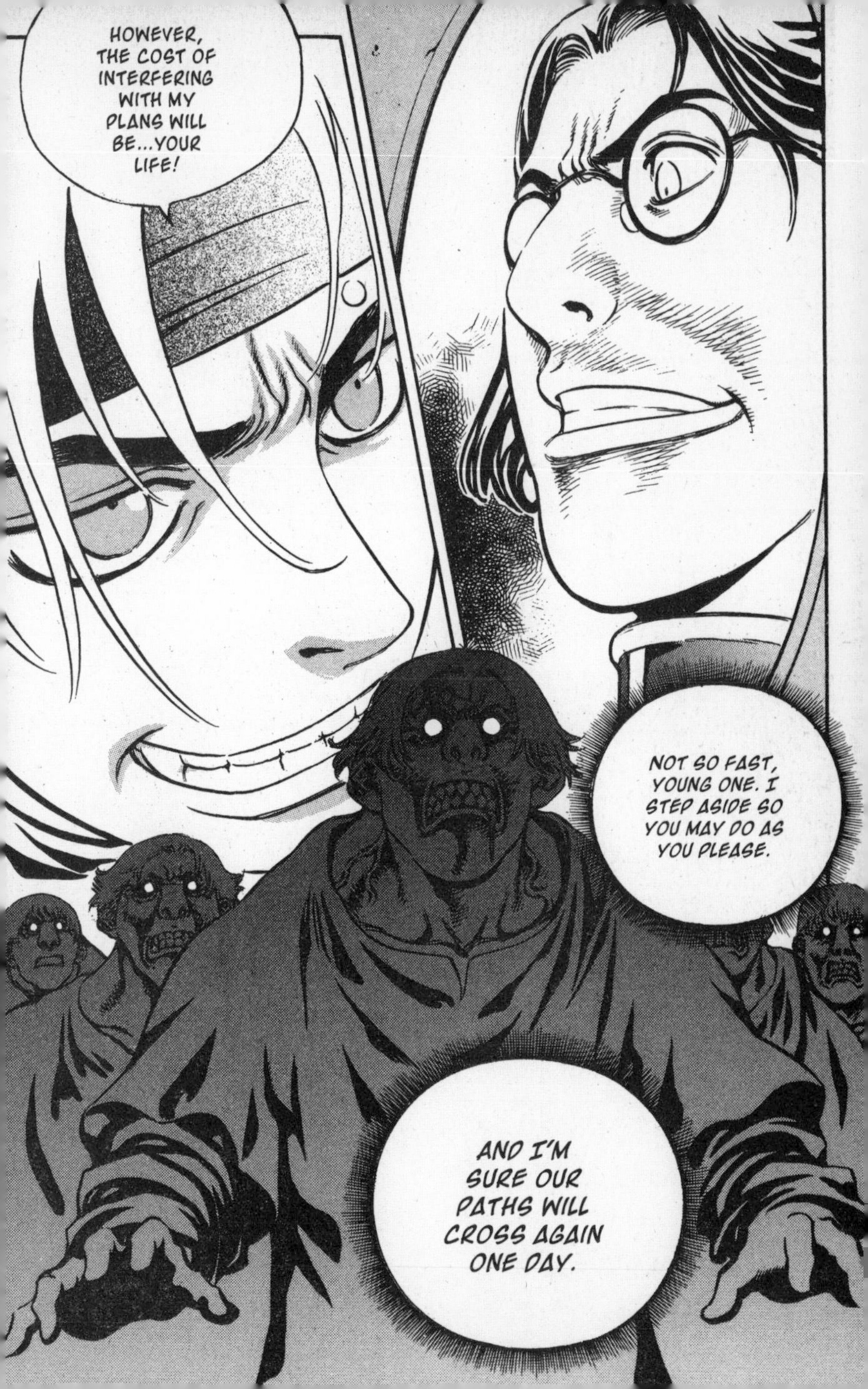
HOWEVER, THE COST OF INTERFERING WITH MY PLANS WILL BE...YOUR LIFE!
NOT SO FAST, YOUNG ONE. I STEP ASIDE SO YOU MAY DO AS YOU PLEASE.
AND I'M SURE OUR PATHS WILL CROSS AGAIN ONE DAY.

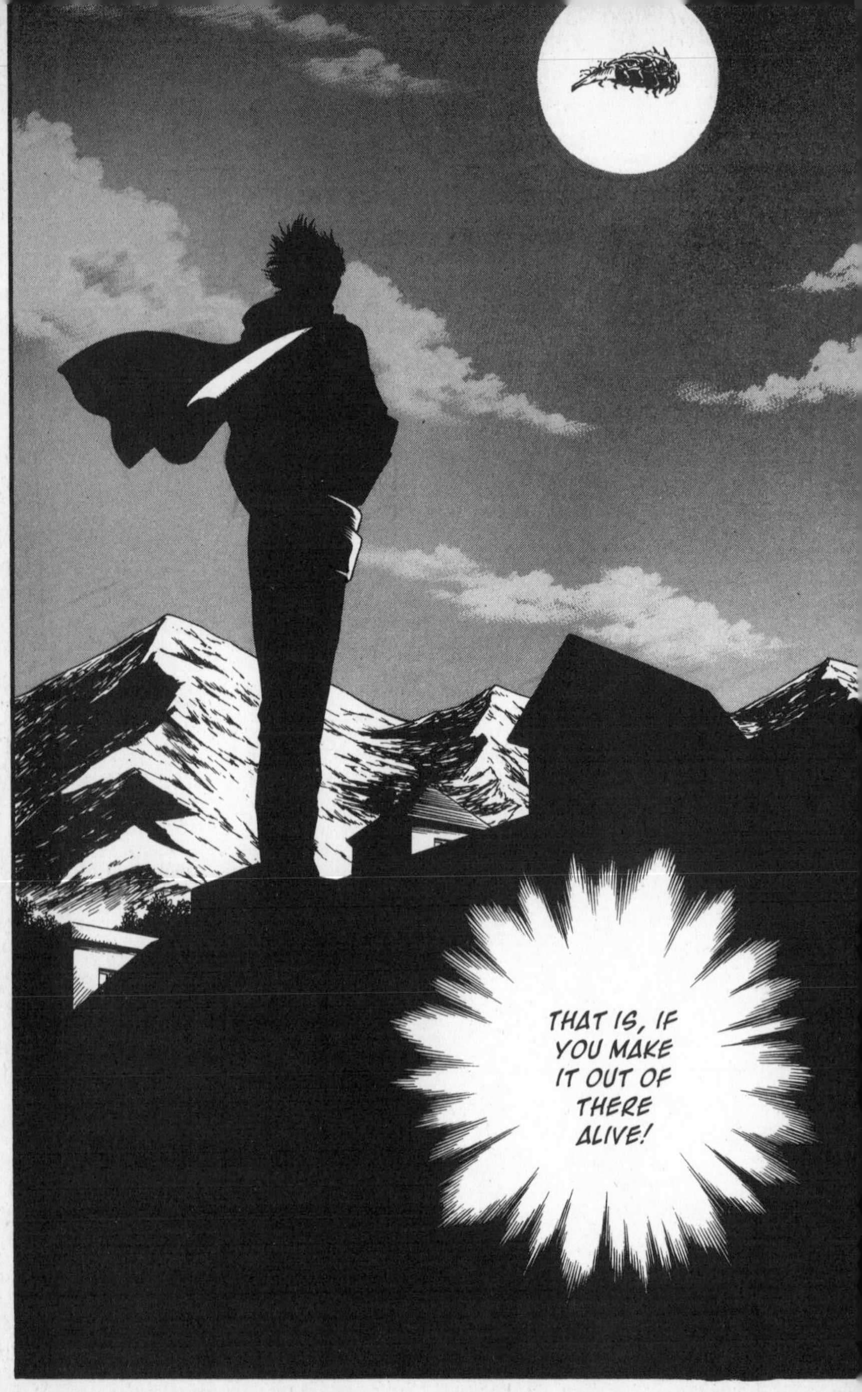
THAT IS, IF YOU MAKE IT OUT OF THERE ALIVE!

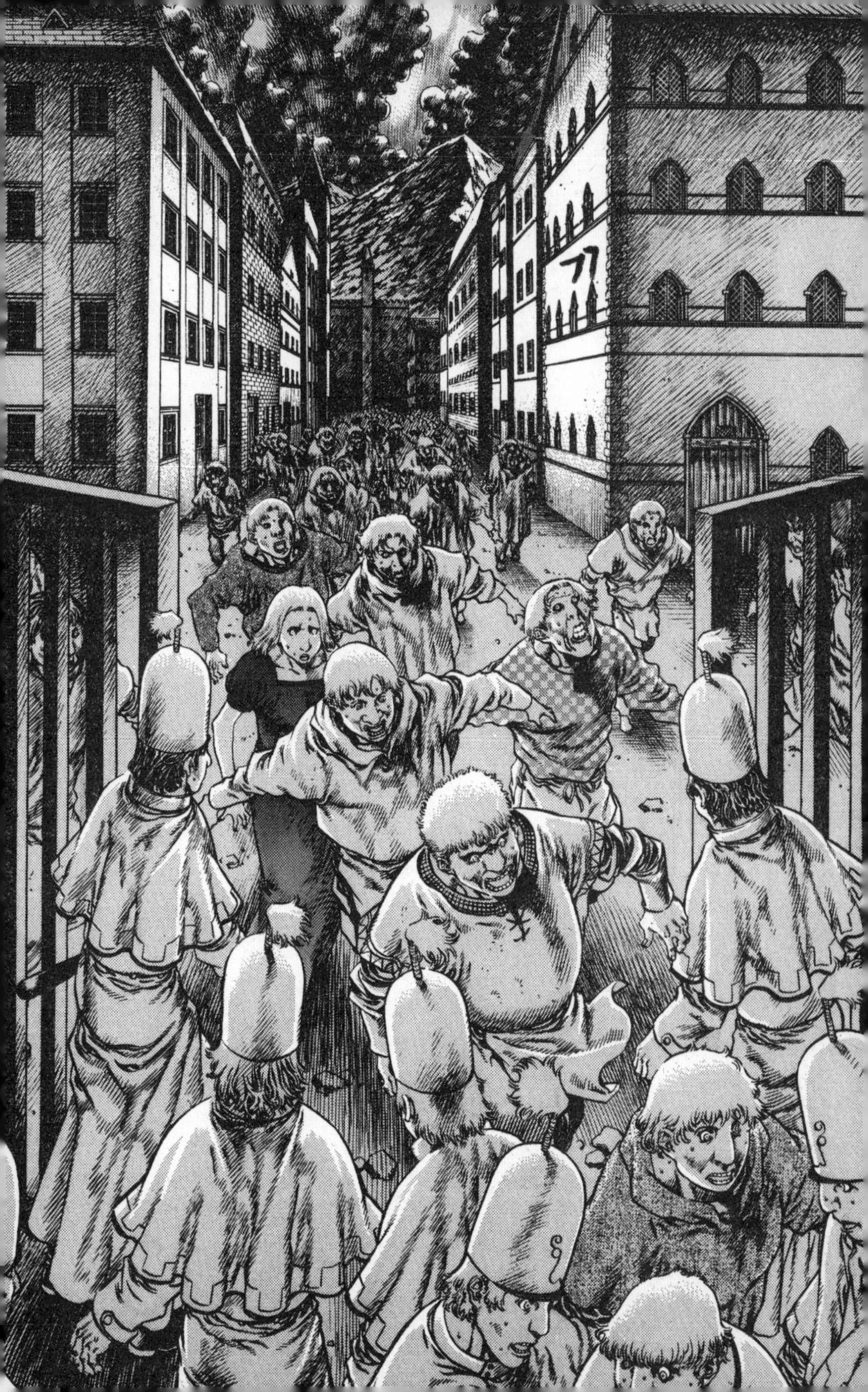
ㄲ

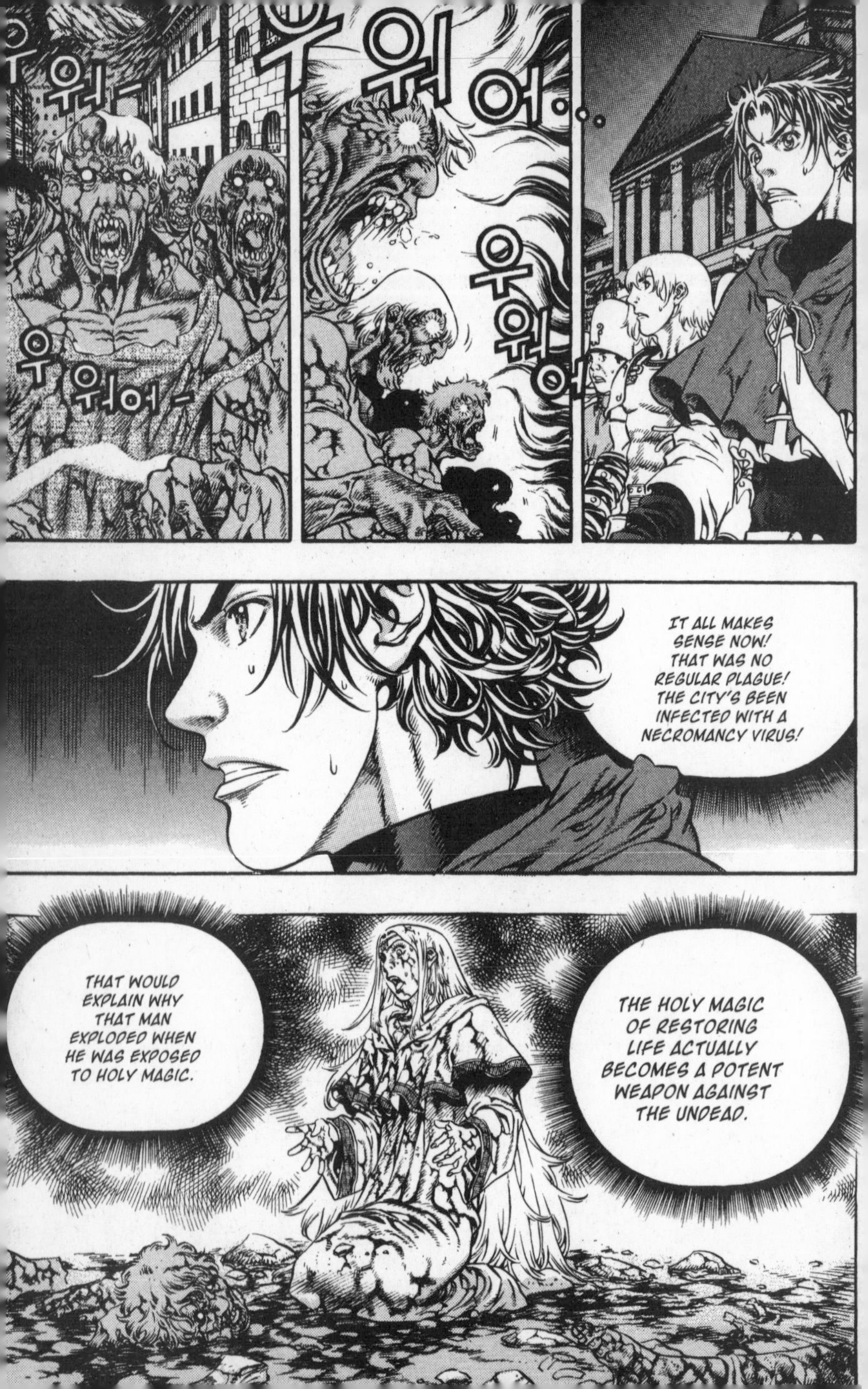
우워-
우워어...
우워어-
우워어
IT ALL MAKES SENSE NOW! THAT WAS NO REGULAR PLAGUE! THE CITY'S BEEN INFECTED WITH A NECROMANCY VIRUS!
THE HOLY MAGIC OF RESTORING LIFE ACTUALLY BECOMES A POTENT WEAPON AGAINST THE UNDEAD.
THAT WOULD EXPLAIN WHY THAT MAN EXPLODED WHEN HE WAS EXPOSED TO HOLY MAGIC.

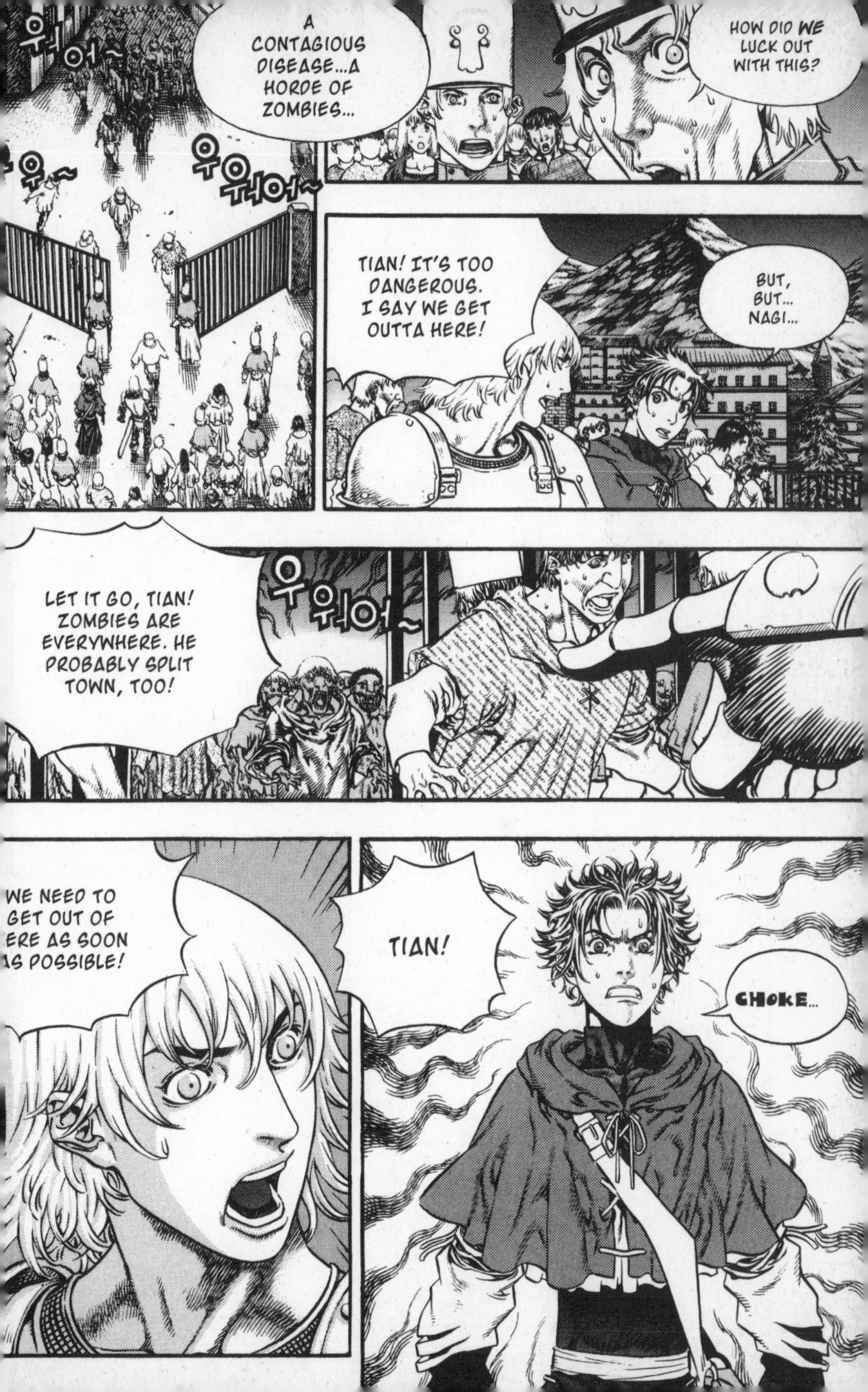
우워어~
A CONTAGIOUS DISEASE...A HORDE OF ZOMBIES...
HOW DID WE LUCK OUT WITH THIS?
TIAN! IT'S TOO DANGEROUS. I SAY WE GET OUTTA HERE!
BUT, BUT... NAGI...
LET IT GO, TIAN! ZOMBIES ARE EVERYWHERE. HE PROBABLY SPLIT TOWN, TOO!
WE NEED TO GET OUT OF ERE AS SOON AS POSSIBLE!
TIAN!
CHOKE...

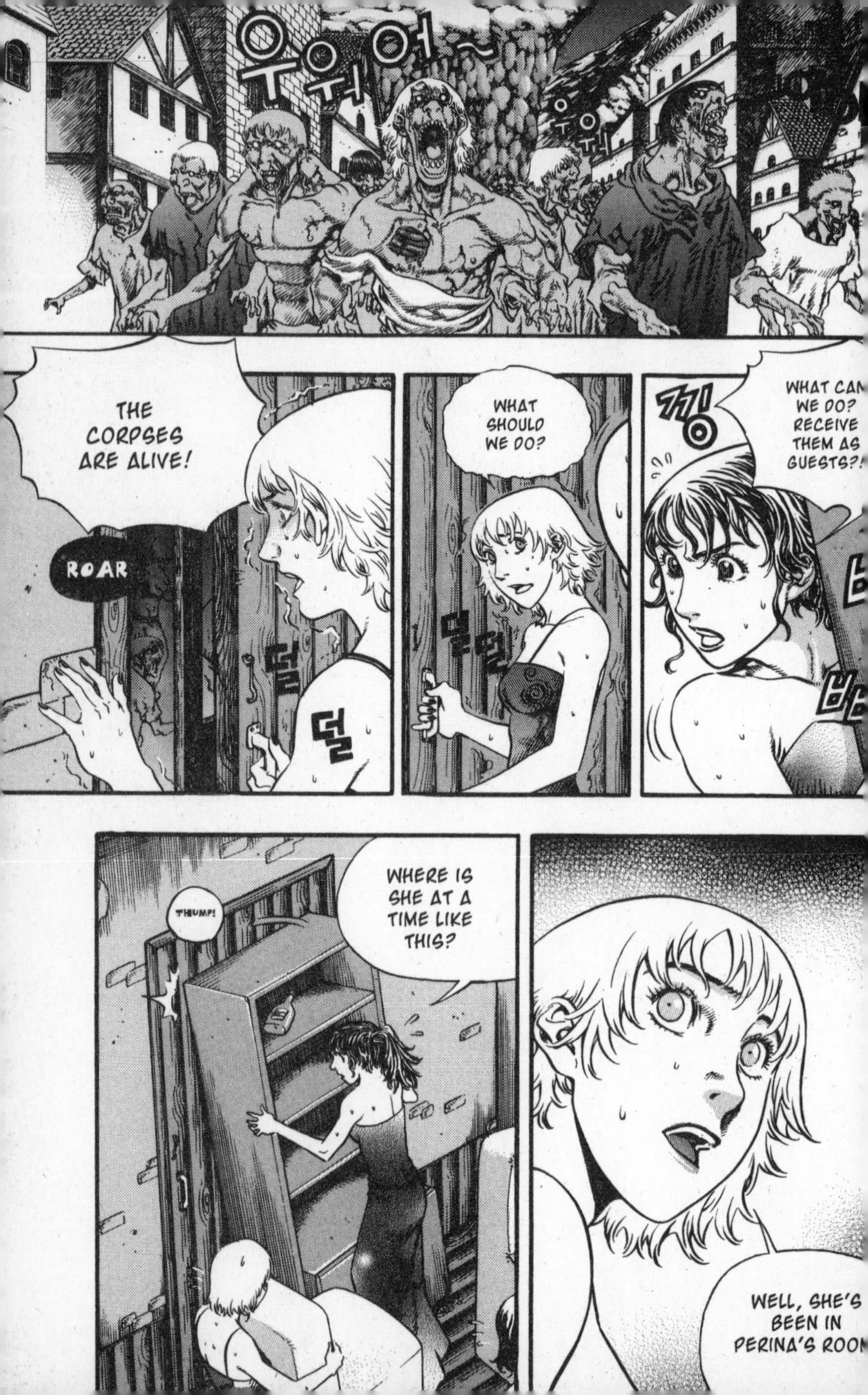

으어어~
으어
THE CORPSES ARE ALIVE!
ROAR
덜
덜
WHAT SHOULD WE DO?
덜덜
WHAT CAN WE DO? RECEIVE THEM AS GUESTS?!
끼잉
THUMP!
WHERE IS SHE AT A TIME LIKE THIS?
WELL, SHE'S BEEN IN PERINA'S ROOM

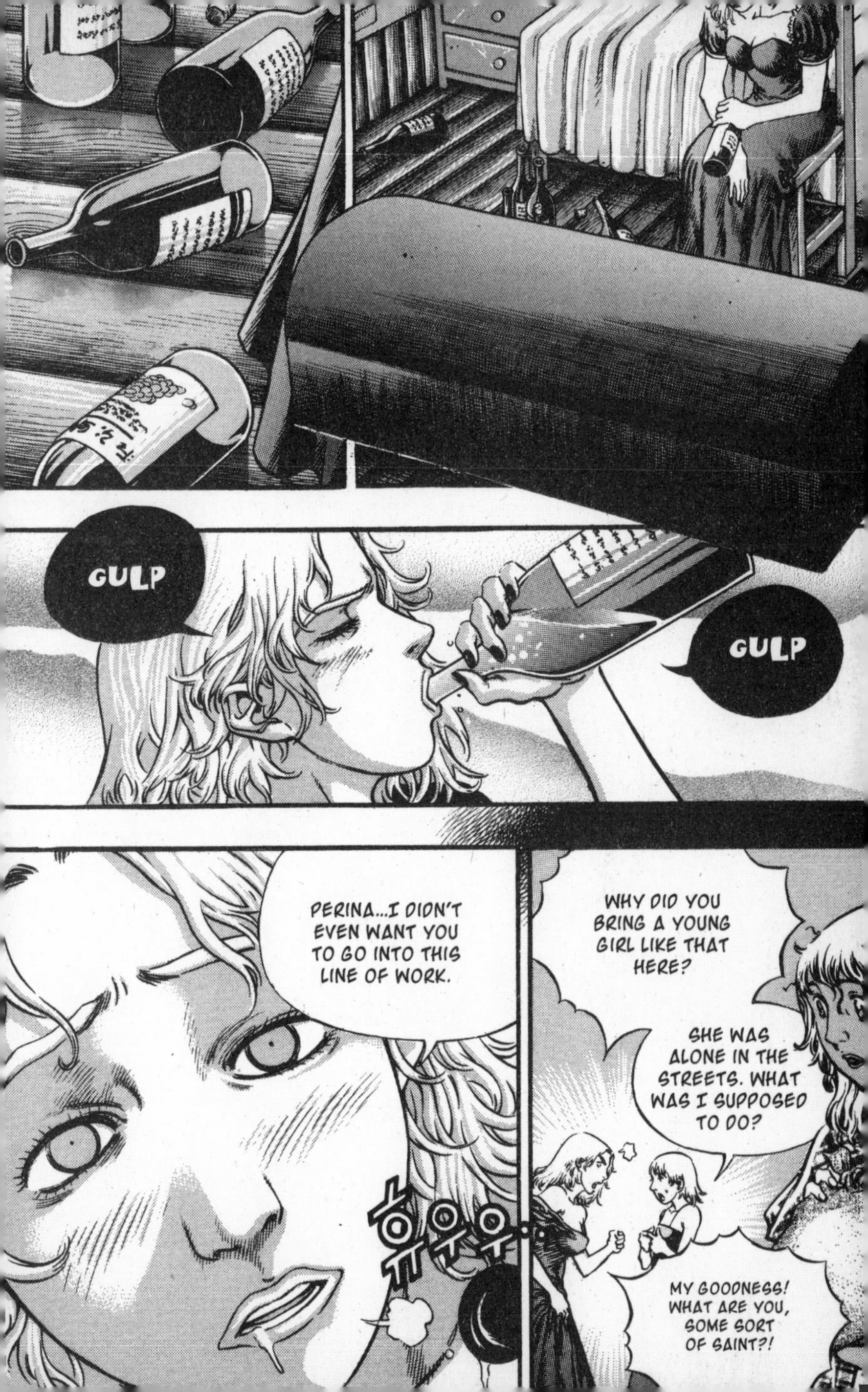
GULP
GULP
PERINA...I DIDN'T EVEN WANT YOU TO GO INTO THIS LINE OF WORK.
WHY DID YOU BRING A YOUNG GIRL LIKE THAT HERE?
SHE WAS ALONE IN THE STREETS. WHAT WAS I SUPPOSED TO DO?
MY GOODNESS! WHAT ARE YOU, SOME SORT OF SAINT?!

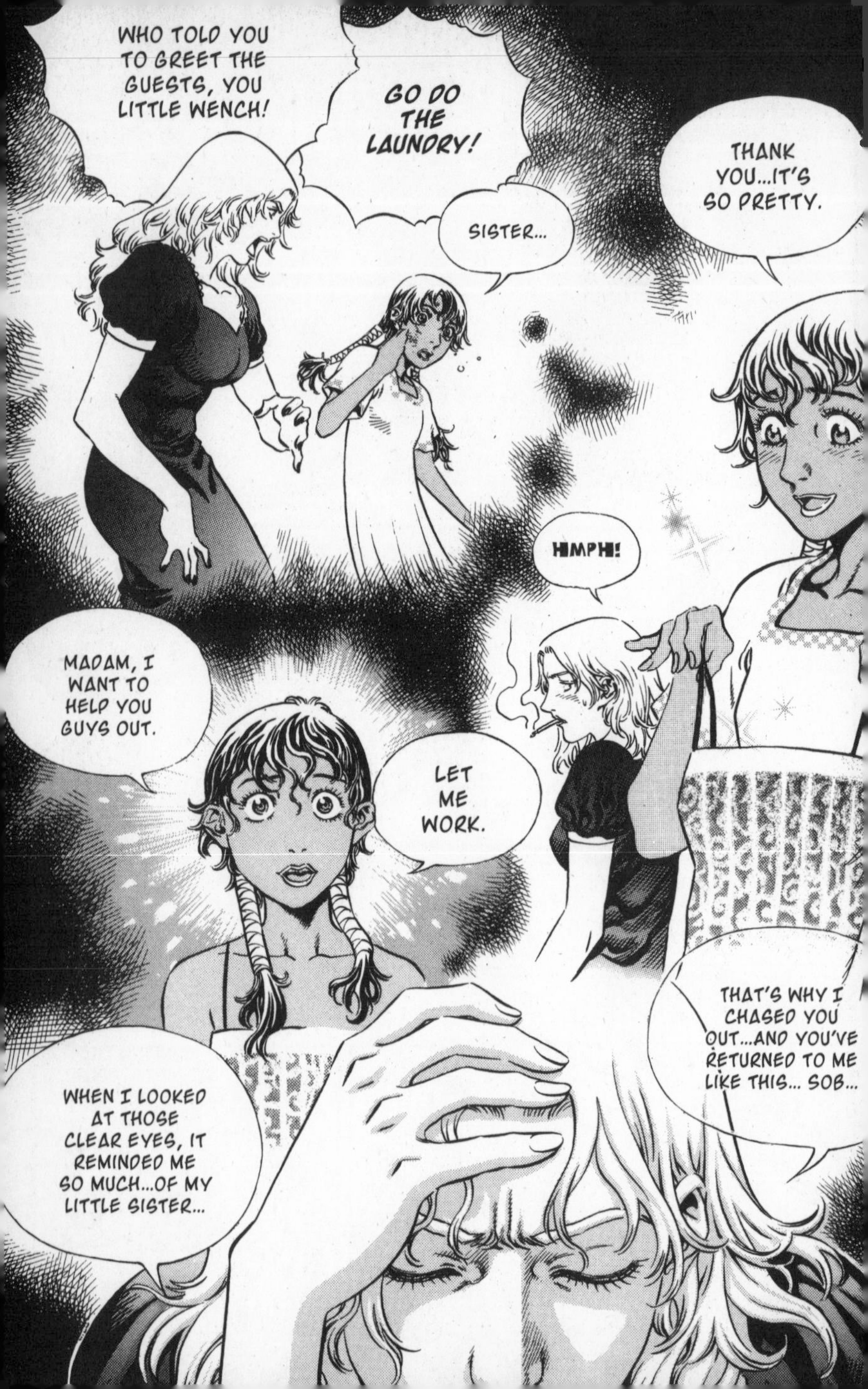
WHO TOLD YOU TO GREET THE GUESTS, YOU LITTLE WENCH!
GO DO THE LAUNDRY!
SISTER...
THANK YOU...IT'S SO PRETTY.
HMPH!
MADAM, I WANT TO HELP YOU GUYS OUT.
LET ME WORK.
THAT'S WHY I CHASED YOU OUT...AND YOU'VE RETURNED TO ME LIKE THIS... SOB...
WHEN I LOOKED AT THOSE CLEAR EYES, IT REMINDED ME SO MUCH...OF MY LITTLE SISTER...

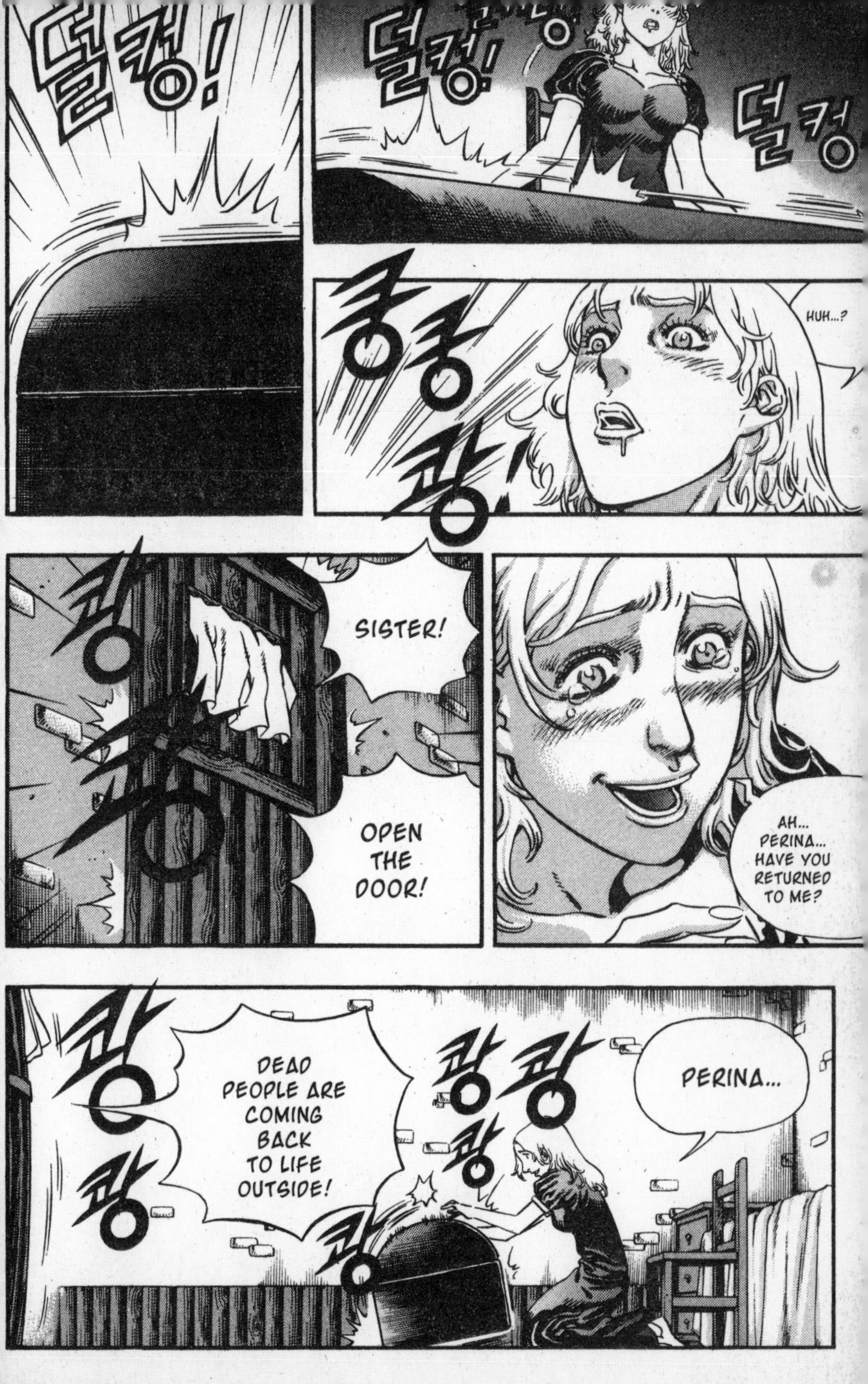

덜컹!
덜컹!
덜컹
쿵쿵
쾅!
HUH...?
쾅
쾅
SISTER!
OPEN THE DOOR!
AH... PERINA... HAVE YOU RETURNED TO ME?
쾅
쾅
DEAD PEOPLE ARE COMING BACK TO LIFE OUTSIDE!
쾅 쾅
쾅
PERINA...
쾅

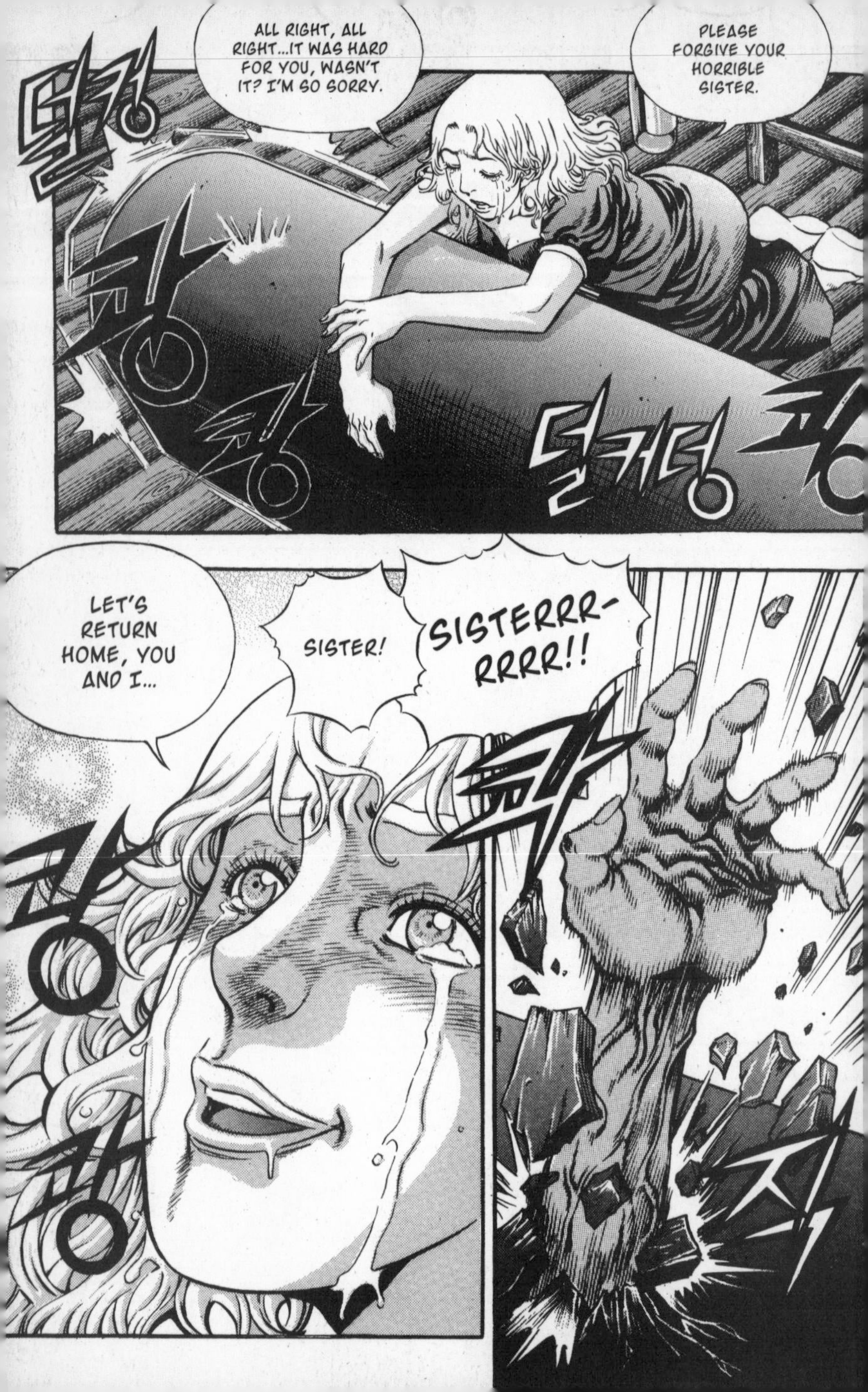
ALL RIGHT, ALL RIGHT...IT WAS HARD FOR YOU, WASN'T IT? I'M SO SORRY.
PLEASE FORGIVE YOUR HORRIBLE SISTER.
LET'S RETURN HOME, YOU AND I...
SISTER!
SISTERRR-RRRR!!

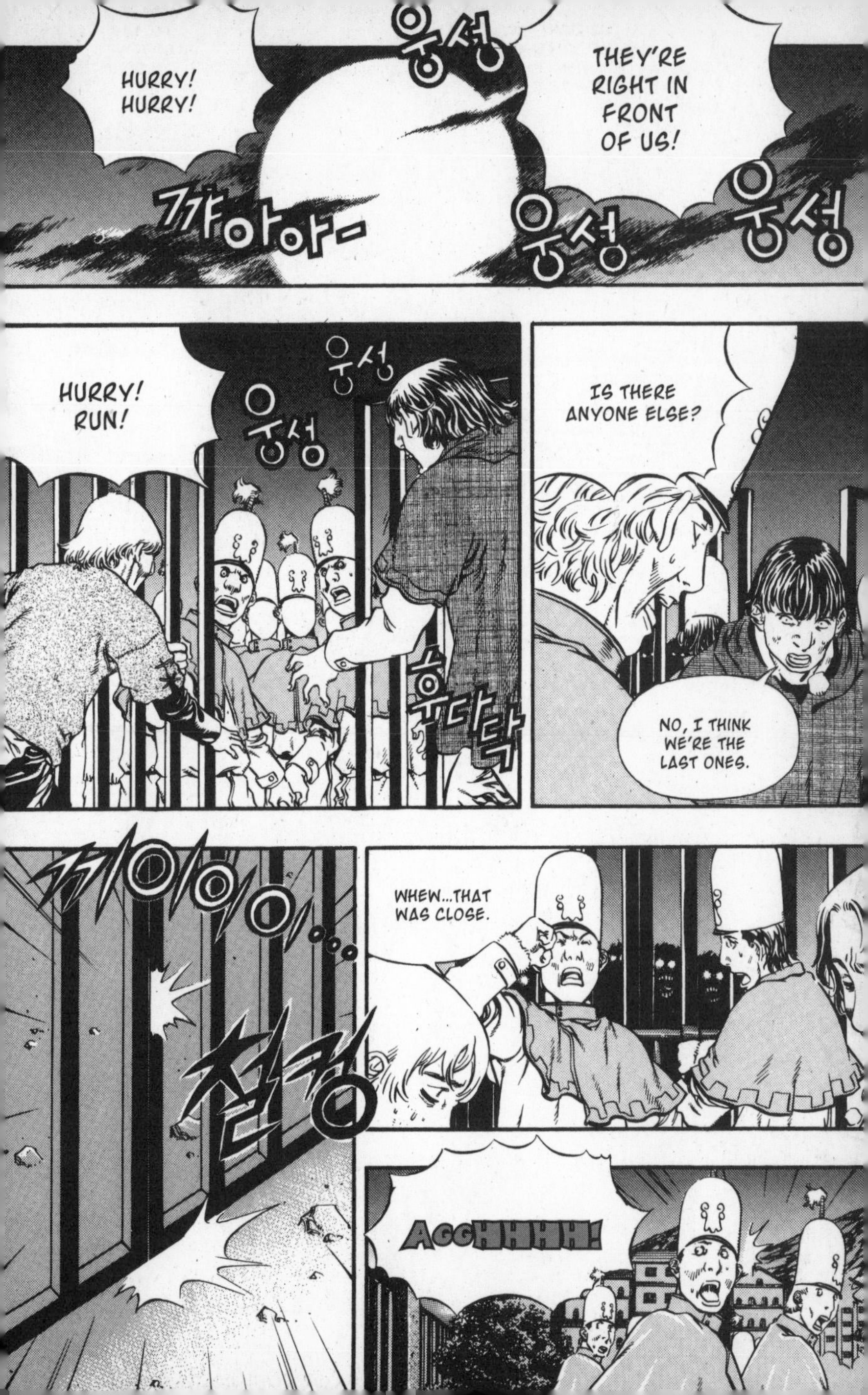

HURRY! HURRY!
웅성
THEY'RE RIGHT IN FRONT OF US!
꺄아아-
웅성
웅성
HURRY! RUN!
웅성
웅성
우다닥
IS THERE ANYONE ELSE?
NO, I THINK WE'RE THE LAST ONES.
끼이이이...
철컹
WHEW...THAT WAS CLOSE.
AGGHHHH!

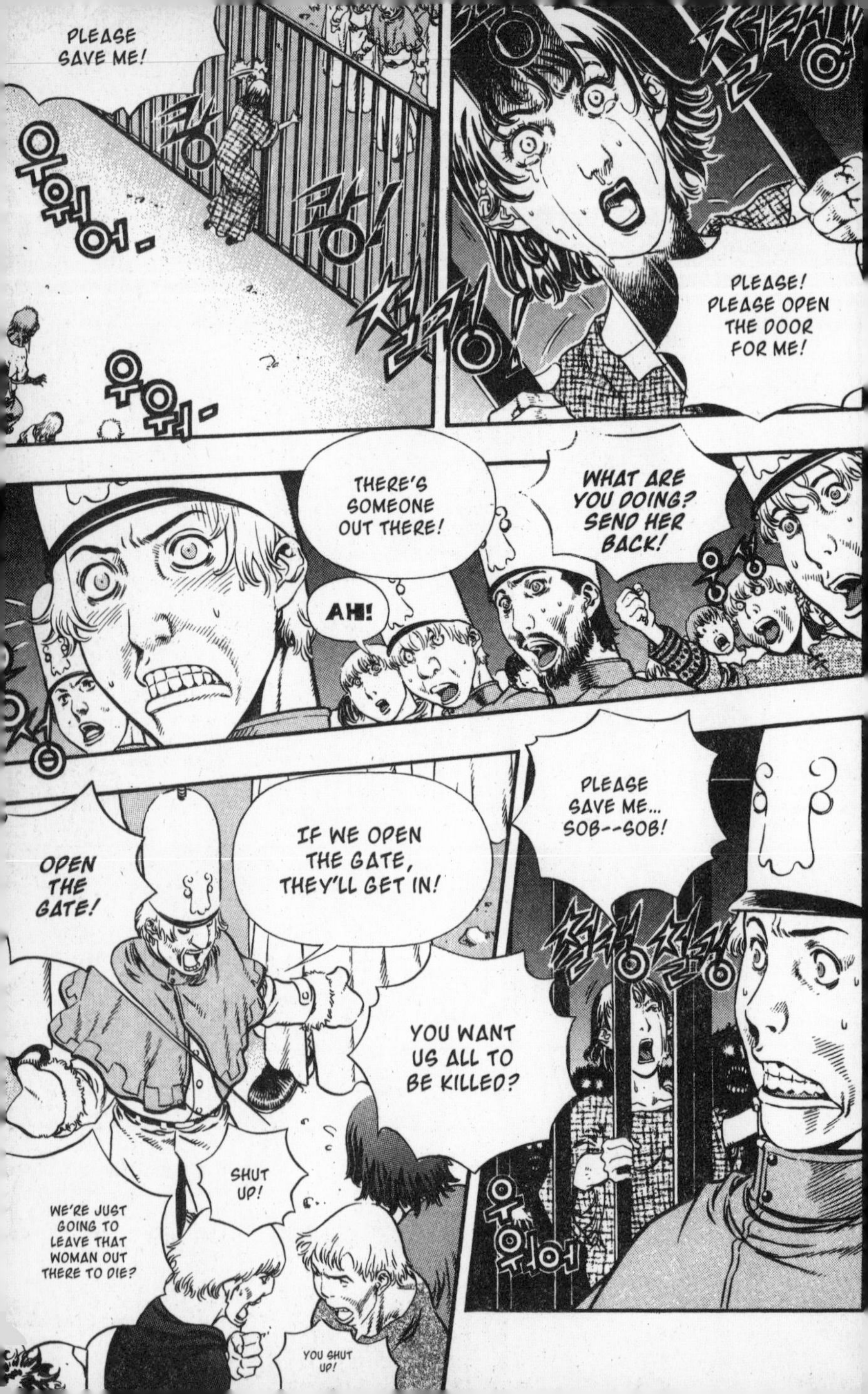
PLEASE SAVE ME!
PLEASE! PLEASE OPEN THE DOOR FOR ME!
THERE'S SOMEONE OUT THERE!
AH!
WHAT ARE YOU DOING? SEND HER BACK!
OPEN THE GATE!
IF WE OPEN THE GATE, THEY'LL GET IN!
PLEASE SAVE ME... SOB--SOB!
YOU WANT US ALL TO BE KILLED?
WE'RE JUST GOING TO LEAVE THAT WOMAN OUT THERE TO DIE?
SHUT UP!
YOU SHUT UP!

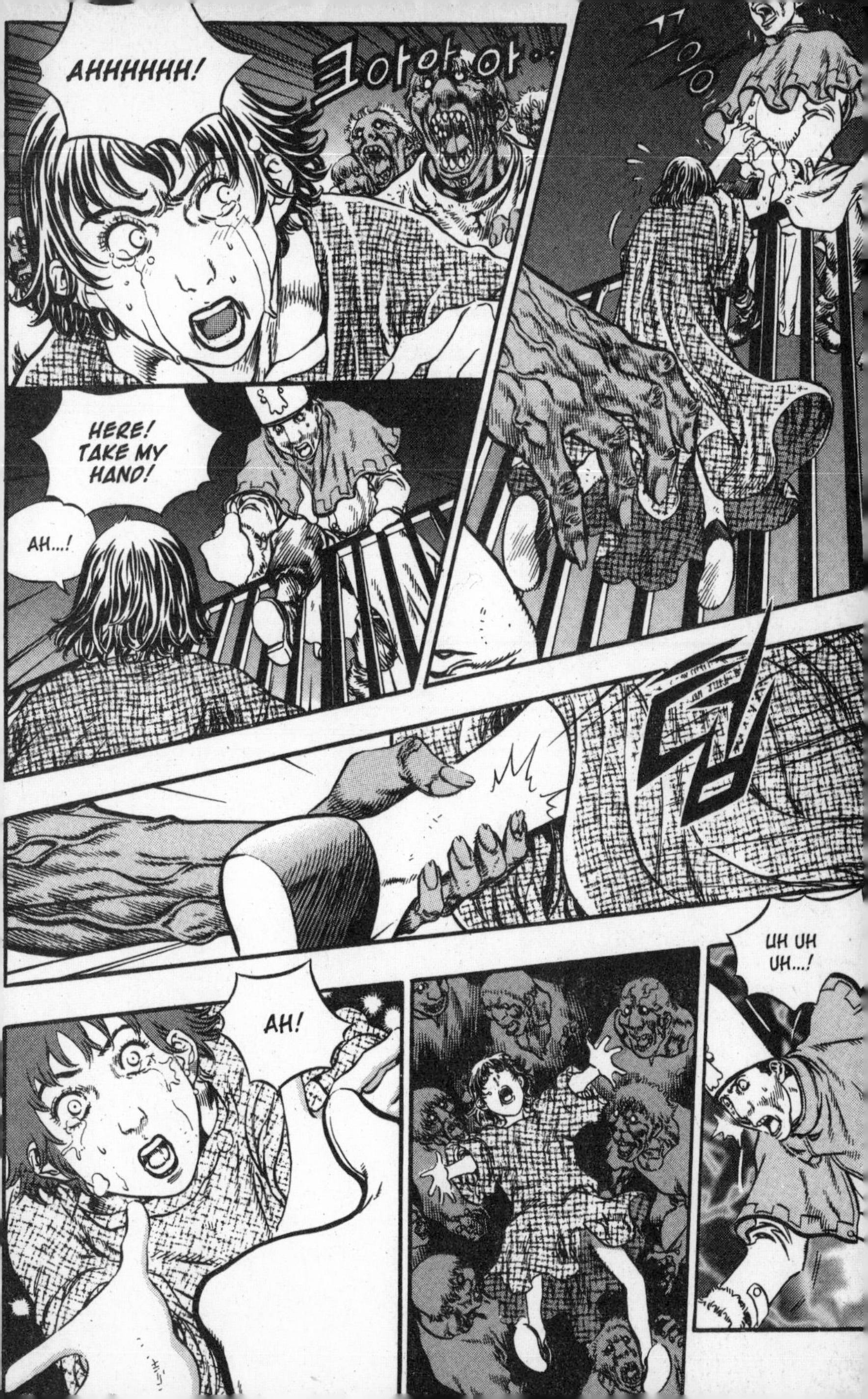
AHHHHHH!
크아아아..
HERE! TAKE MY HAND!
AH...!
AH!
UH UH UH...!

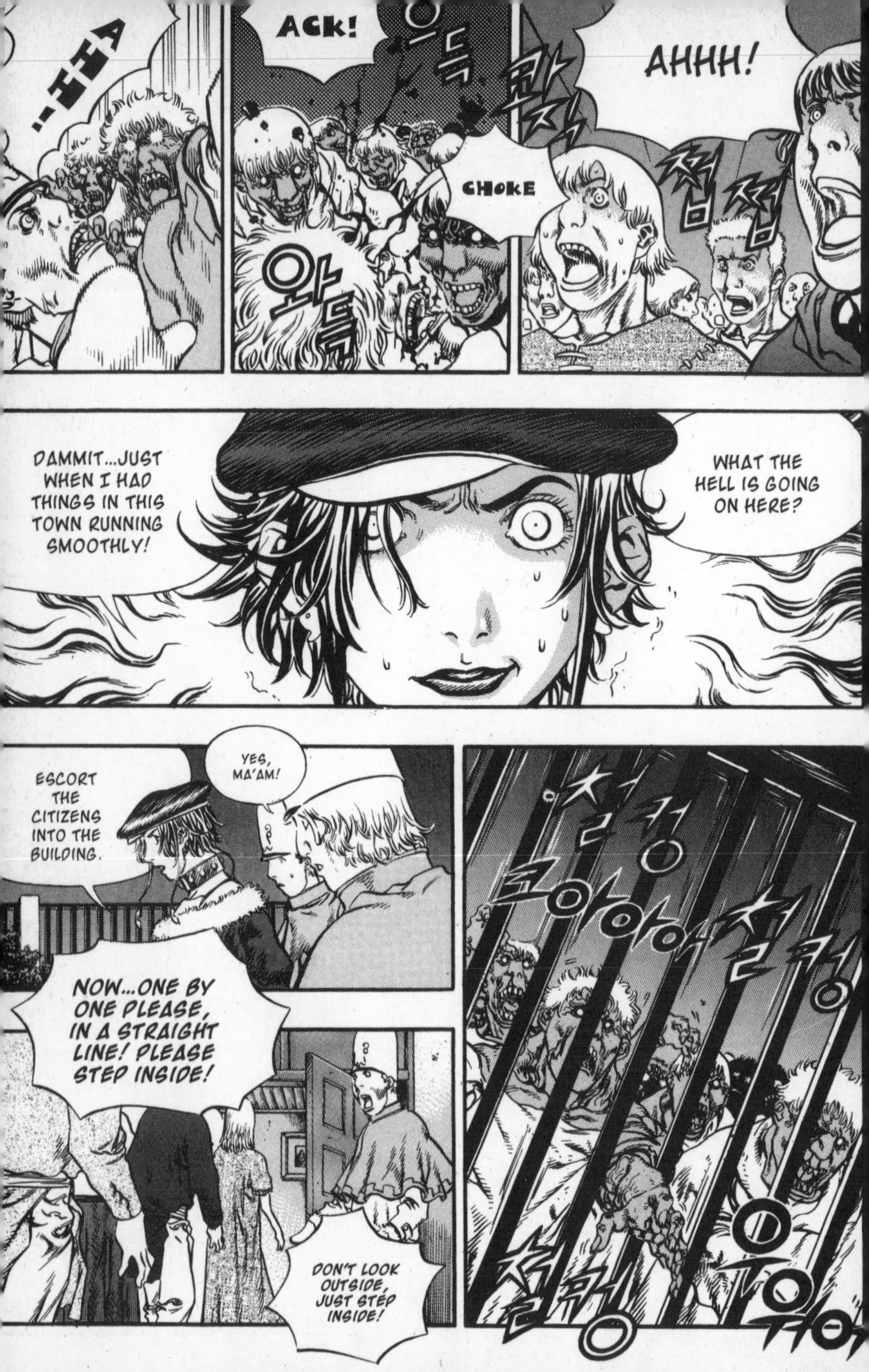

ACK!
CHOKE
AHHH!
DAMMIT...JUST WHEN I HAD THINGS IN THIS TOWN RUNNING SMOOTHLY!
WHAT THE HELL IS GOING ON HERE?
ESCORT THE CITIZENS INTO THE BUILDING.
YES, MA'AM!
NOW...ONE BY ONE PLEASE, IN A STRAIGHT LINE! PLEASE STEP INSIDE!
DON'T LOOK OUTSIDE, JUST STEP INSIDE!

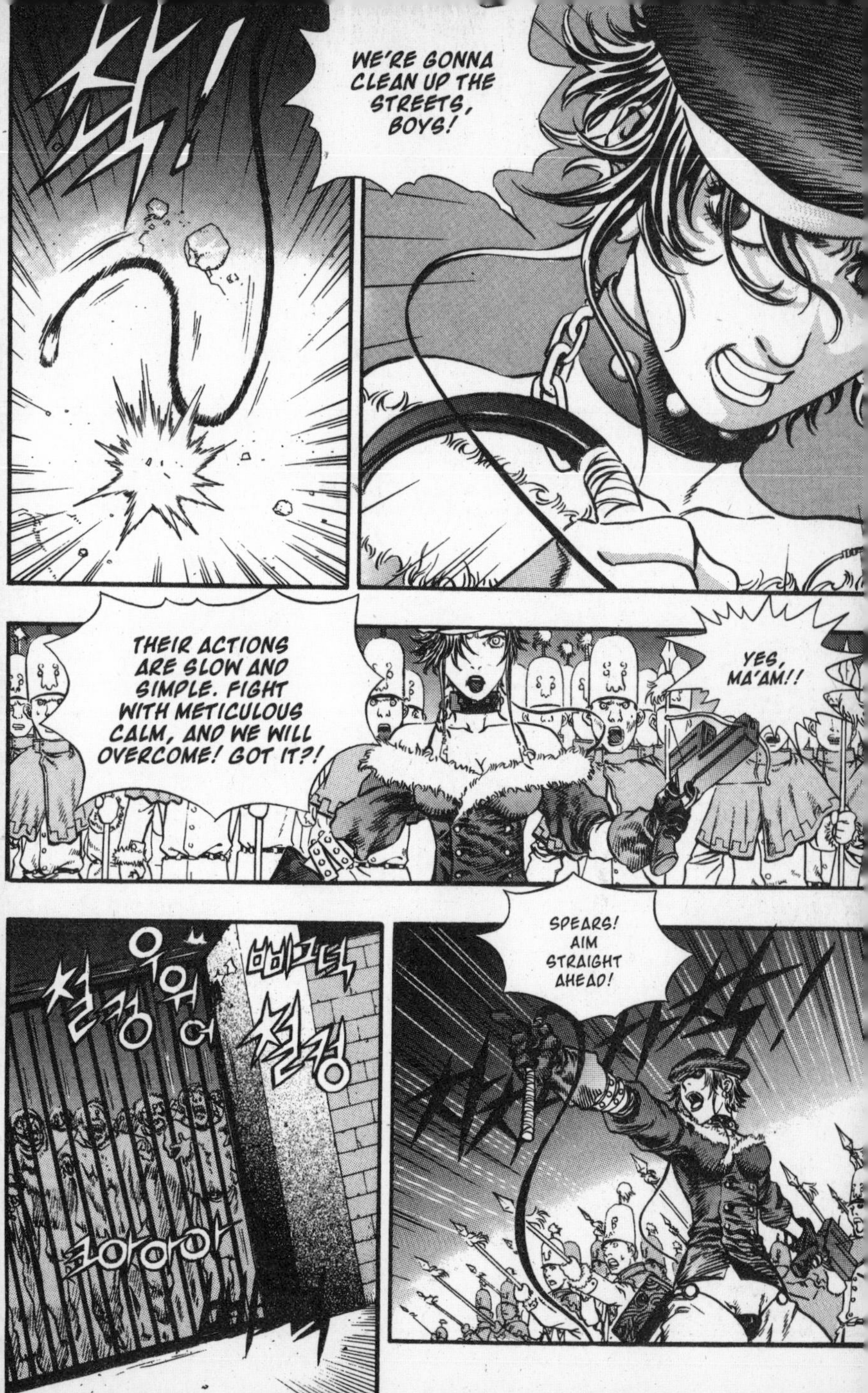
WE'RE GONNA CLEAN UP THE STREETS, BOYS!
THEIR ACTIONS ARE SLOW AND SIMPLE. FIGHT WITH METICULOUS CALM, AND WE WILL OVERCOME! GOT IT?!
YES, MA'AM!!
SPEARS! AIM STRAIGHT AHEAD!

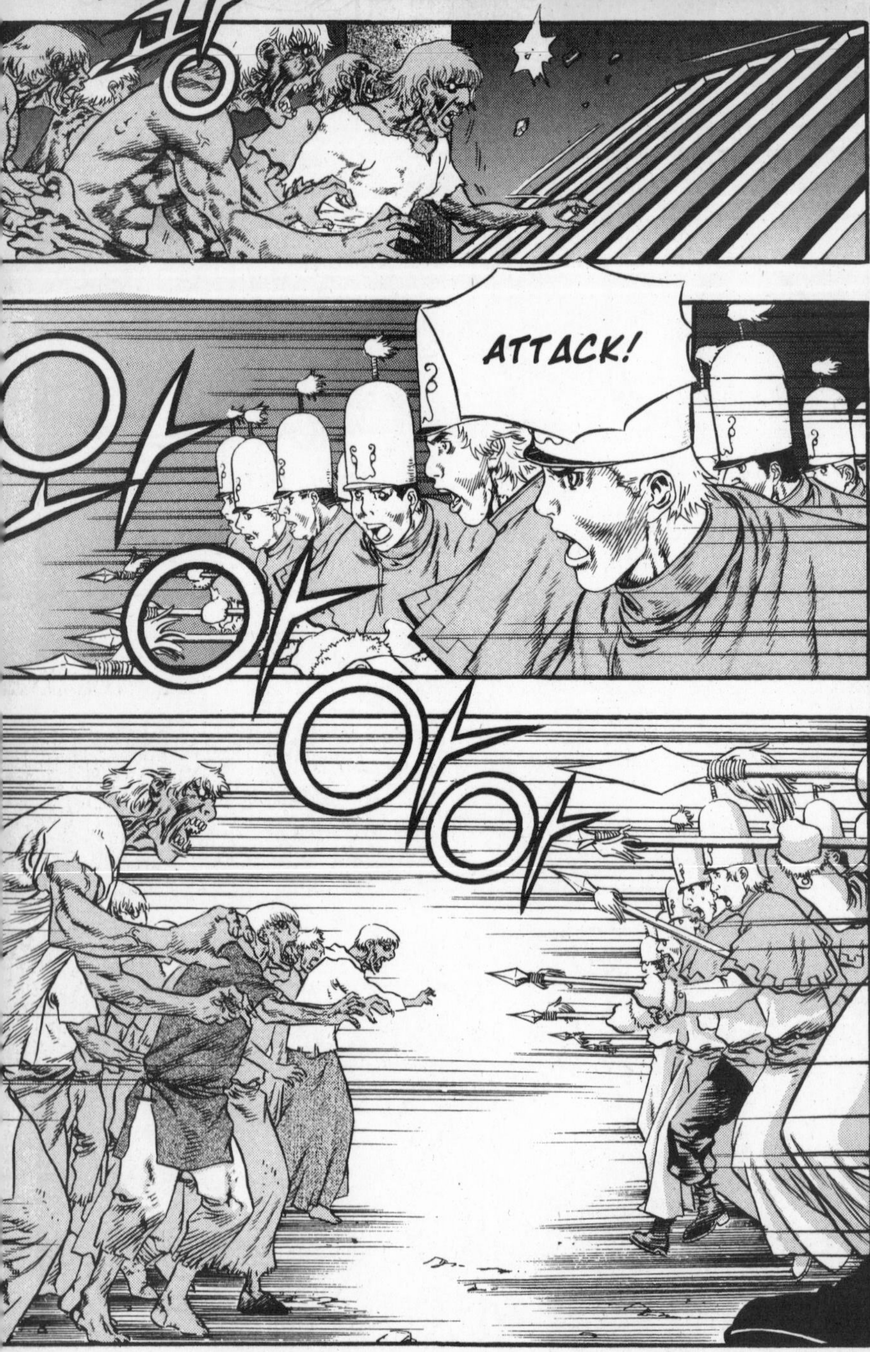
ATTACK!

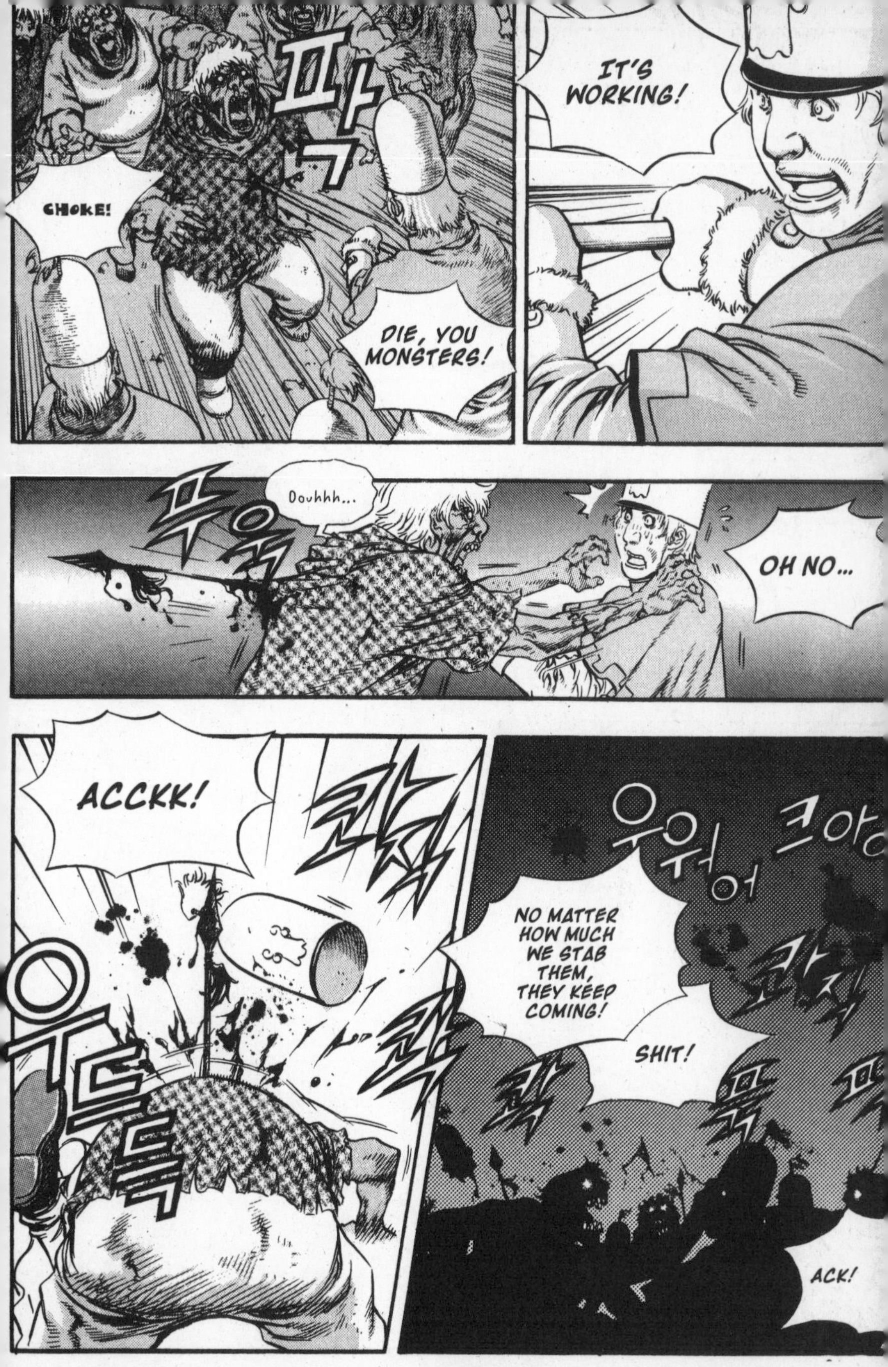
CHOKE!
DIE, YOU MONSTERS!
IT'S WORKING!
Douhhh...
OH NO...
ACCKK!
NO MATTER HOW MUCH WE STAB THEM, THEY KEEP COMING!
SHIT!
ACK!

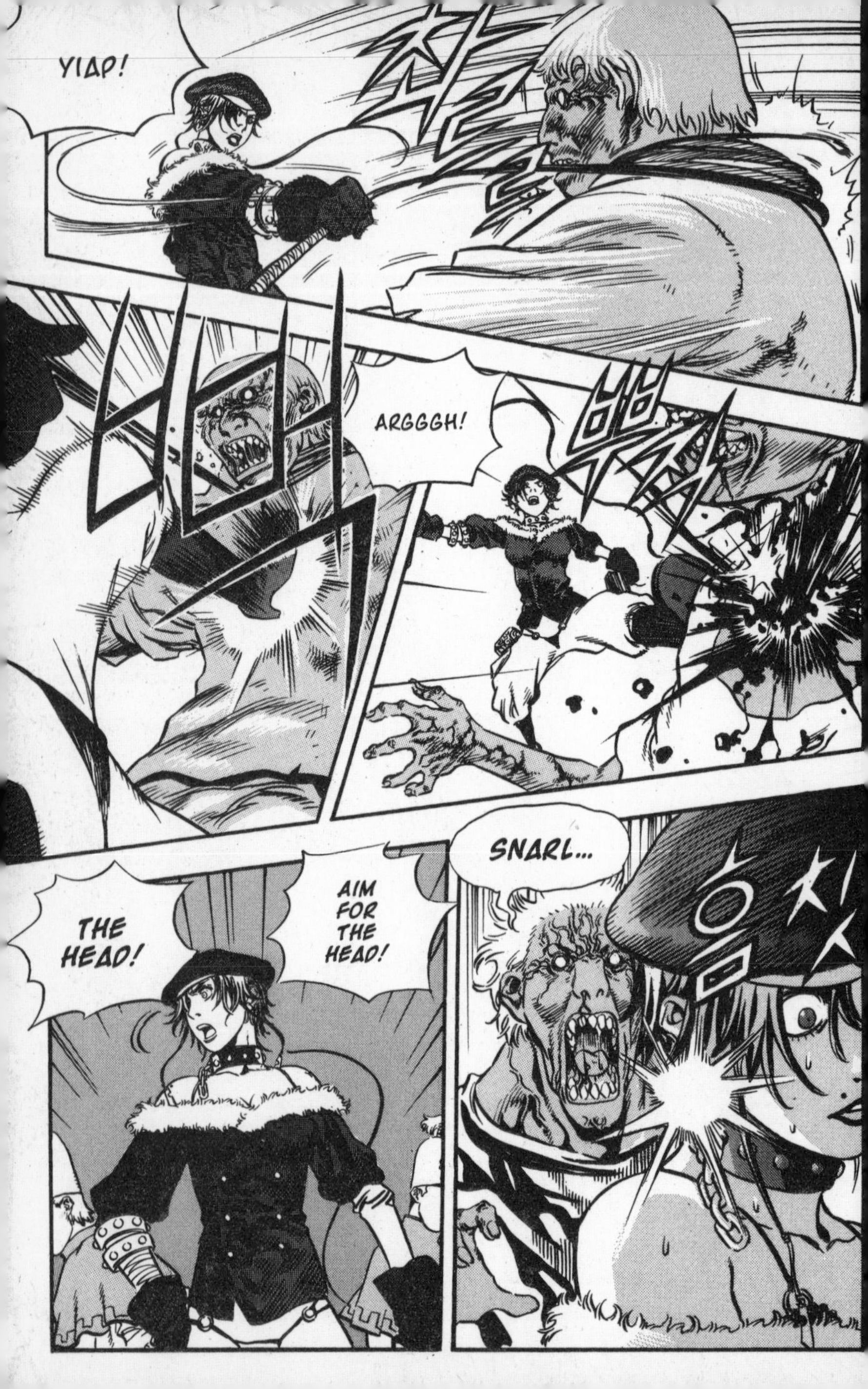
YIAP!
ARGGGH!
SNARL...
AIM FOR THE HEAD!
THE HEAD!

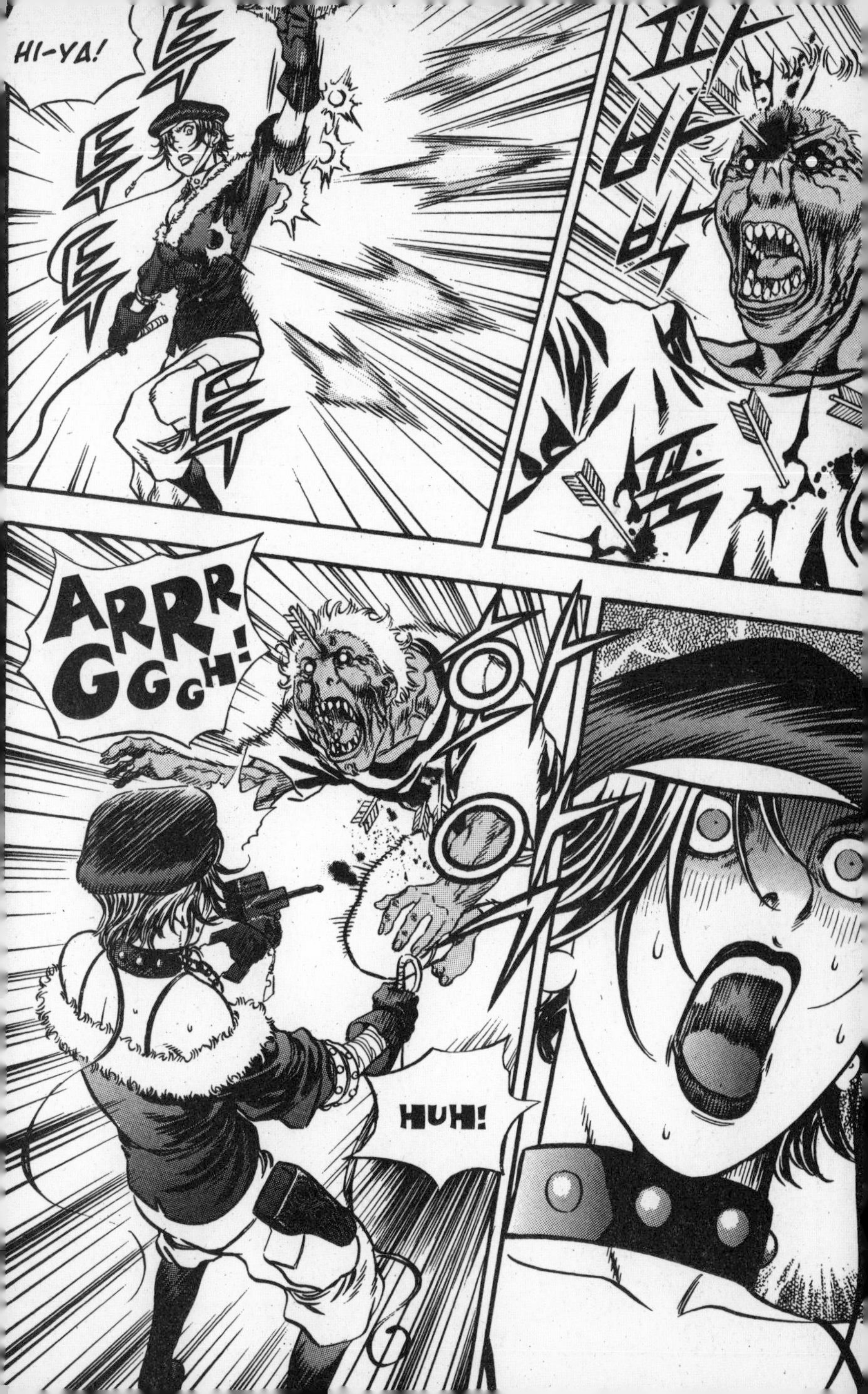
HI-YA!
ARRRGGGGH!
HUH!

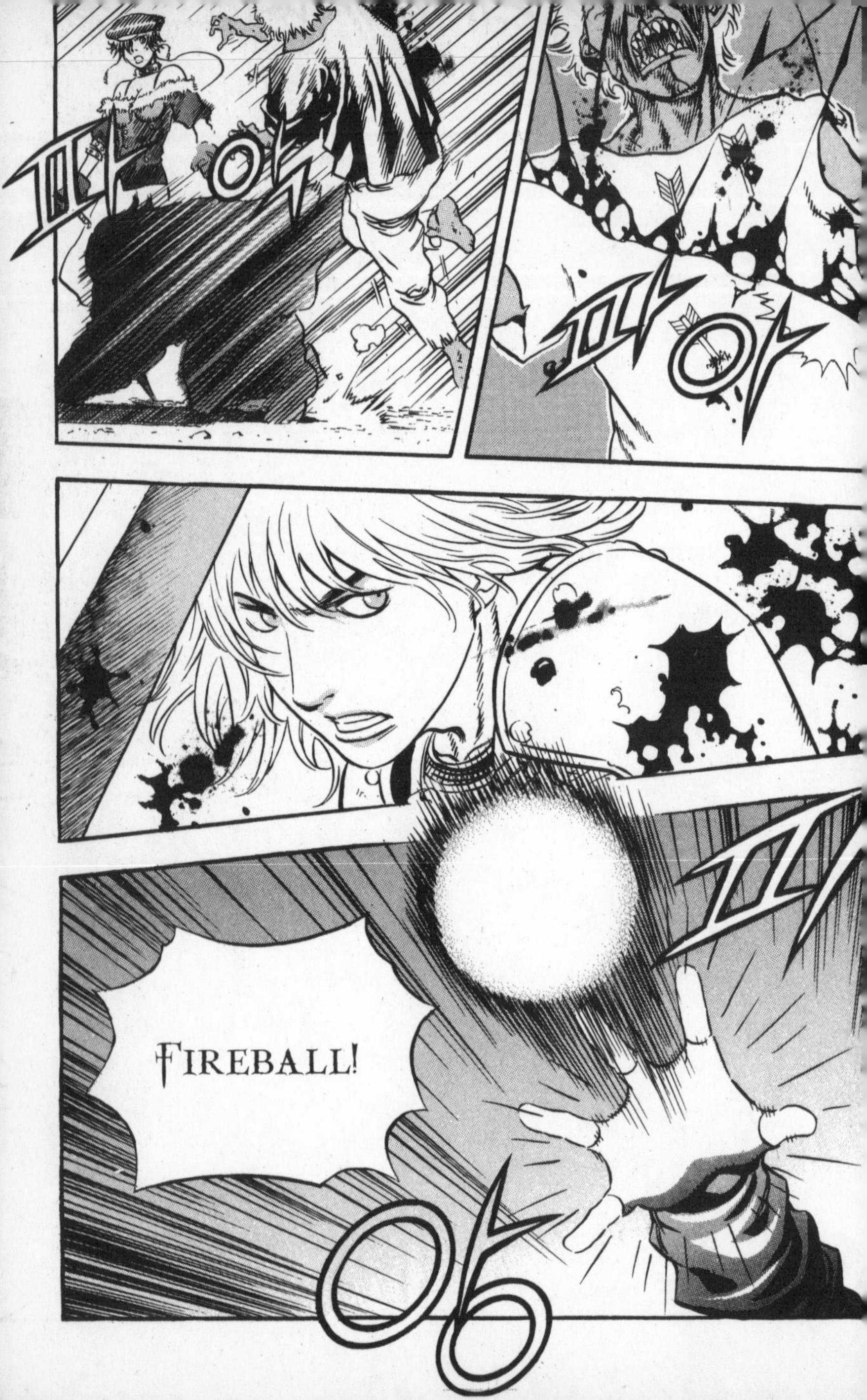
FIREBALL!

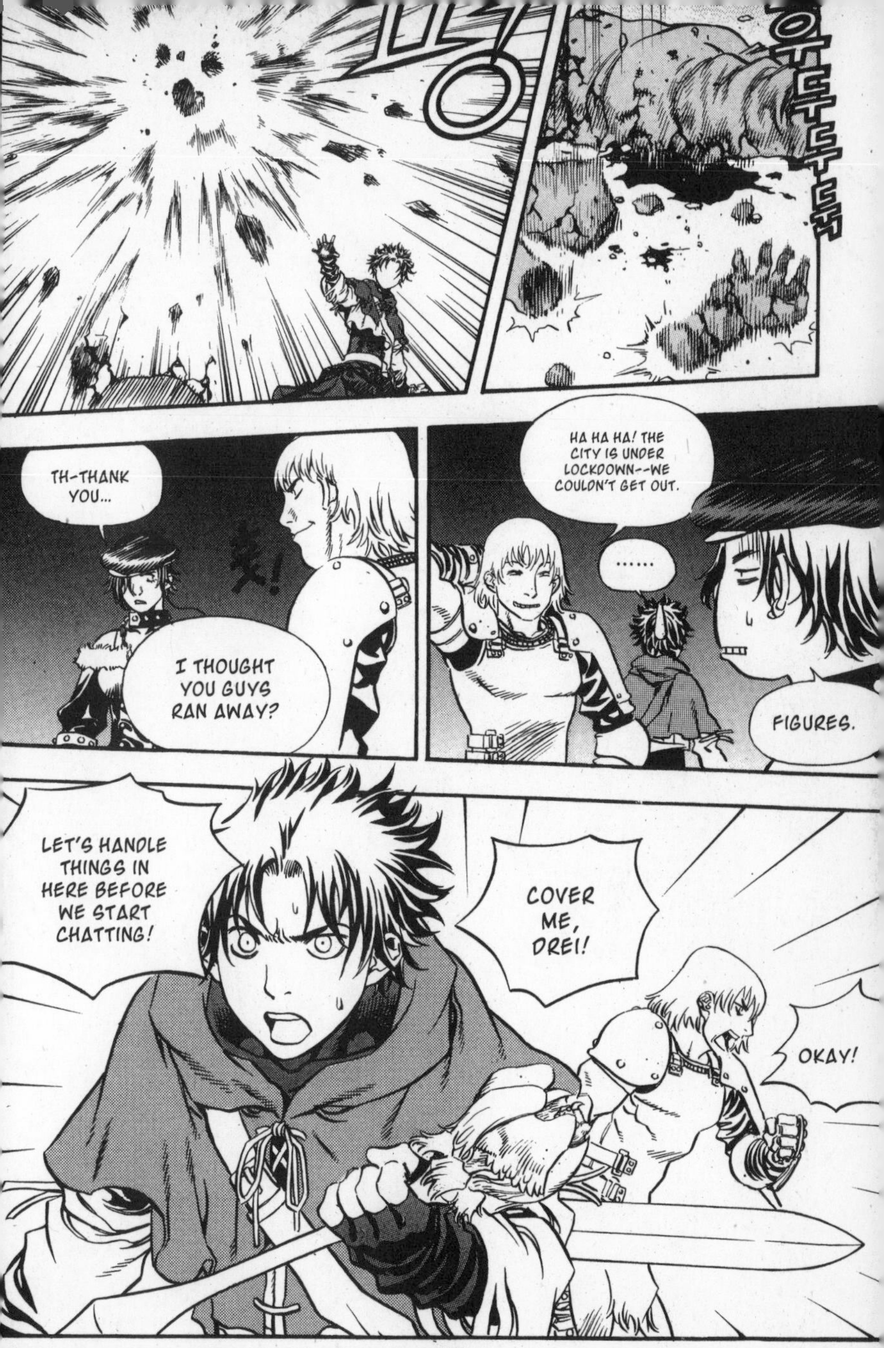

TH-THANK YOU...
I THOUGHT YOU GUYS RAN AWAY?
HA HA HA! THE CITY IS UNDER LOCKDOWN--WE COULDN'T GET OUT.
......
FIGURES.
LET'S HANDLE THINGS IN HERE BEFORE WE START CHATTING!
COVER ME, DREI!
OKAY!

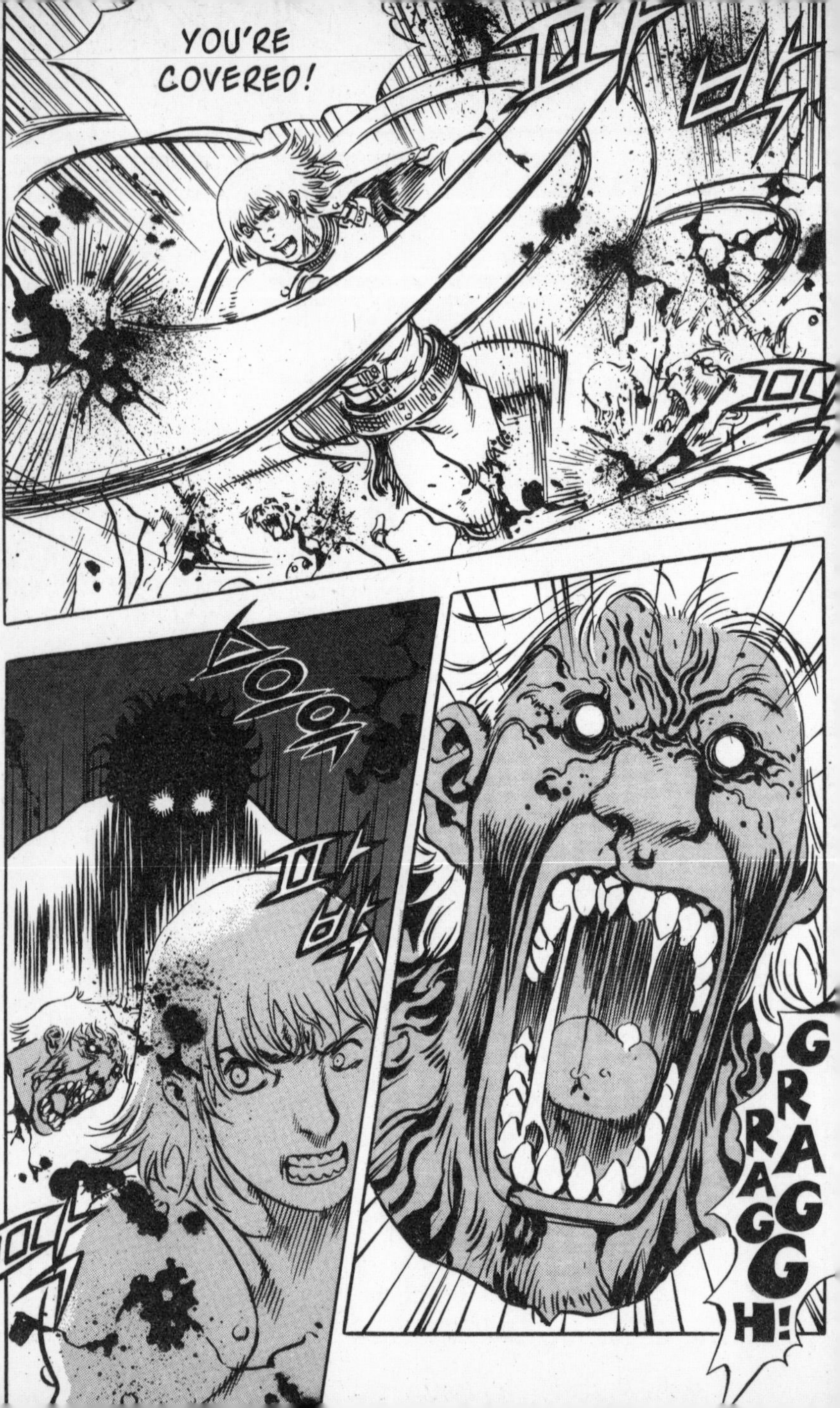
YOU'RE COVERED!
GRAGGH!
RAGG

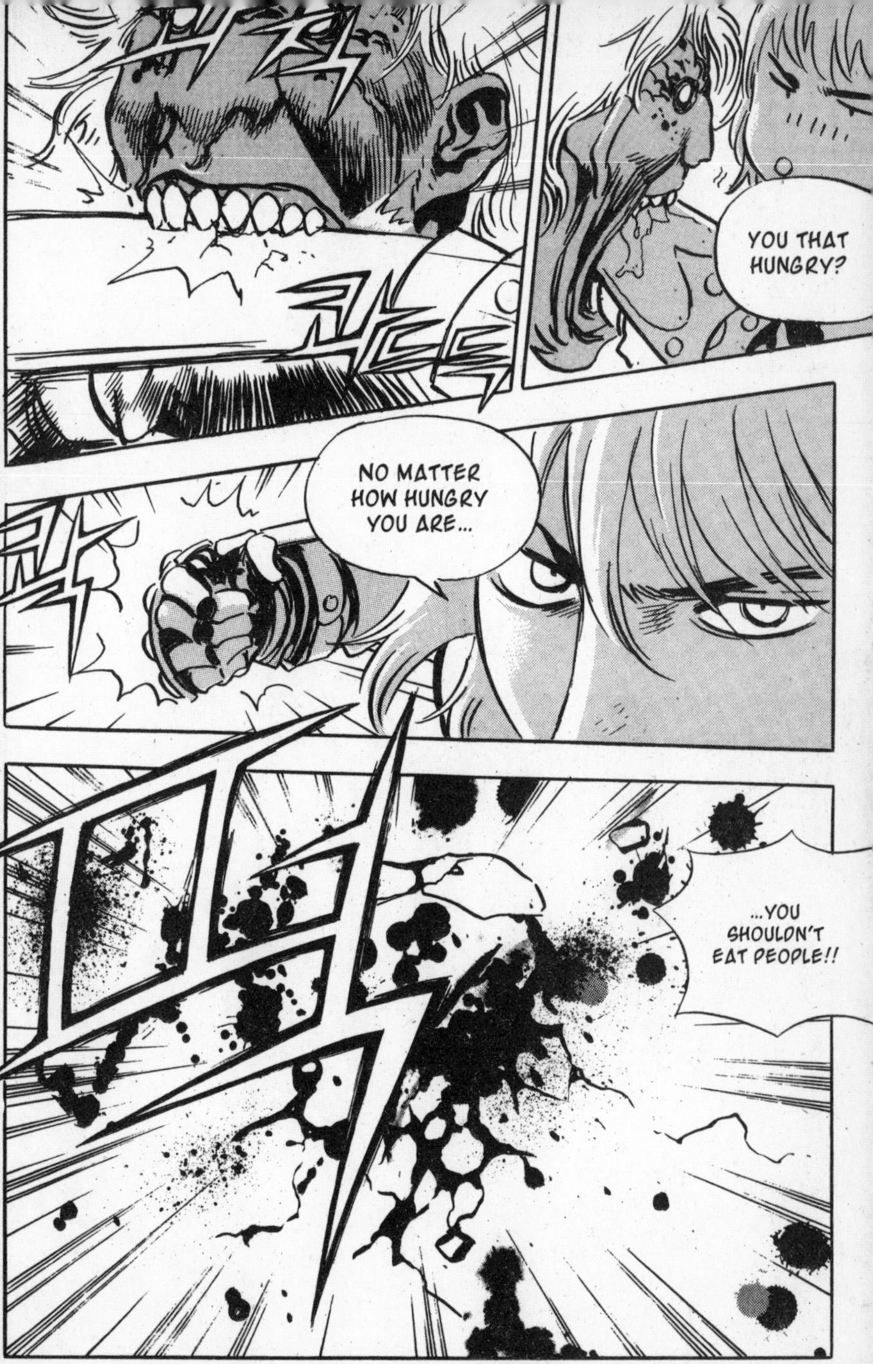
YOU THAT HUNGRY?
NO MATTER HOW HUNGRY YOU ARE...
...YOU SHOULDN'T EAT PEOPLE!!

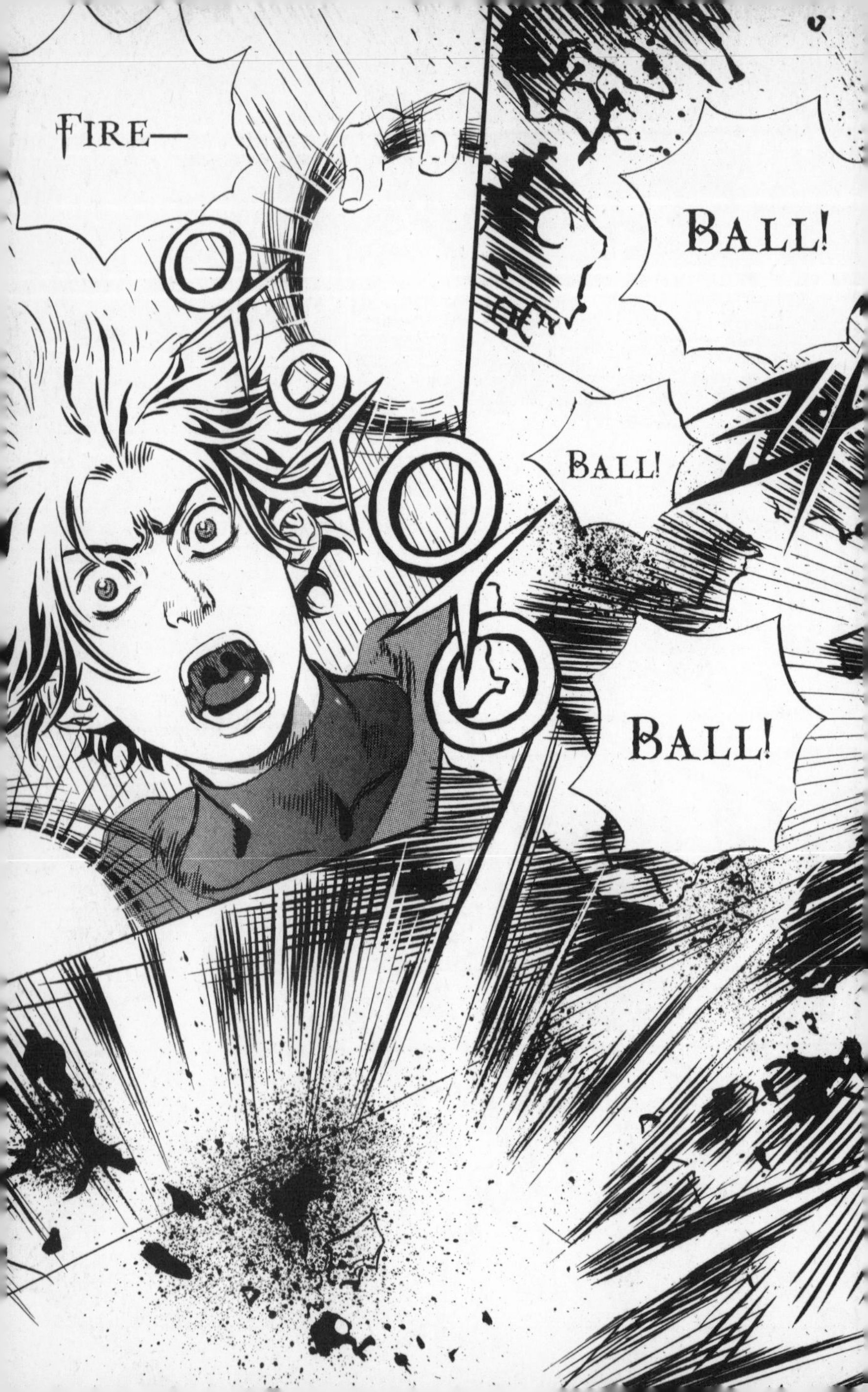
FIRE—
BALL!
BALL!
BALL!

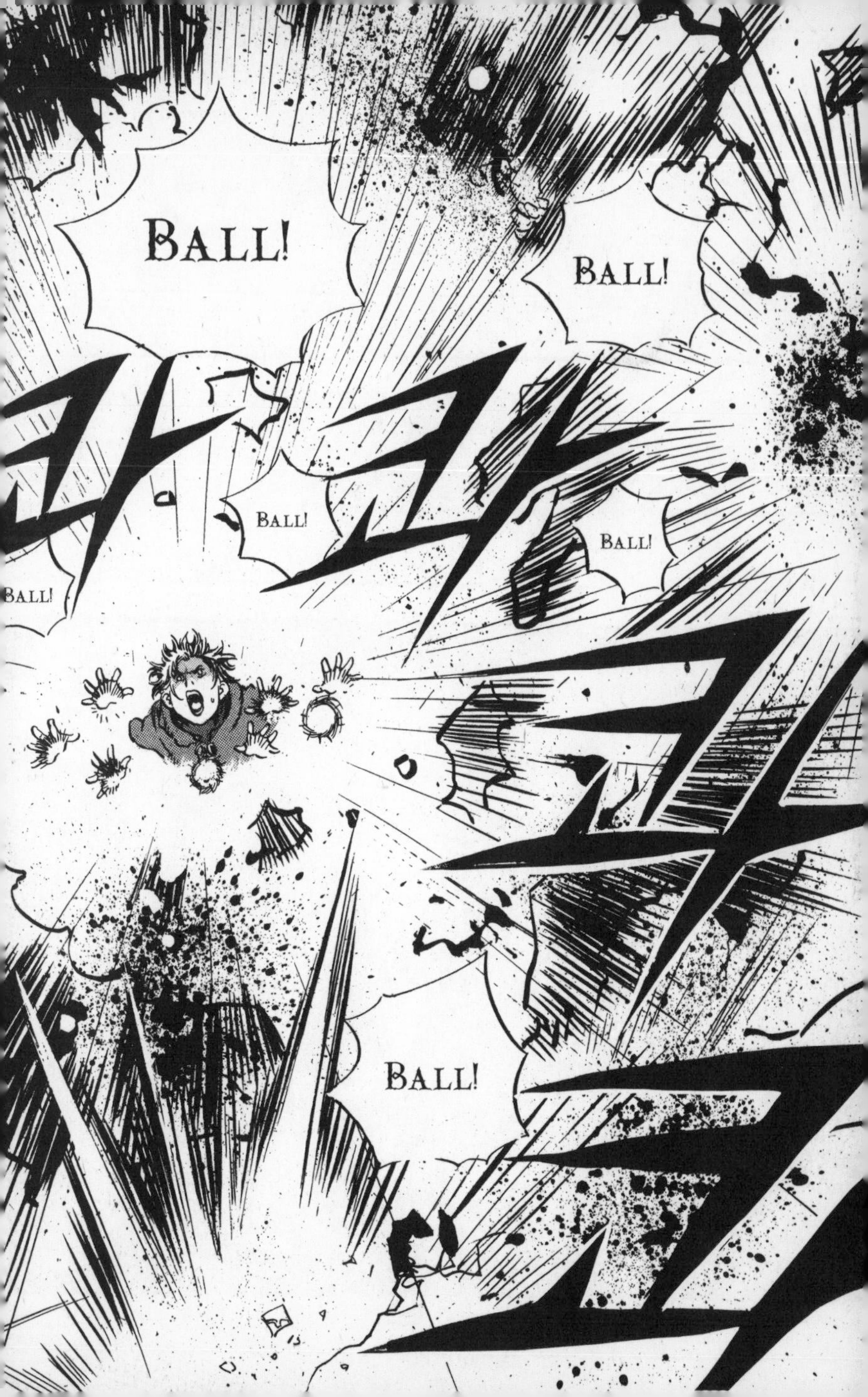
BALL!
BALL!
BALL!
BALL!
BALL!
BALL!

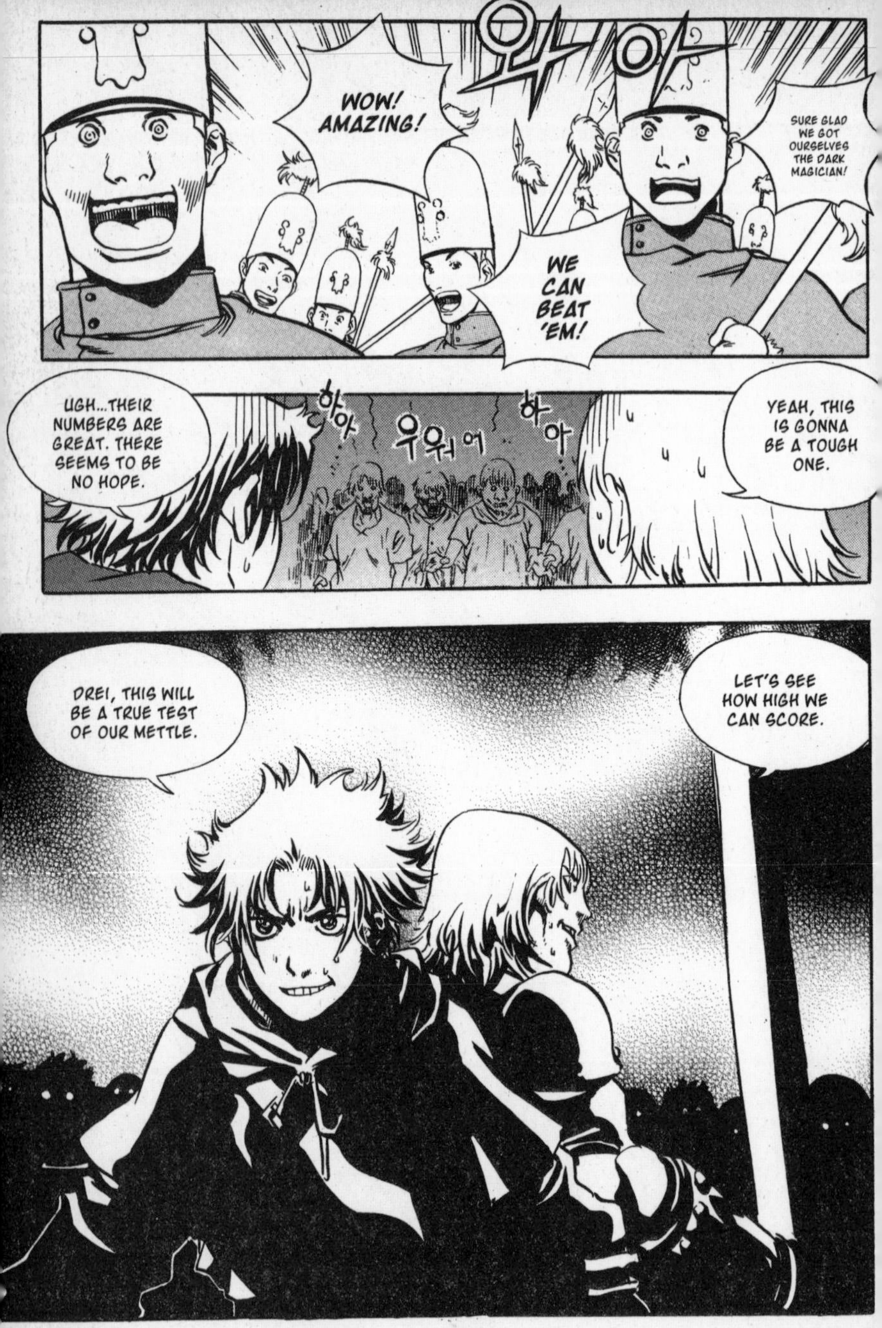
와아
WOW! AMAZING!
SURE GLAD WE GOT OURSELVES THE DARK MAGICIAN!
WE CAN BEAT 'EM!
UGH...THEIR NUMBERS ARE GREAT. THERE SEEMS TO BE NO HOPE.
하아
우워어
하아
YEAH, THIS IS GONNA BE A TOUGH ONE.
DREI, THIS WILL BE A TRUE TEST OF OUR METTLE.
LET'S SEE HOW HIGH WE CAN SCORE.

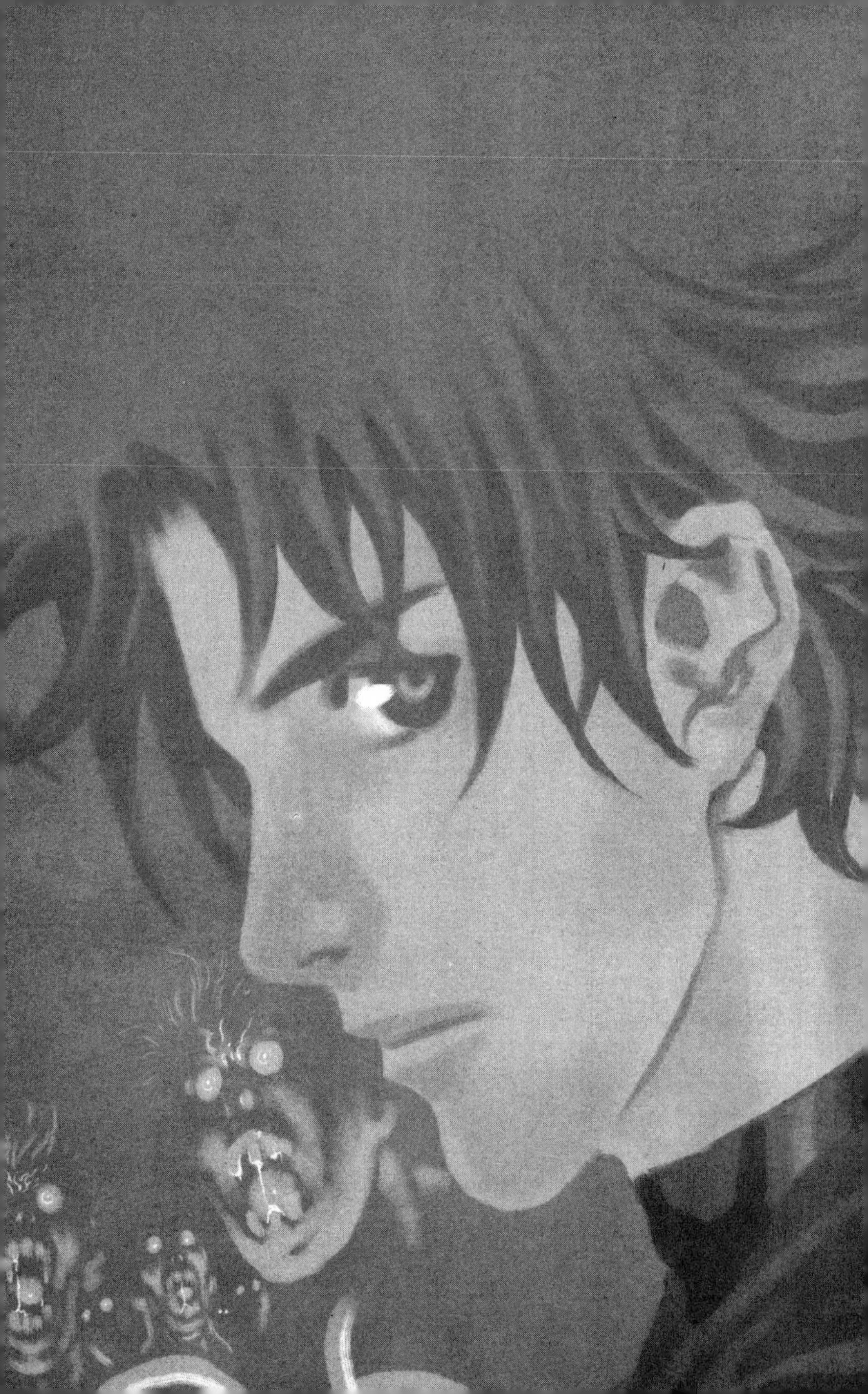

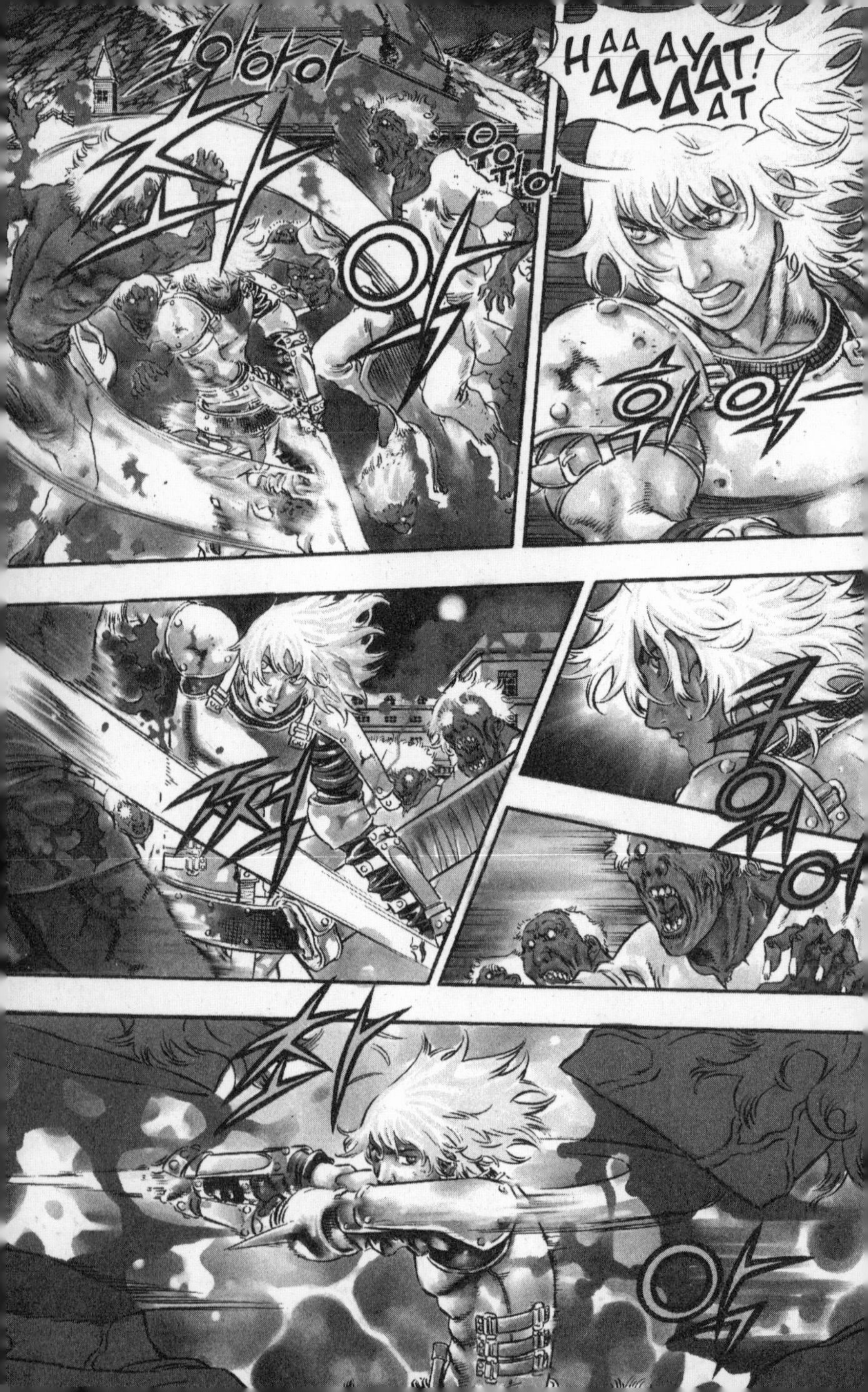
HAAAAYAAAAT!

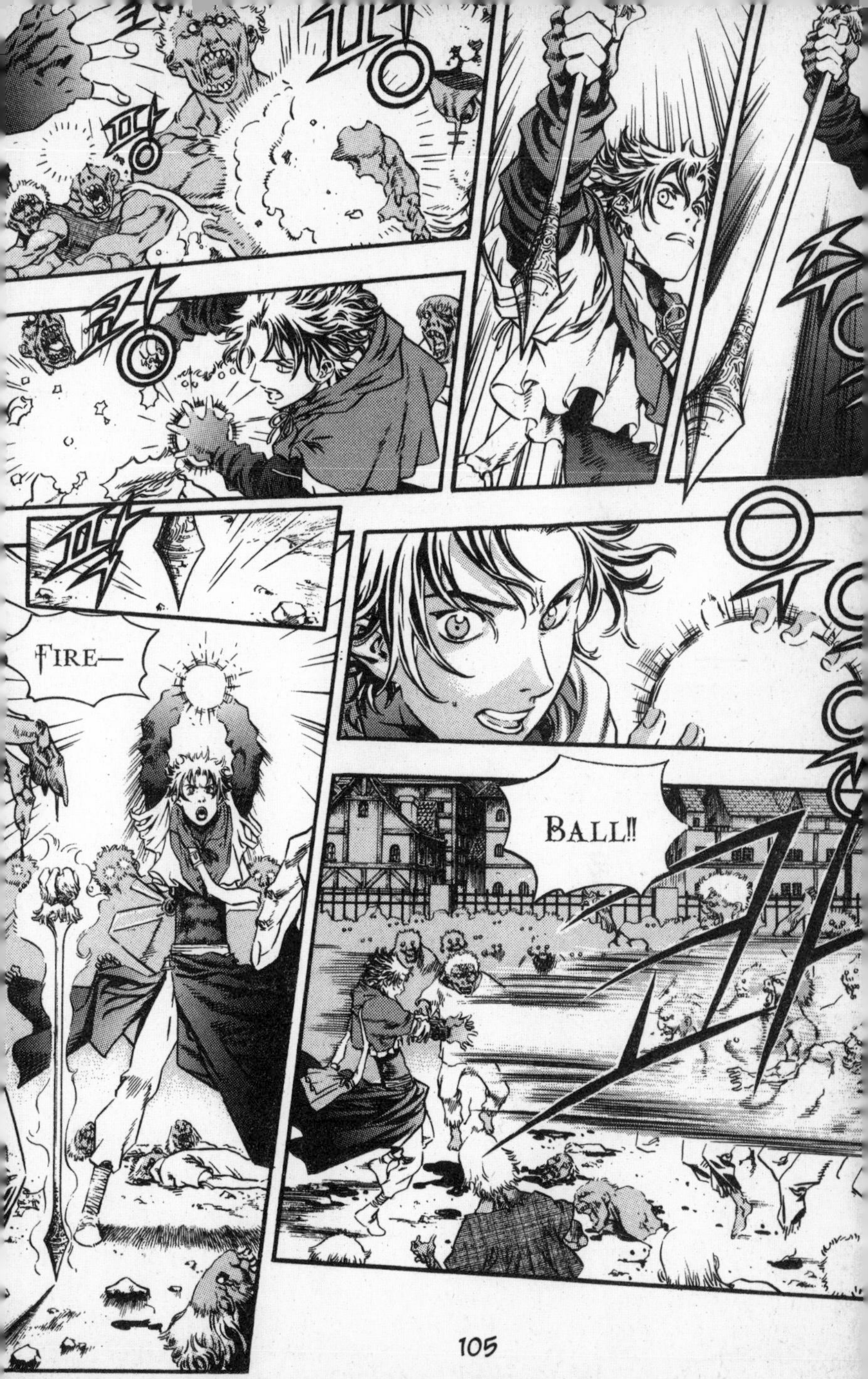
FIRE—
BALL!!

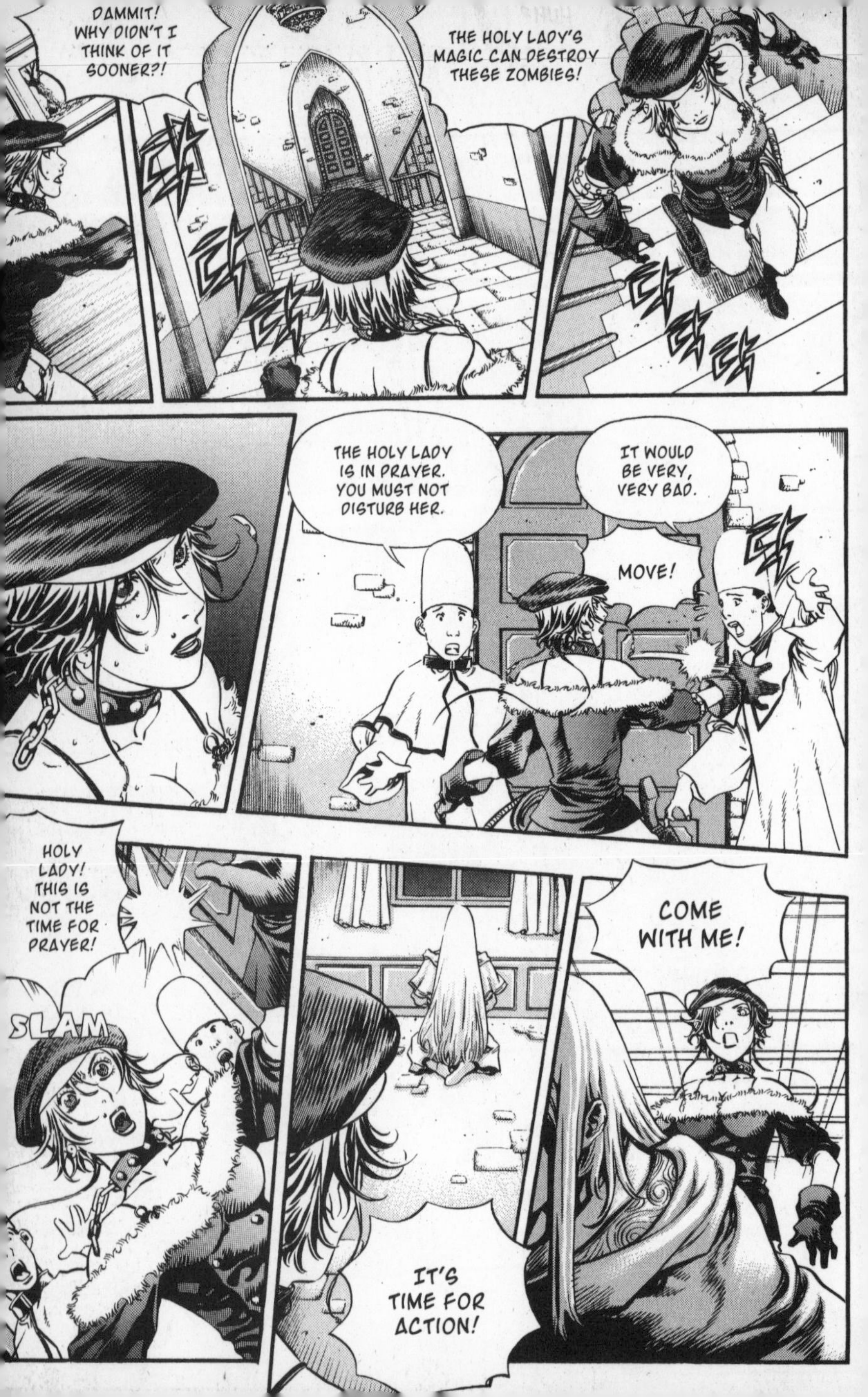
DAMMIT! WHY DIDN'T I THINK OF IT SOONER?!
THE HOLY LADY'S MAGIC CAN DESTROY THESE ZOMBIES!
THE HOLY LADY IS IN PRAYER. YOU MUST NOT DISTURB HER.
IT WOULD BE VERY, VERY BAD.
MOVE!
HOLY LADY! THIS IS NOT THE TIME FOR PRAYER!
SLAM
COME WITH ME!
IT'S TIME FOR ACTION!

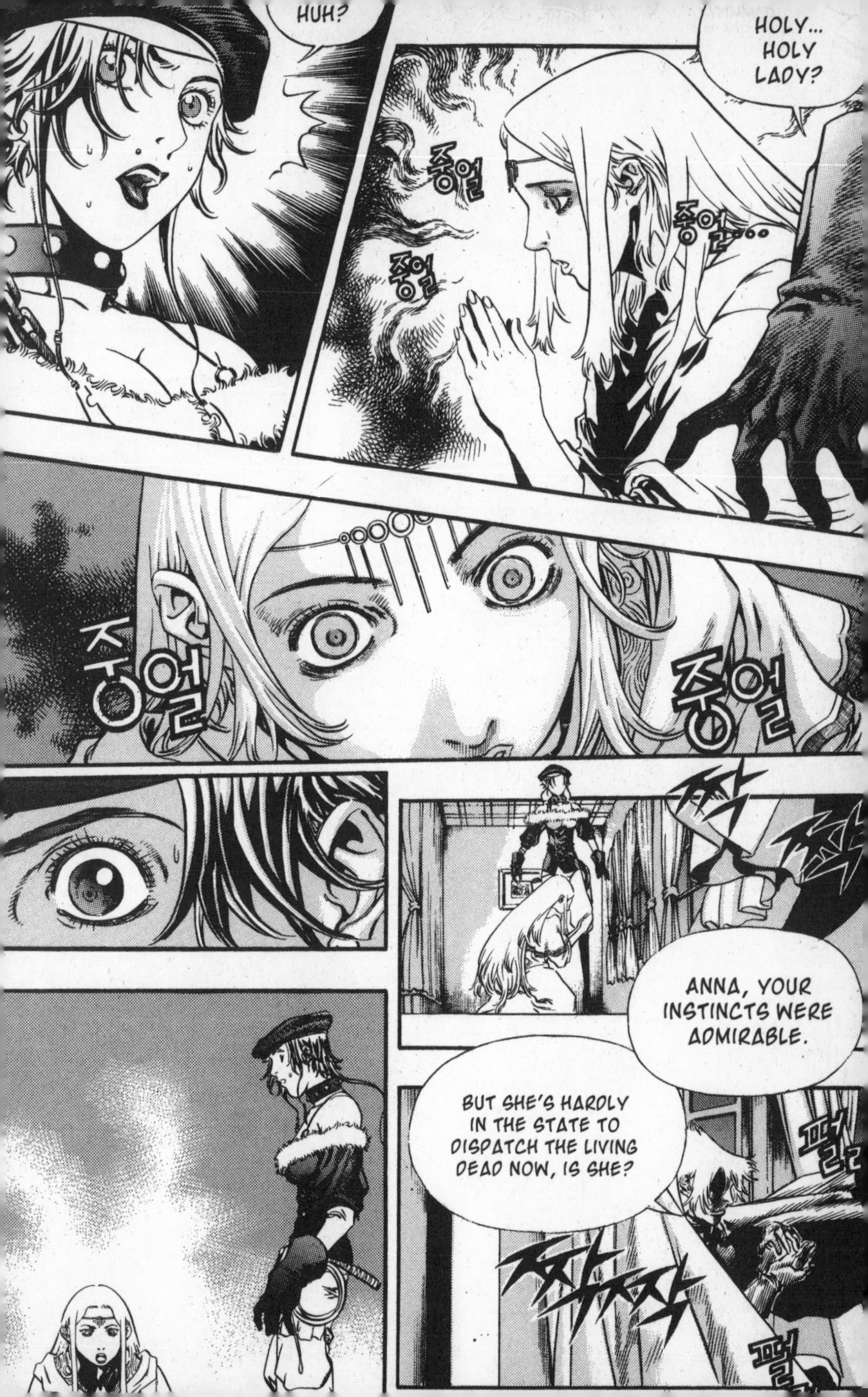
HUH?
HOLY... HOLY LADY?
중얼
중얼
중얼...
중얼
중얼
ANNA, YOUR INSTINCTS WERE ADMIRABLE.
BUT SHE'S HARDLY IN THE STATE TO DISPATCH THE LIVING DEAD NOW, IS SHE?

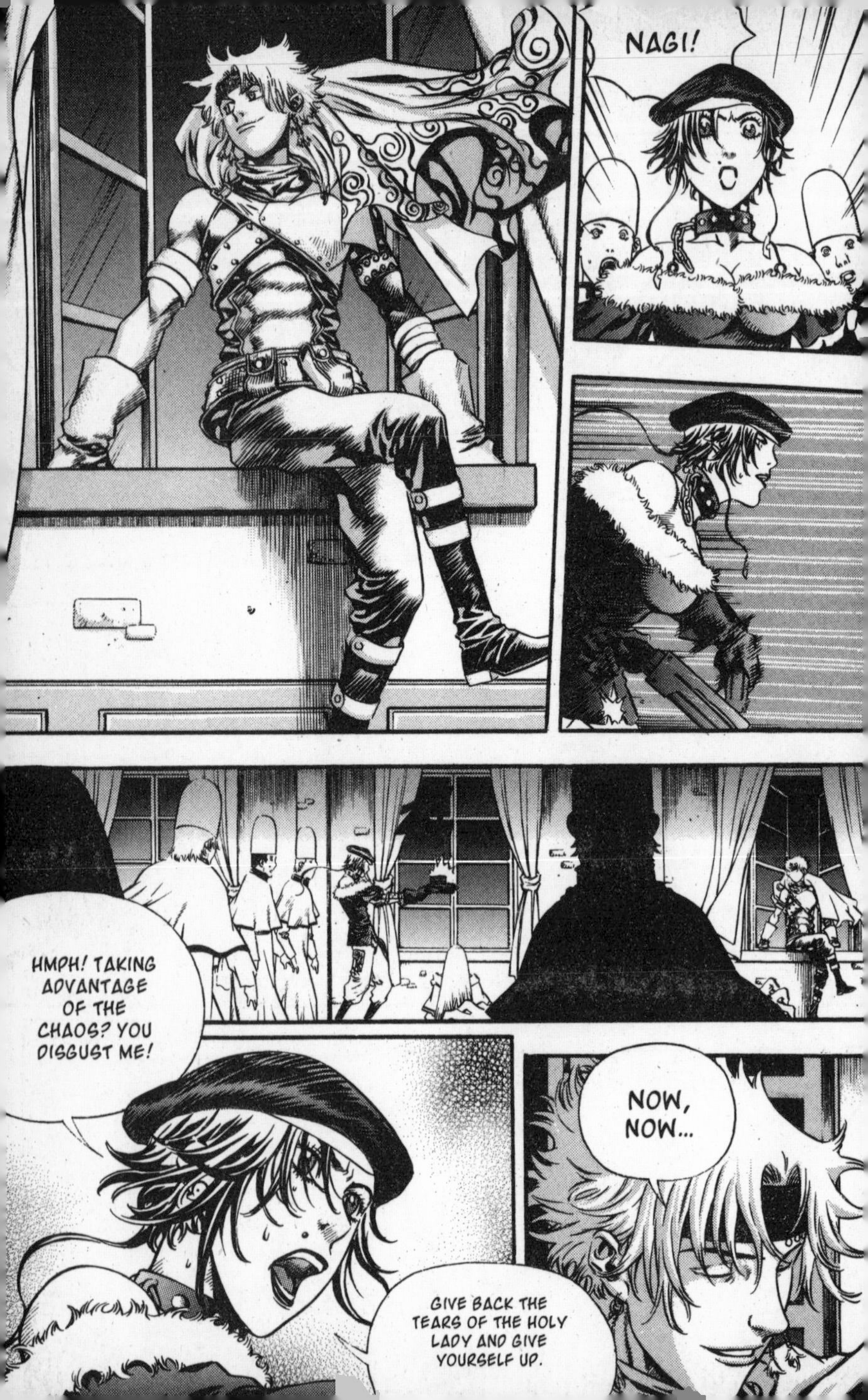
NAGI!
HMPH! TAKING ADVANTAGE OF THE CHAOS? YOU DISGUST ME!
GIVE BACK THE TEARS OF THE HOLY LADY AND GIVE YOURSELF UP.
NOW, NOW...

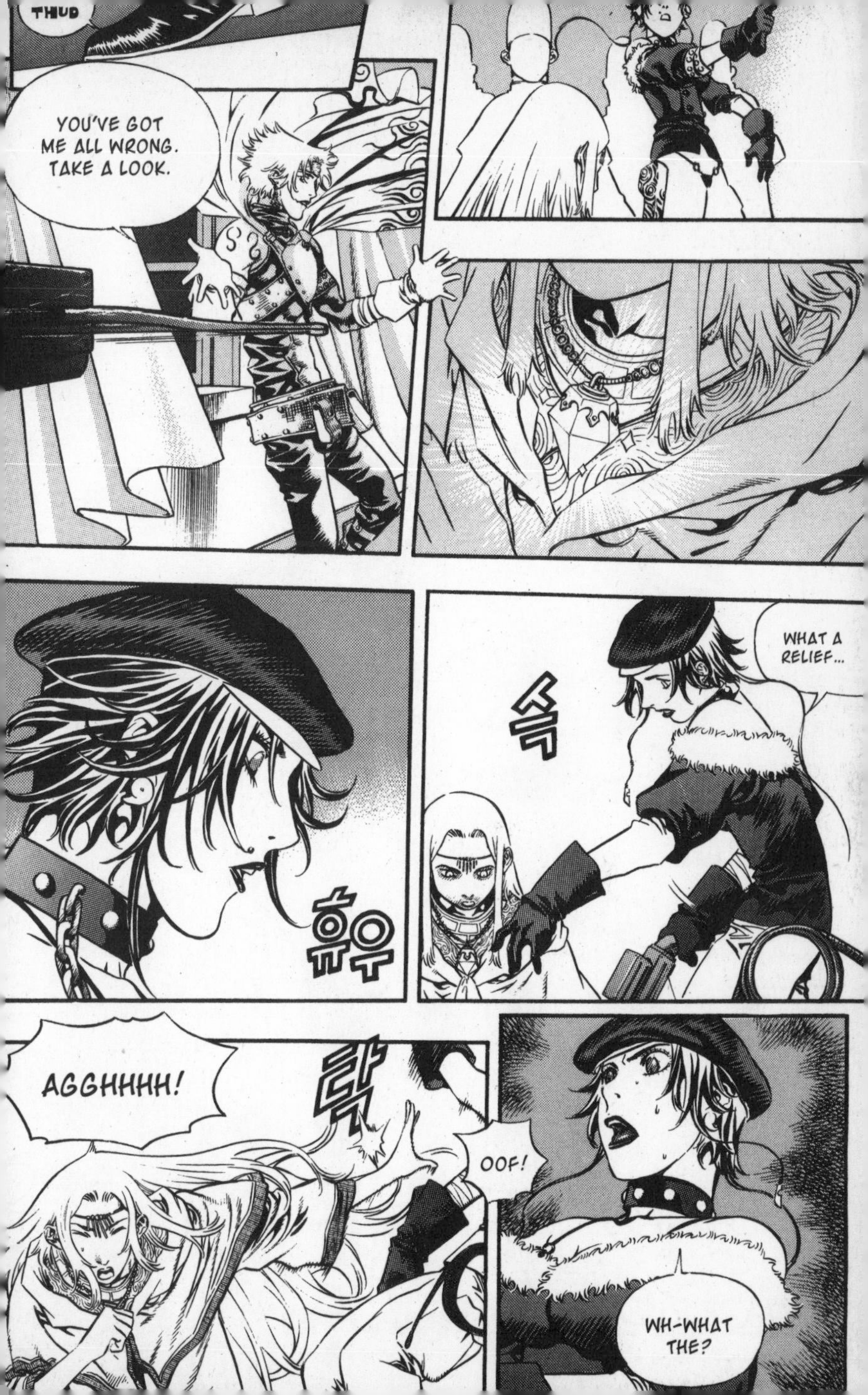
THUD
YOU'VE GOT ME ALL WRONG. TAKE A LOOK.
WHAT A RELIEF...
AGGHHHH!
OOF!
WH-WHAT THE?

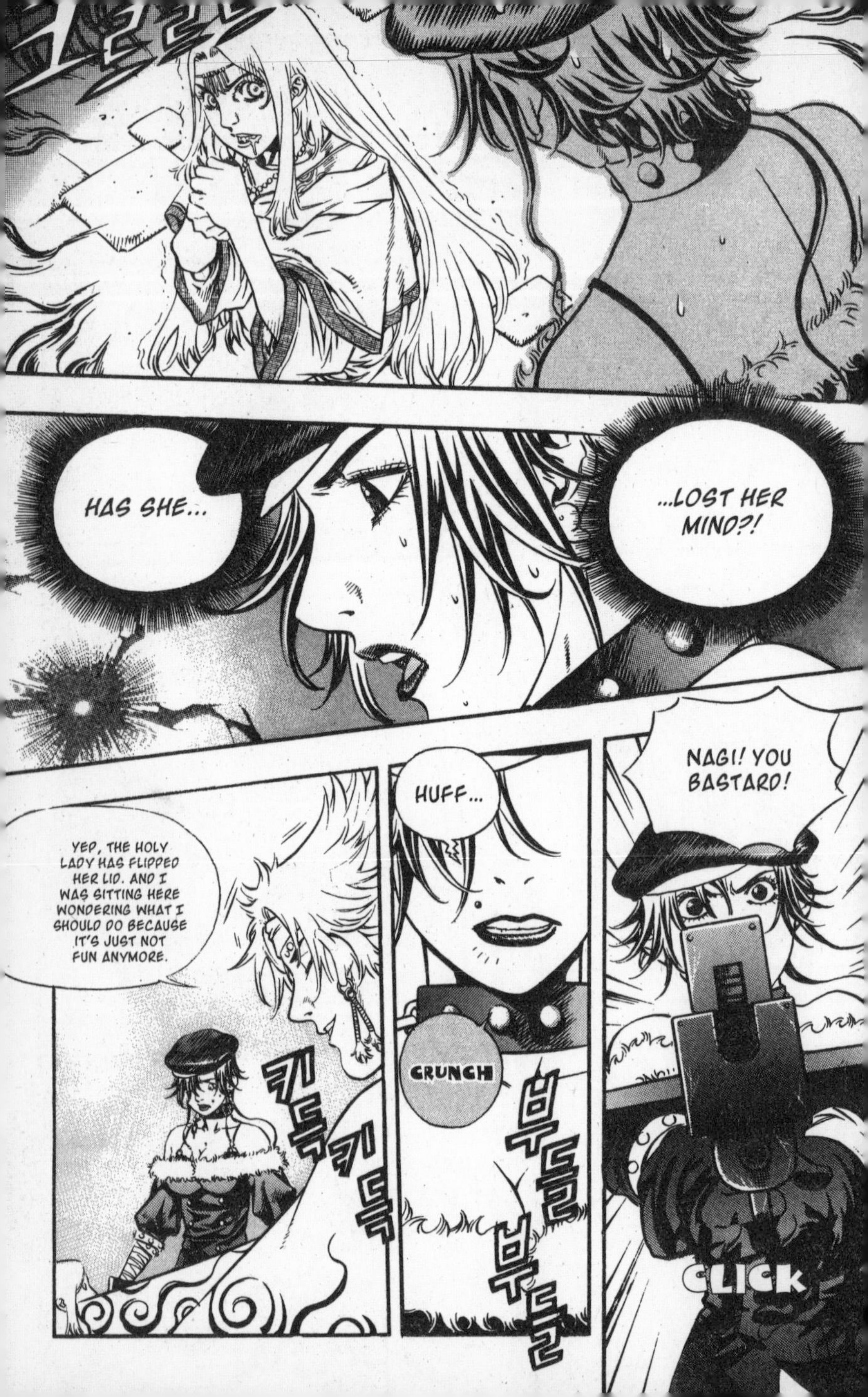
HAS SHE...
...LOST HER MIND?!
NAGI! YOU BASTARD!
HUFF...
YEP, THE HOLY LADY HAS FLIPPED HER LID. AND I WAS SITTING HERE WONDERING WHAT I SHOULD DO BECAUSE IT'S JUST NOT FUN ANYMORE.
CRUNCH
CLICK

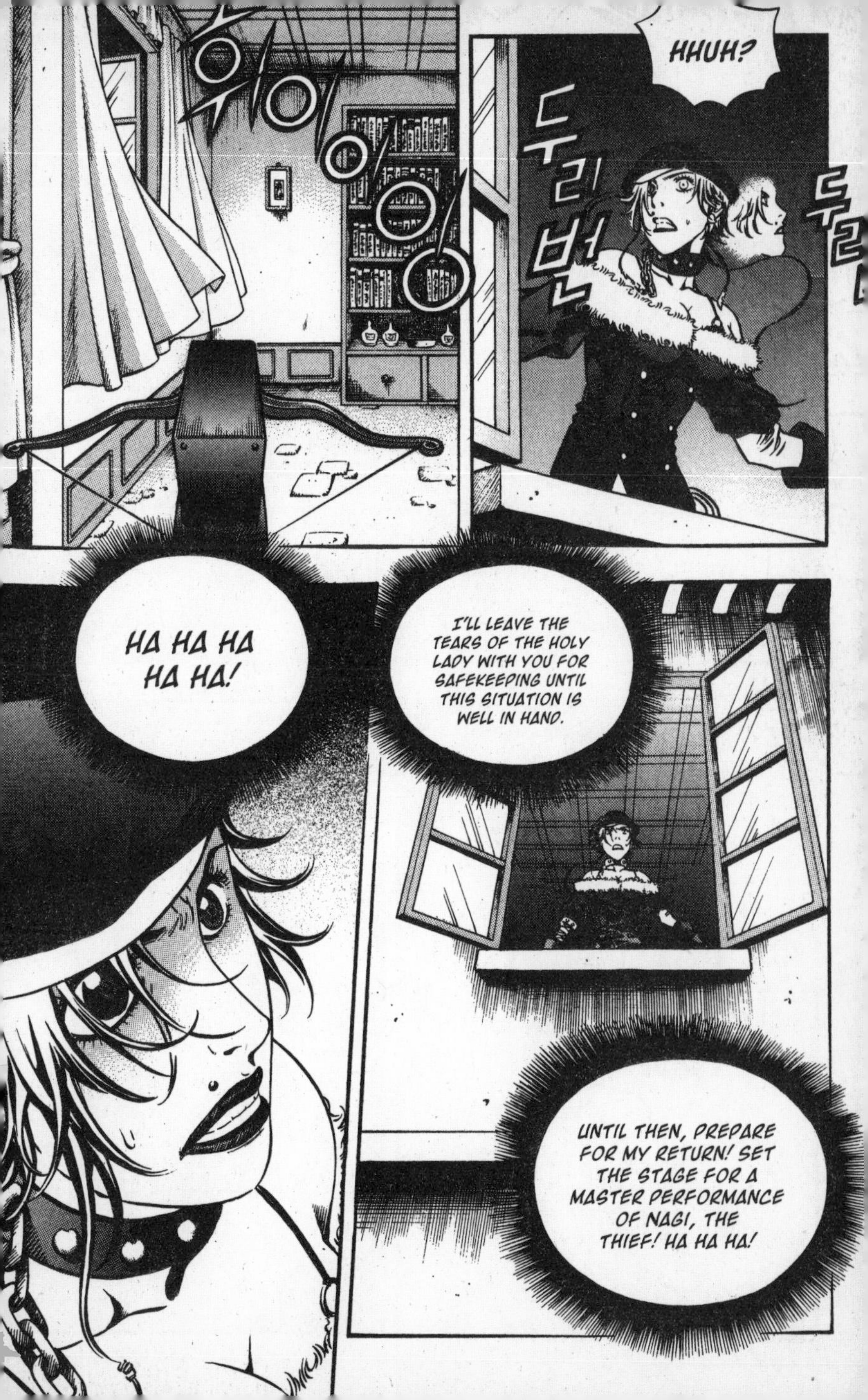
HHUH?
HA HA HA HA HA!
I'LL LEAVE THE TEARS OF THE HOLY LADY WITH YOU FOR SAFEKEEPING UNTIL THIS SITUATION IS WELL IN HAND.
UNTIL THEN, PREPARE FOR MY RETURN! SET THE STAGE FOR A MASTER PERFORMANCE OF NAGI, THE THIEF! HA HA HA!

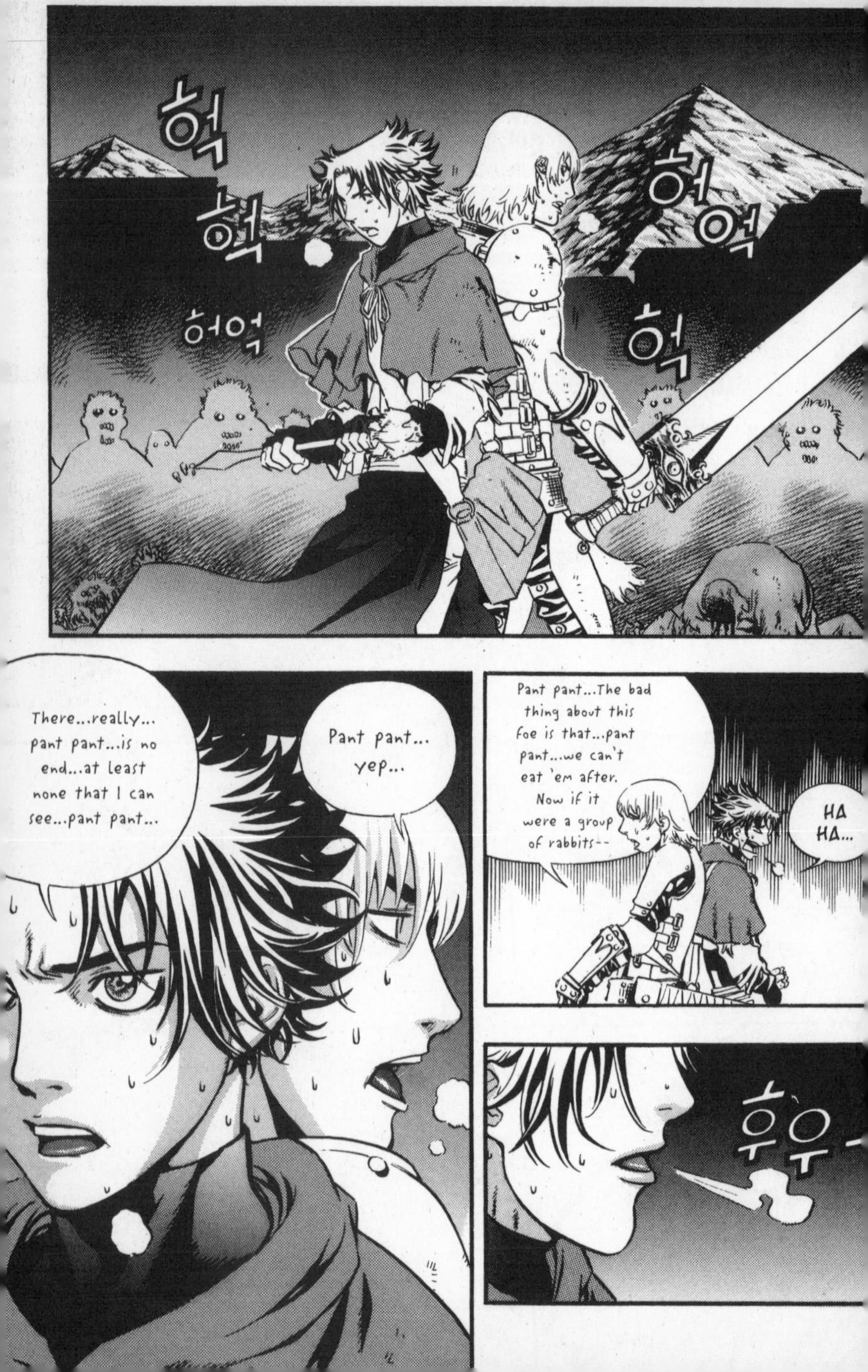

헉
헉
헉억
헉억
헉
There...really... pant pant...is no end...at least none that I can see...pant pant...
Pant pant... yep...
Pant pant...The bad thing about this foe is that...pant pant...we can't eat 'em after. Now if it were a group of rabbits--
HA HA...
후우-

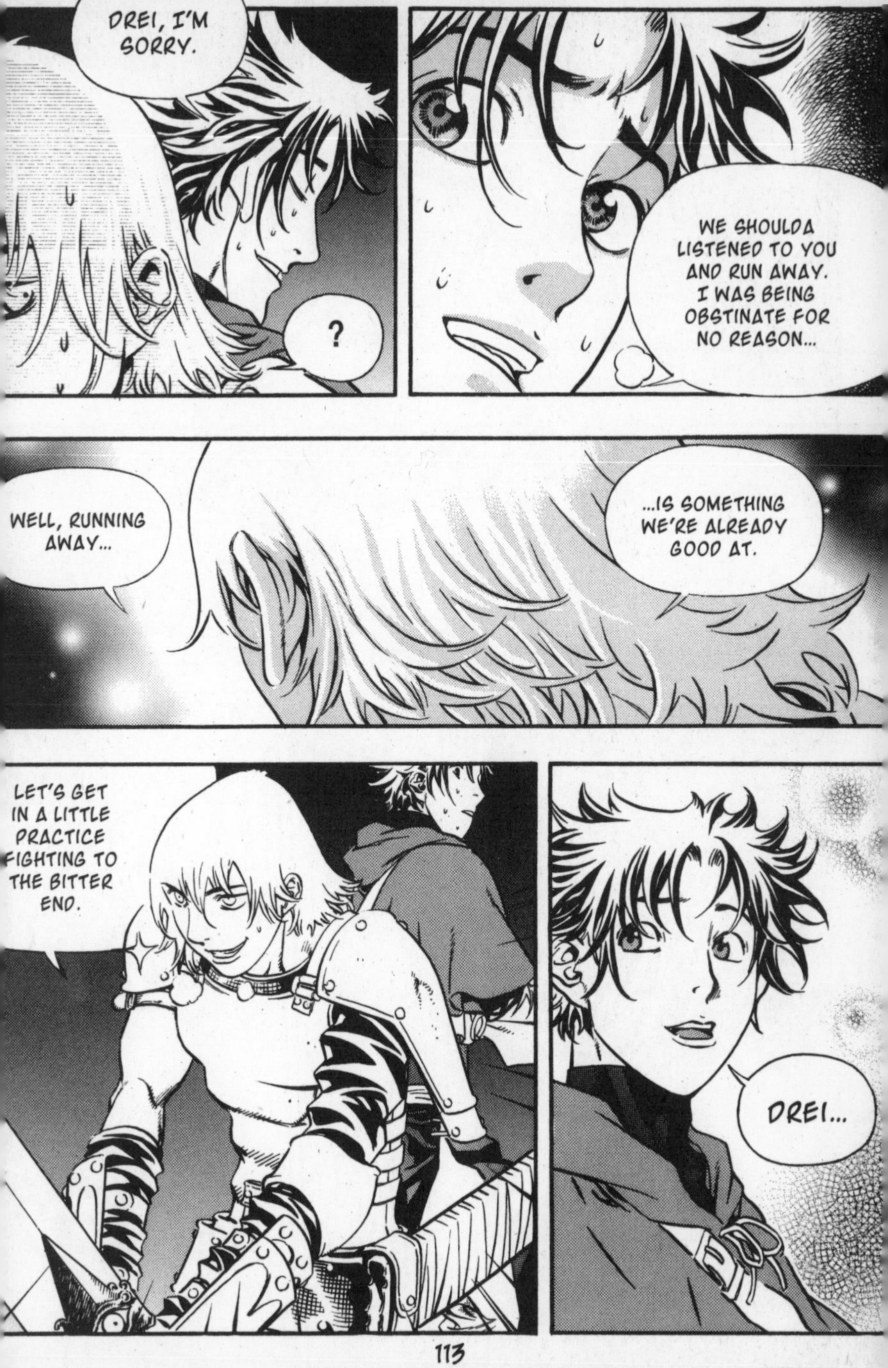
DREI, I'M SORRY.
?
WE SHOULDA LISTENED TO YOU AND RUN AWAY. I WAS BEING OBSTINATE FOR NO REASON...
WELL, RUNNING AWAY...
...IS SOMETHING WE'RE ALREADY GOOD AT.
LET'S GET IN A LITTLE PRACTICE FIGHTING TO THE BITTER END.
DREI...

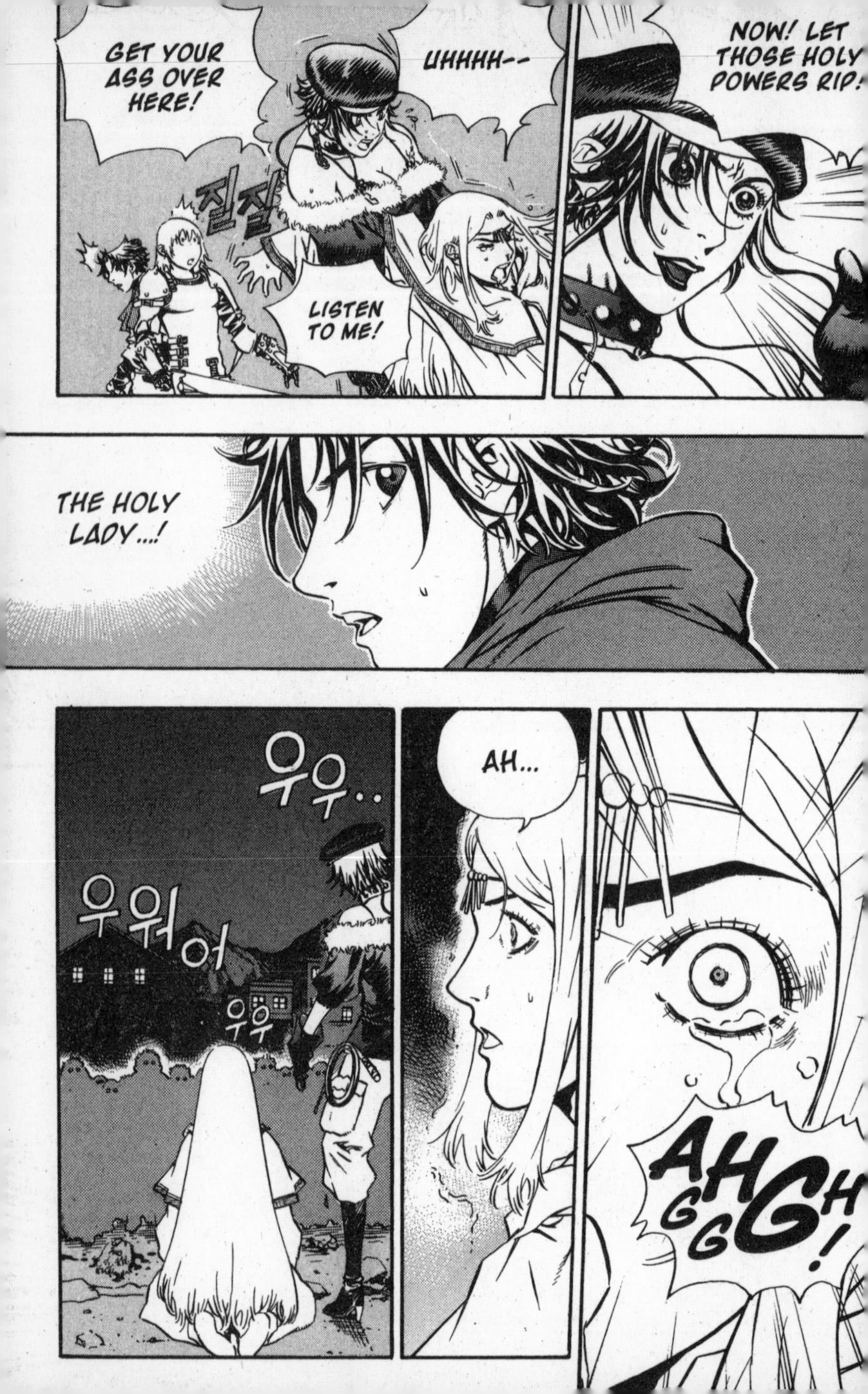
GET YOUR ASS OVER HERE!
UHHHH--
질질
LISTEN TO ME!
NOW! LET THOSE HOLY POWERS RIP!
THE HOLY LADY...!
우우..
우워어
우우
AH...
AHGGGH!

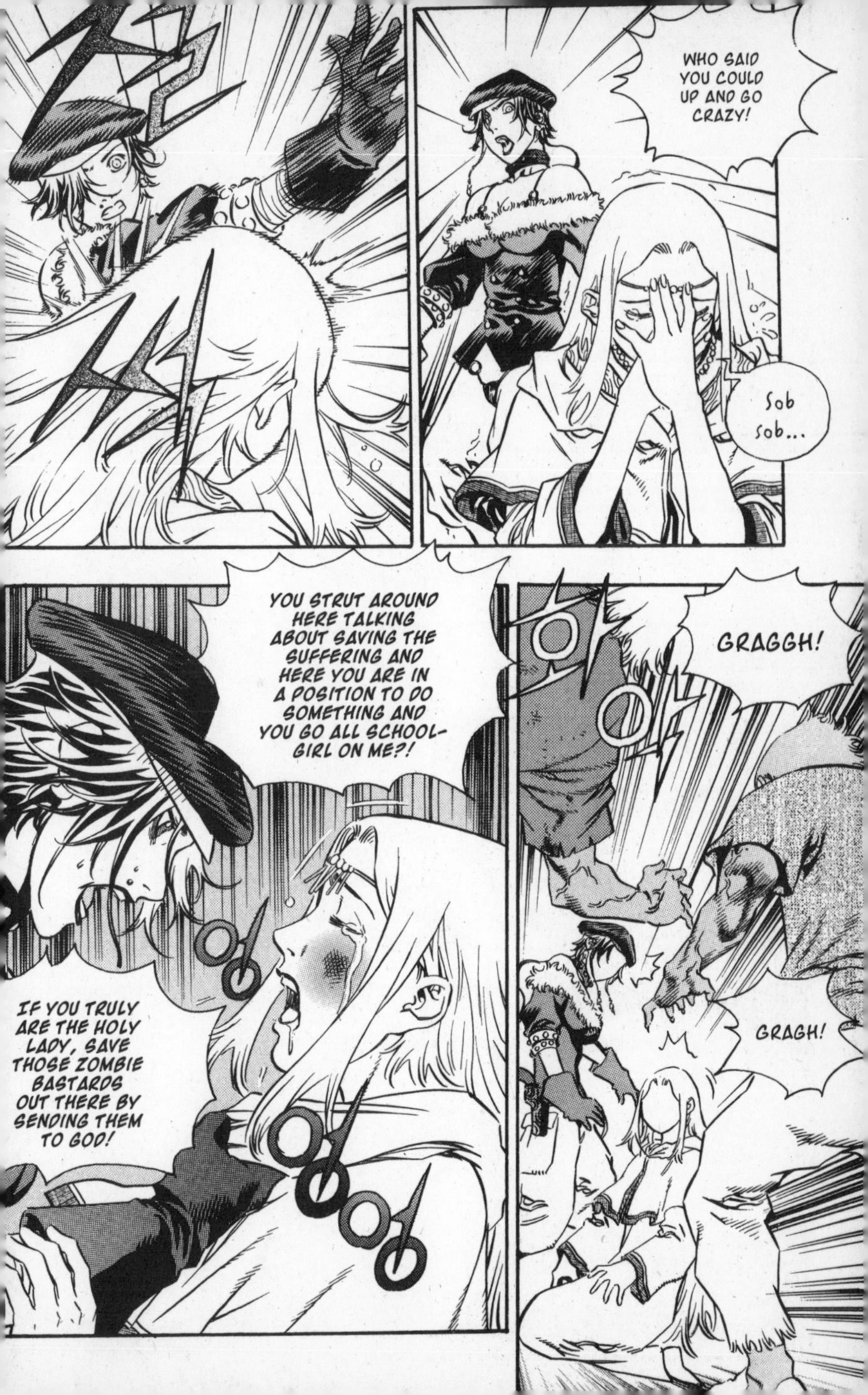
WHO SAID YOU COULD UP AND GO CRAZY!
Sob sob...
YOU STRUT AROUND HERE TALKING ABOUT SAVING THE SUFFERING AND HERE YOU ARE IN A POSITION TO DO SOMETHING AND YOU GO ALL SCHOOL-GIRL ON ME?!
IF YOU TRULY ARE THE HOLY LADY, SAVE THOSE ZOMBIE BASTARDS OUT THERE BY SENDING THEM TO GOD!
GRAGGH!
GRAGH!

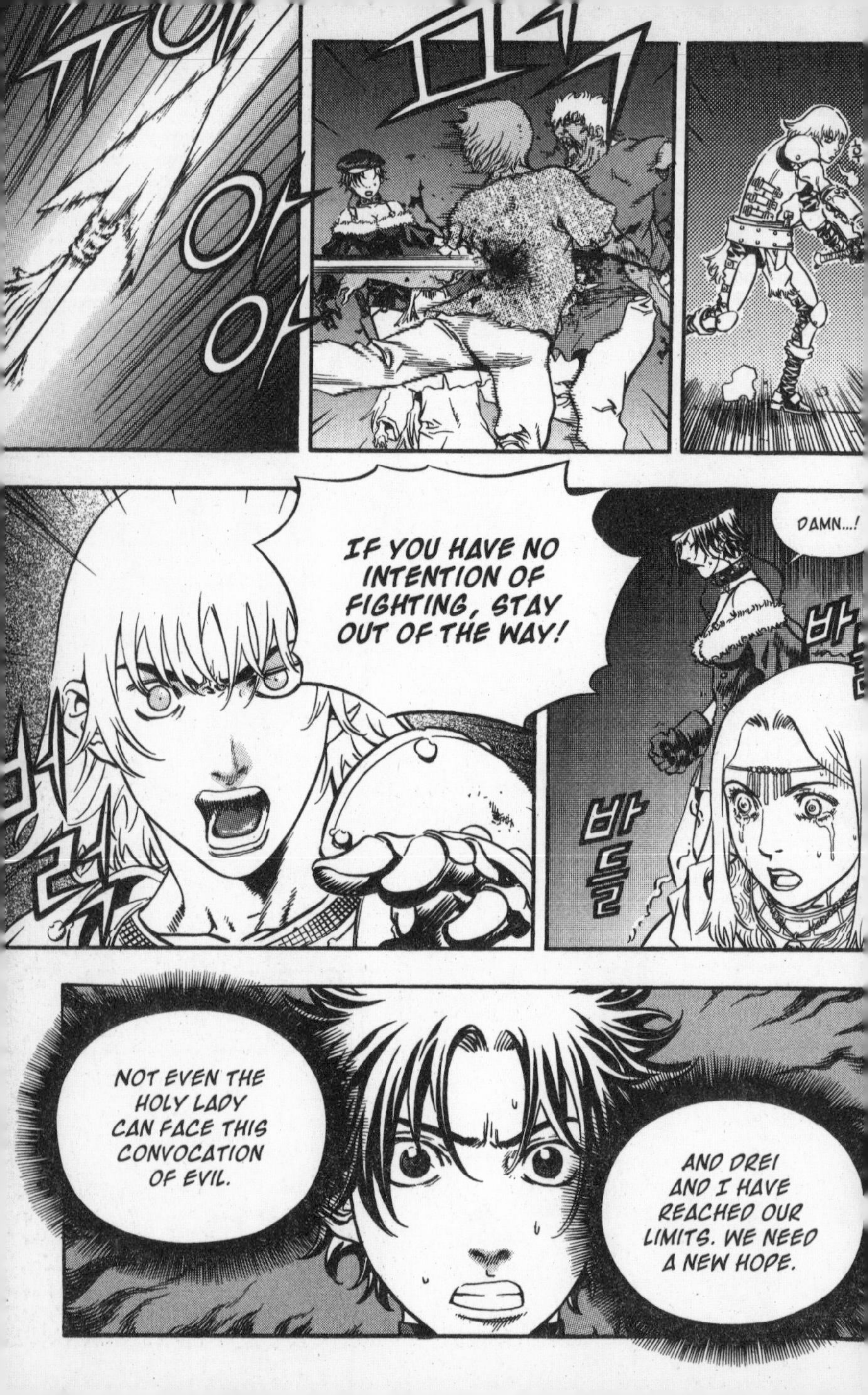
IF YOU HAVE NO INTENTION OF FIGHTING, STAY OUT OF THE WAY!
DAMN...!
NOT EVEN THE HOLY LADY CAN FACE THIS CONVOCATION OF EVIL.
AND DREI AND I HAVE REACHED OUR LIMITS. WE NEED A NEW HOPE.

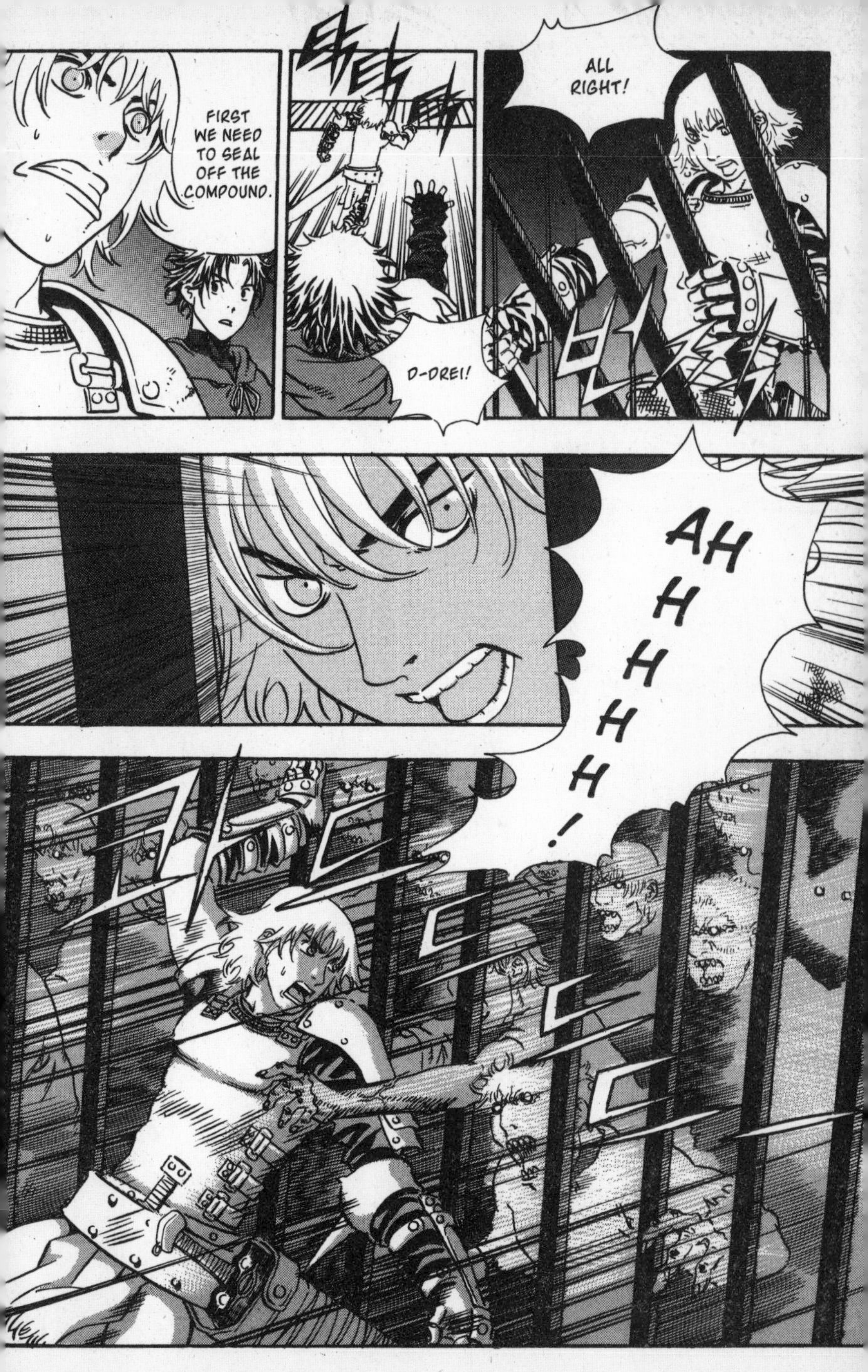
ALL RIGHT!
FIRST WE NEED TO SEAL OFF THE COMPOUND.
D-DREI!
AHHHHHH!

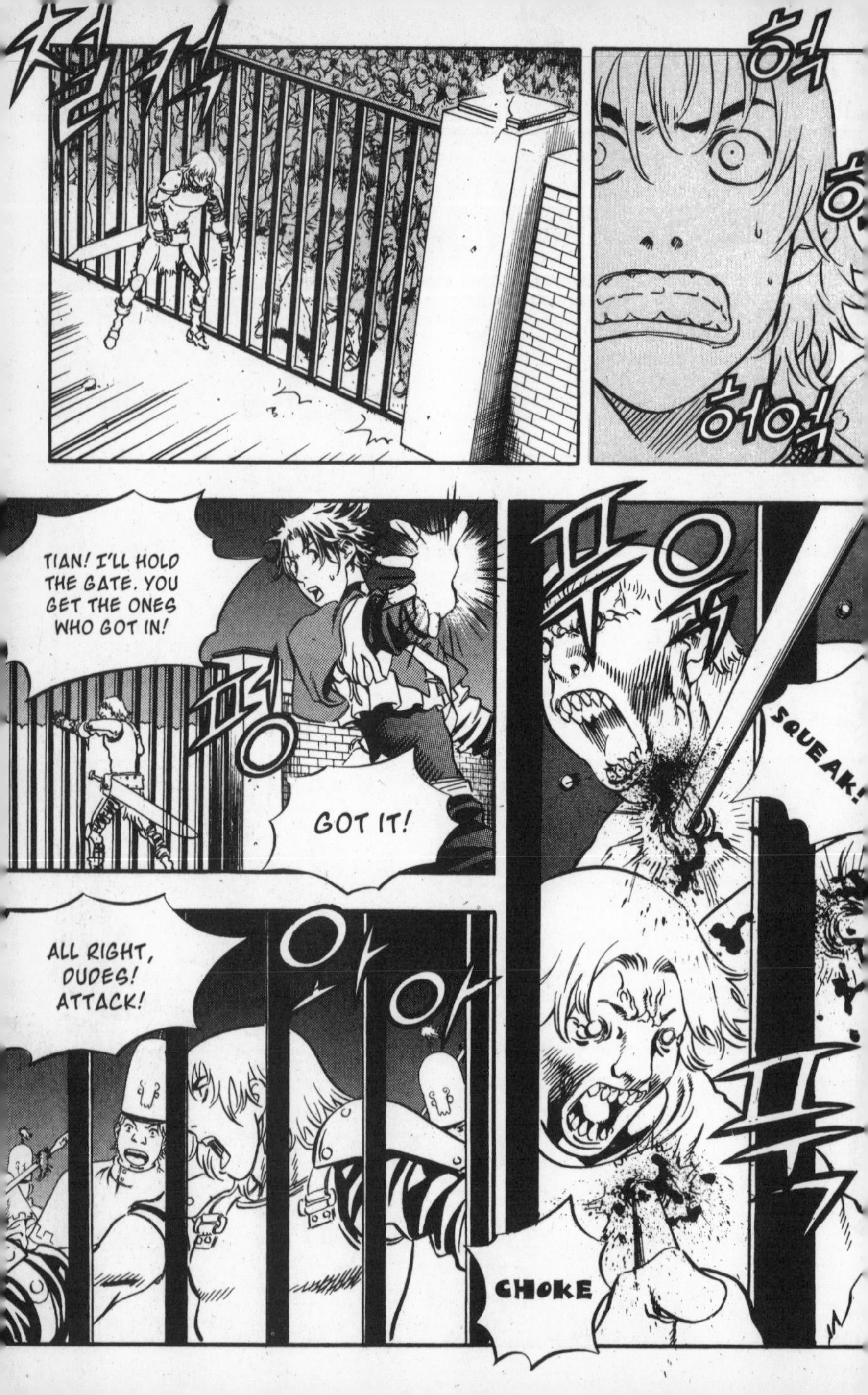
TIAN! I'LL HOLD THE GATE. YOU GET THE ONES WHO GOT IN!
GOT IT!
SQUEAK!
ALL RIGHT, DUDES! ATTACK!
CHOKE

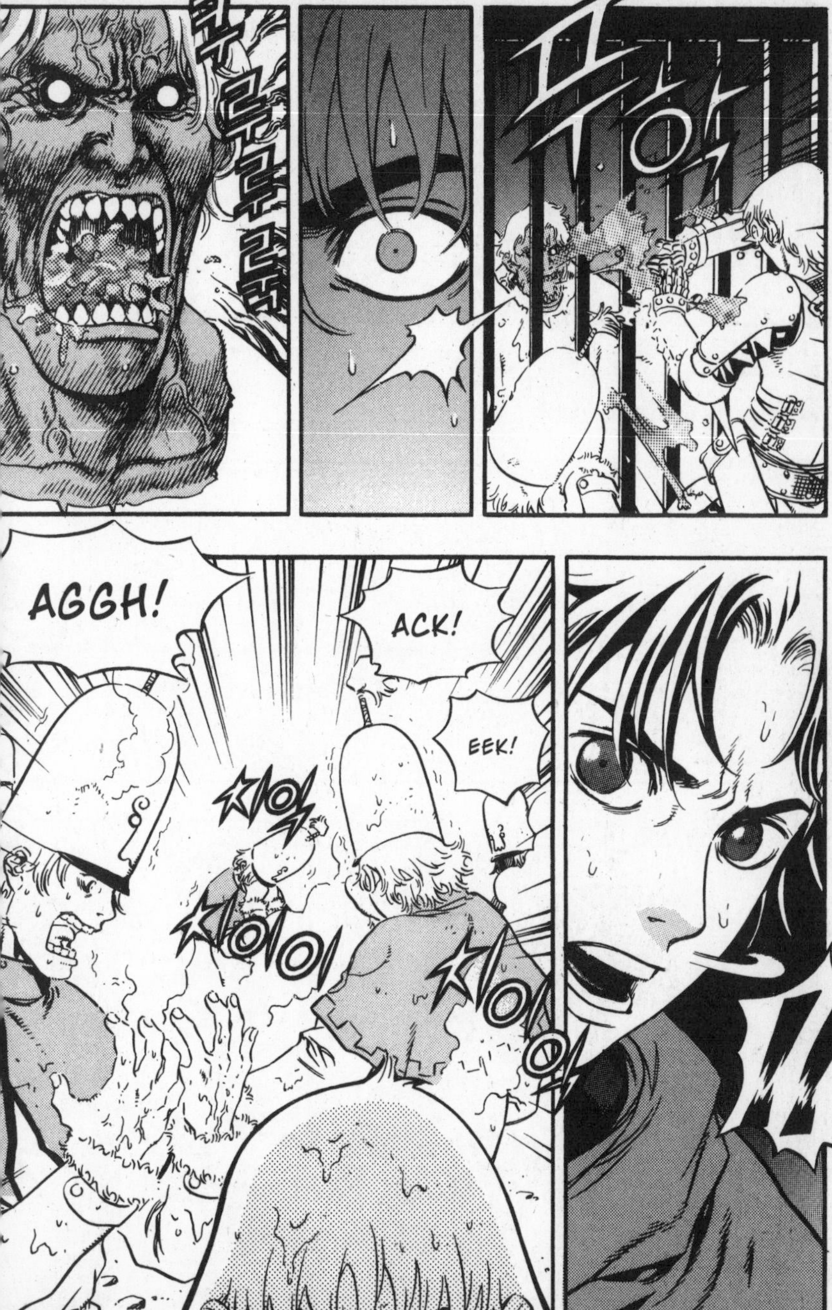
AGGH!
ACK!
EEK!

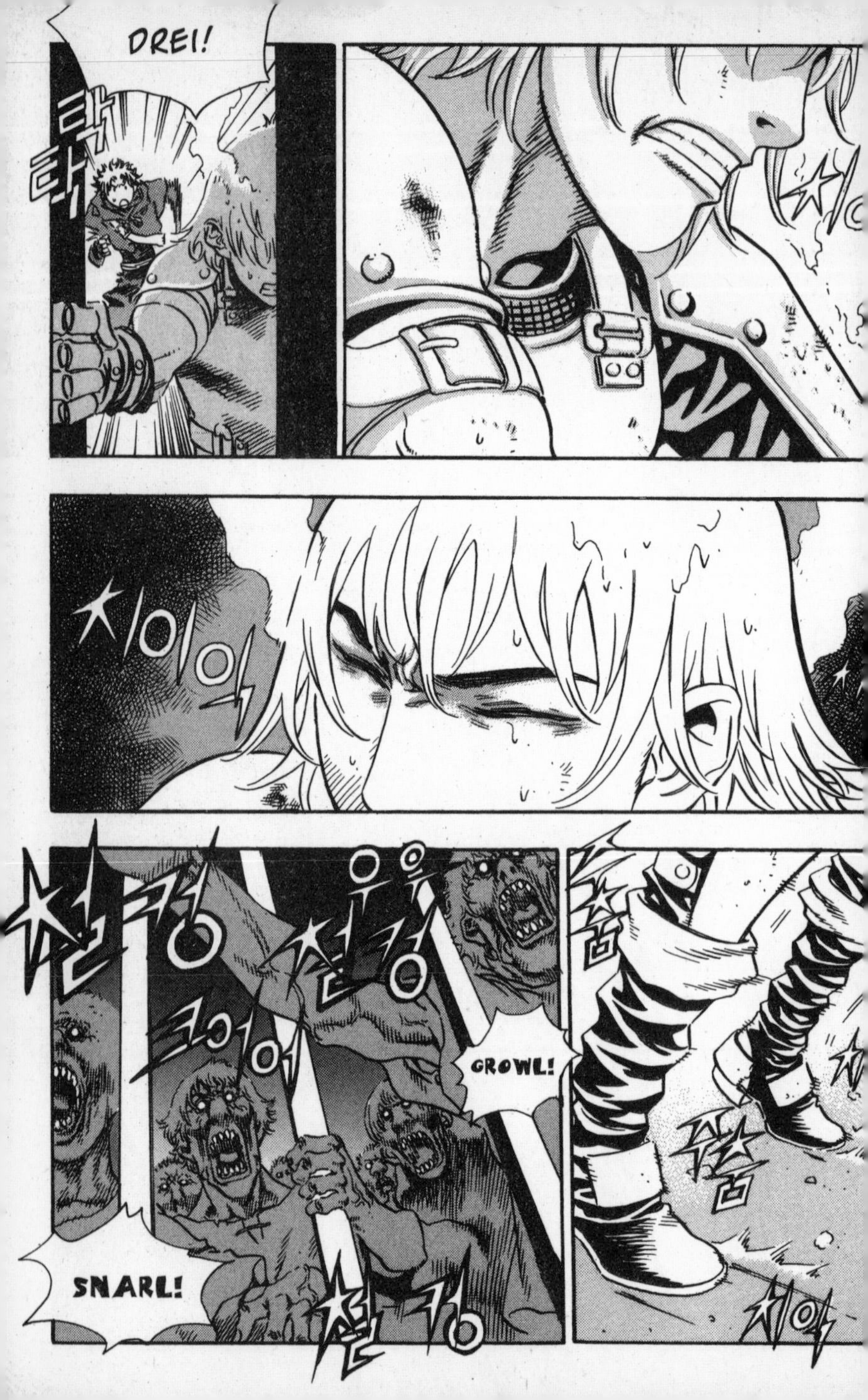
DREI!
GROWL!
SNARL!

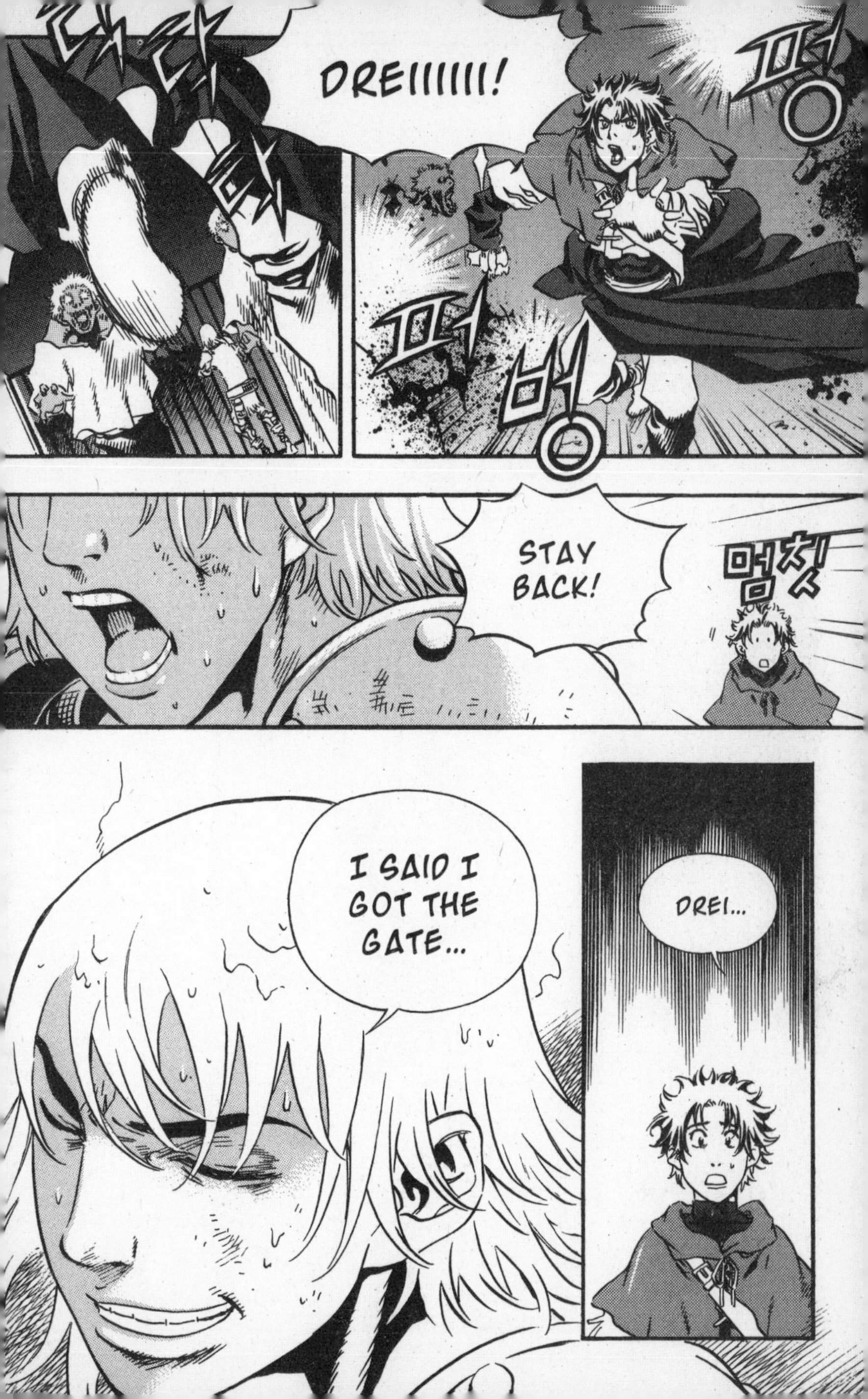
DREIIIIIII!
STAY BACK!
멈칫!
I SAID I GOT THE GATE...
DREI...

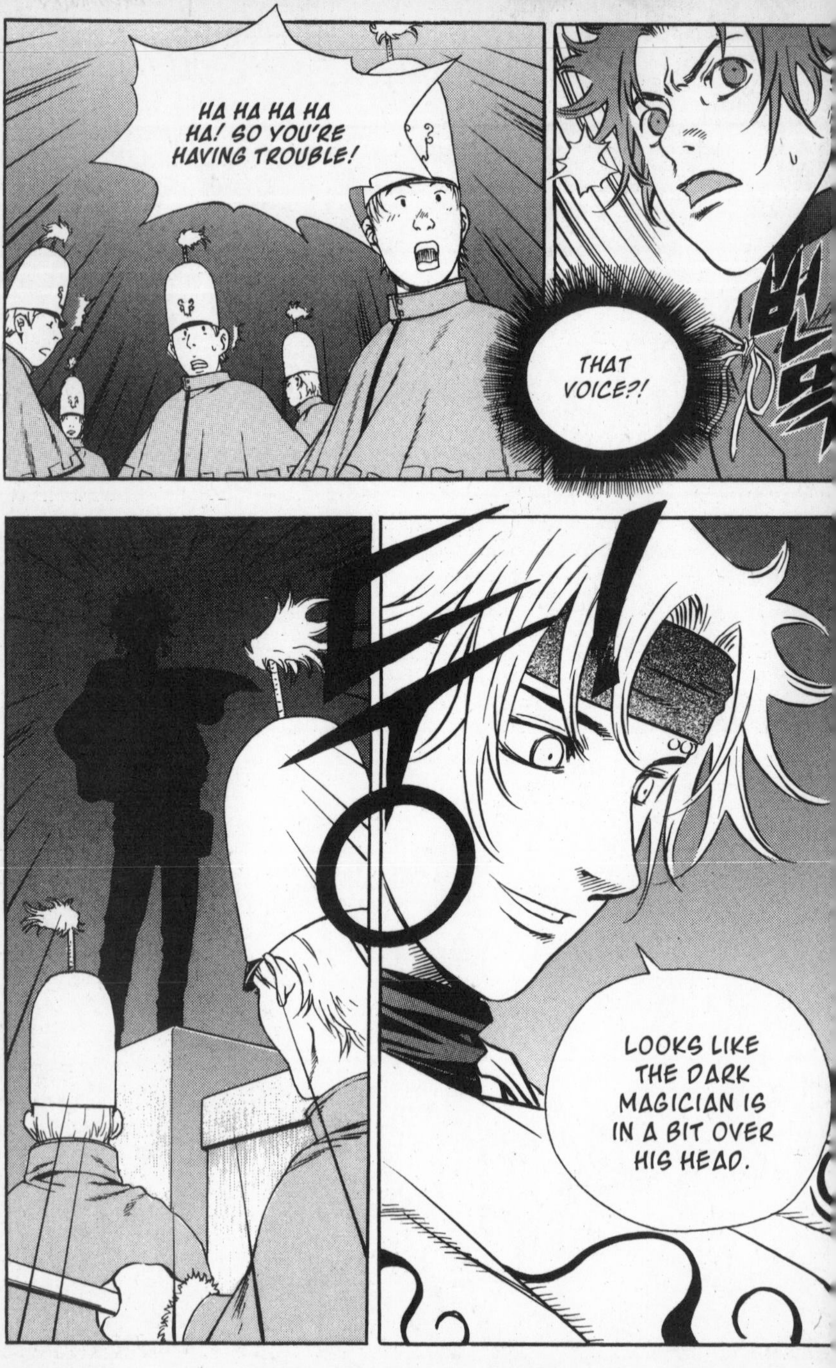
HA HA HA HA HA! SO YOU'RE HAVING TROUBLE!
THAT VOICE?!
LOOKS LIKE THE DARK MAGICIAN IS IN A BIT OVER HIS HEAD.

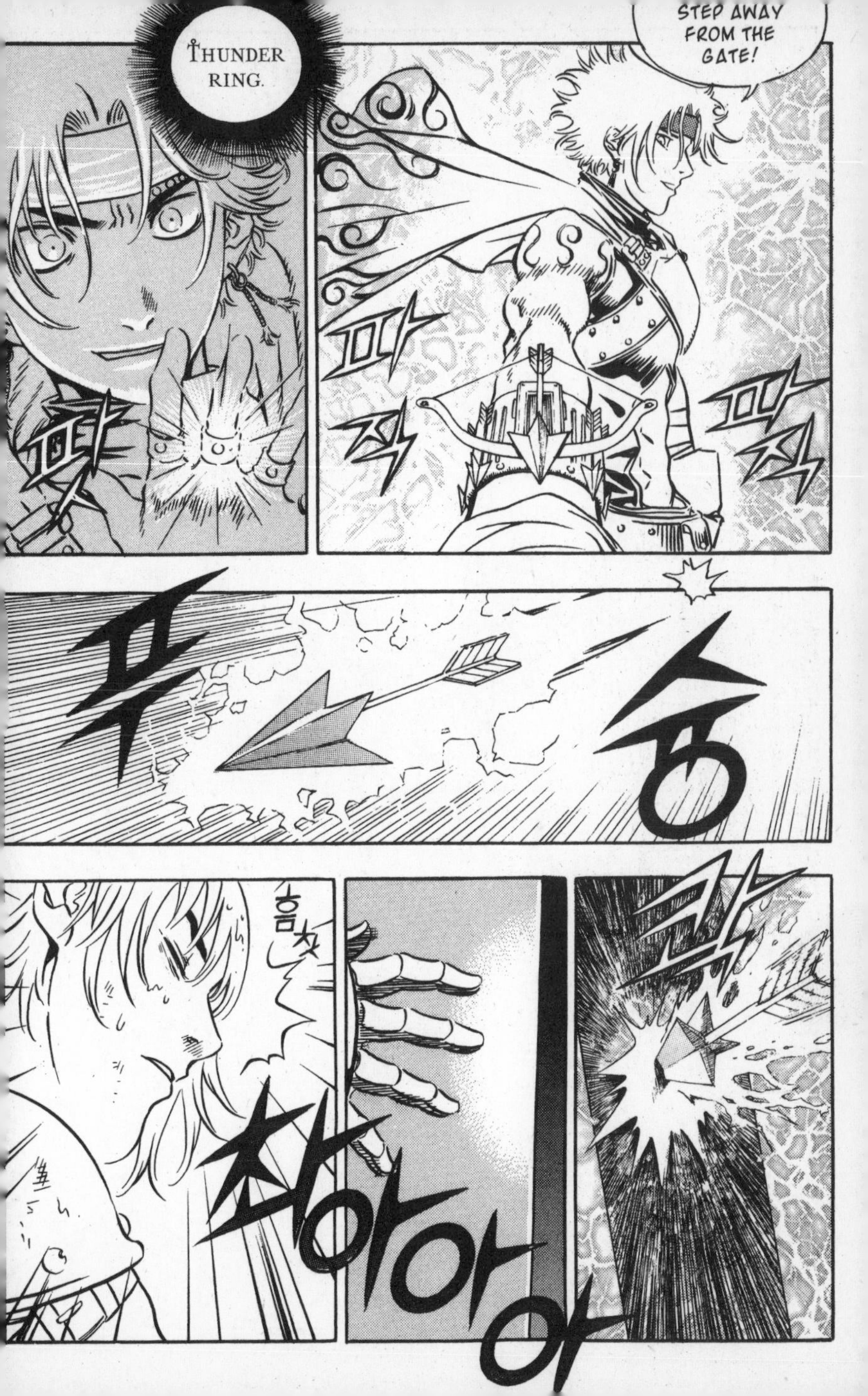
STEP AWAY FROM THE GATE!
THUNDER RING.

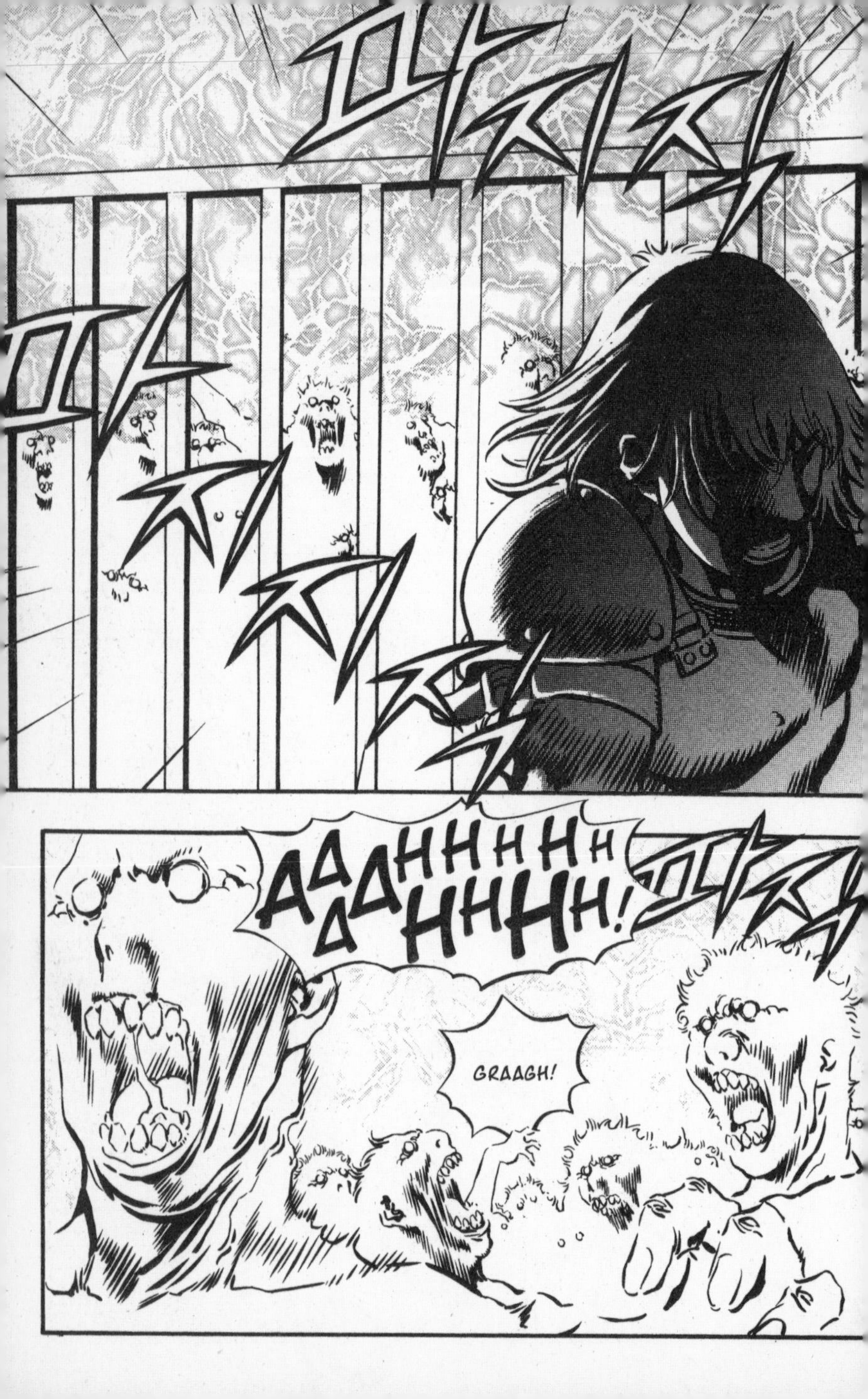
AAAHHHHHH
AHHHHH!
GRAAGH!

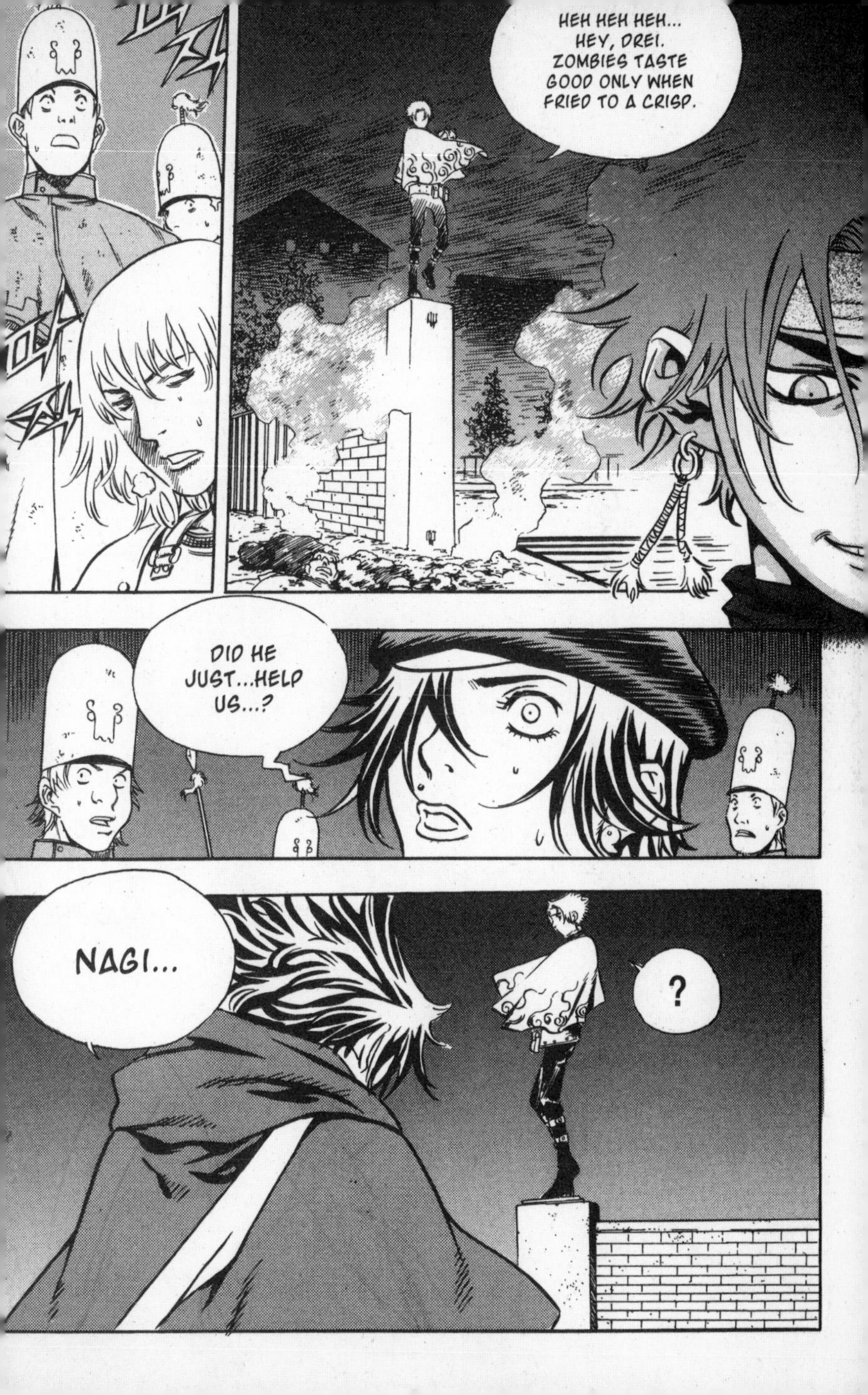
HEH HEH HEH... HEY, DREI. ZOMBIES TASTE GOOD ONLY WHEN FRIED TO A CRISP.
DID HE JUST...HELP US...?
NAGI...
?

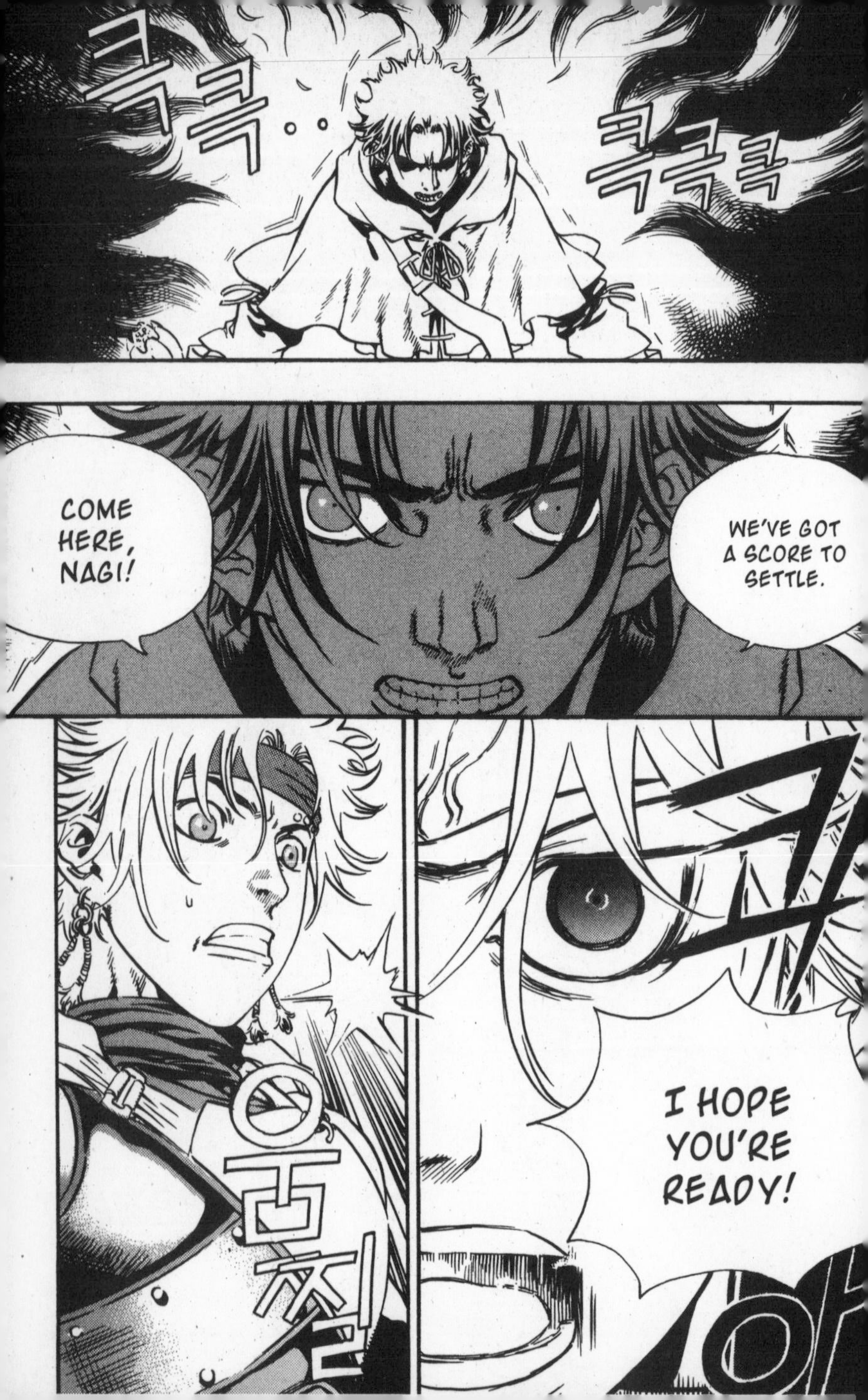
큭큭...
큭큭큭
COME HERE, NAGI!
WE'VE GOT A SCORE TO SETTLE.
I HOPE YOU'RE READY!

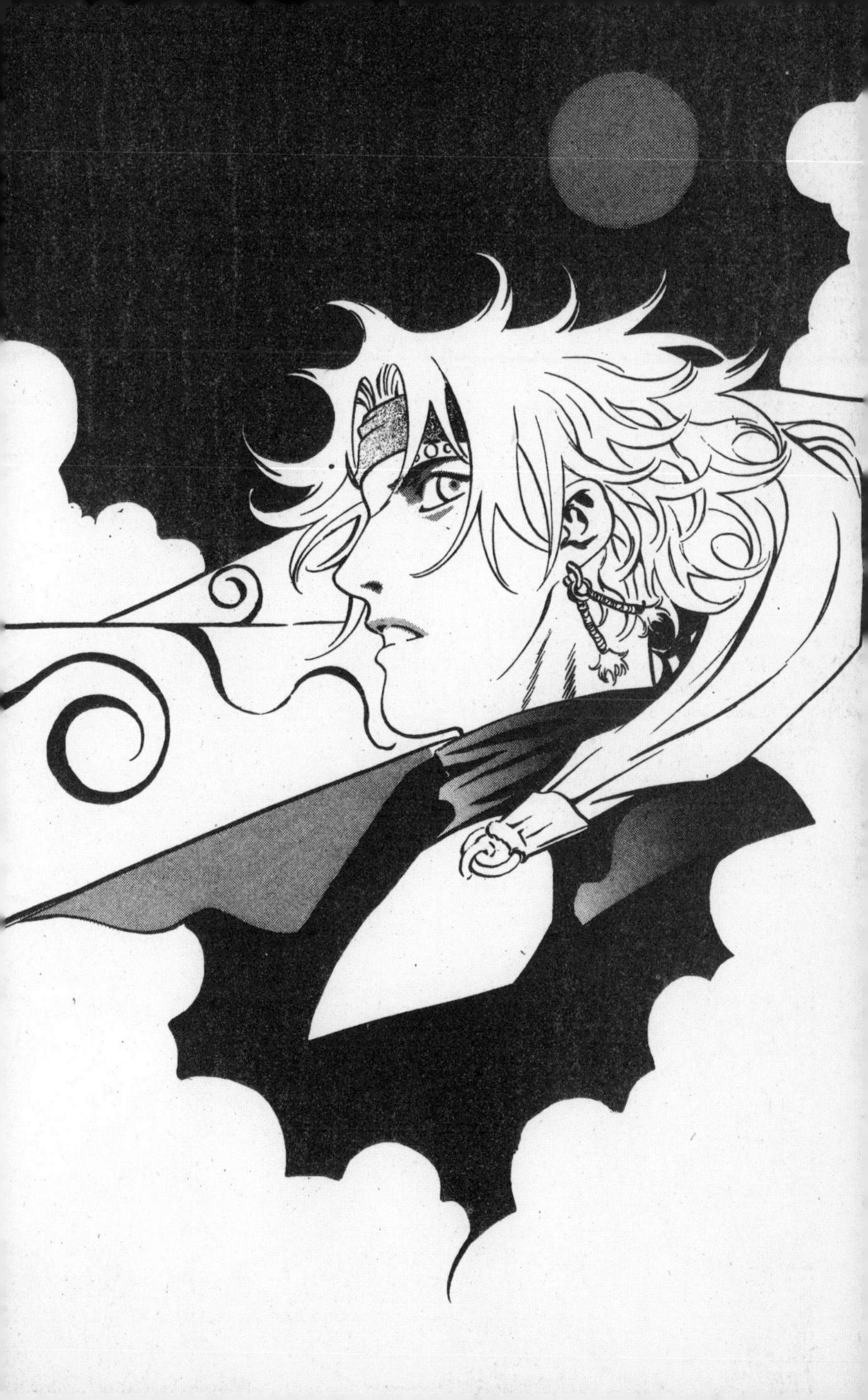

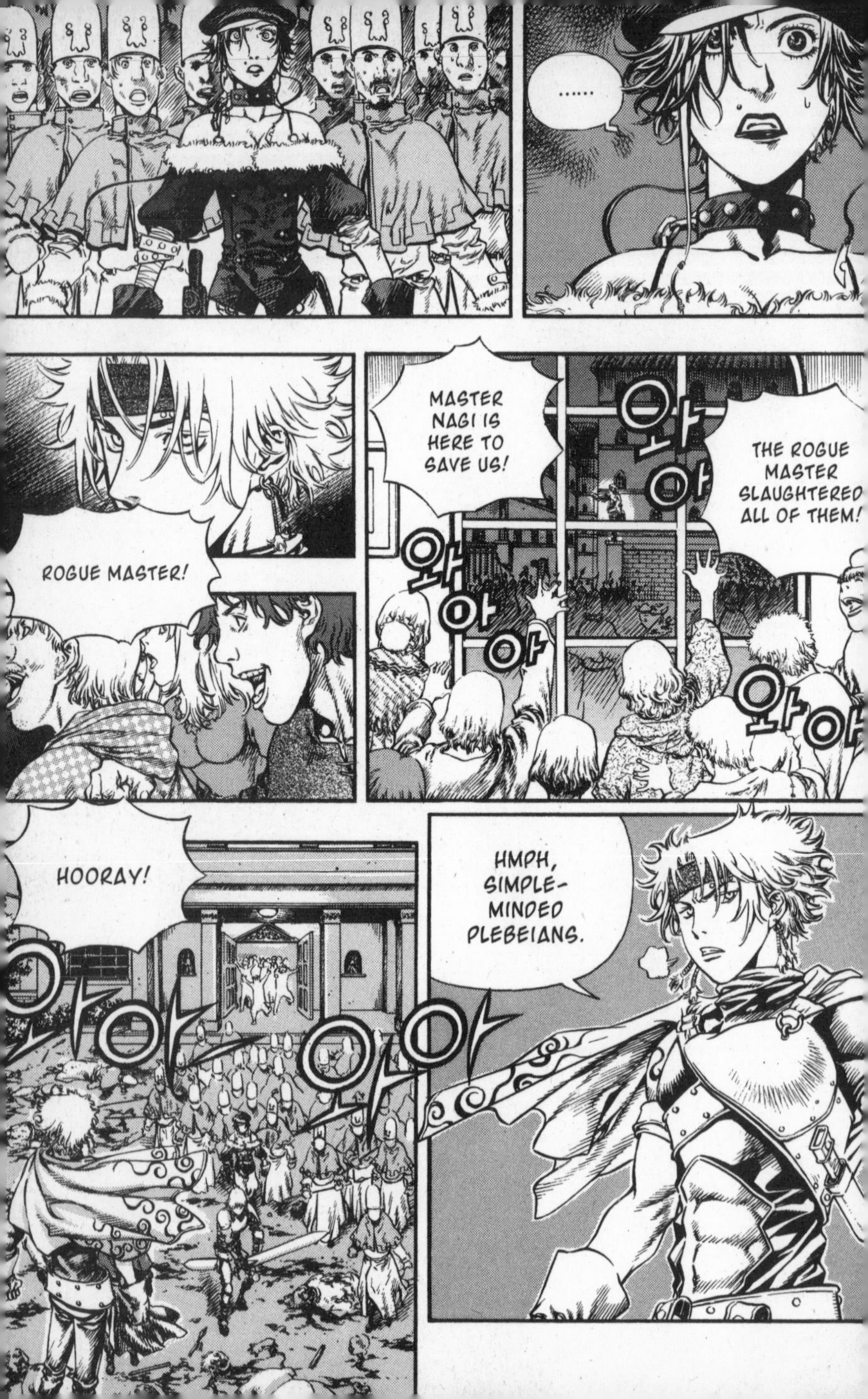
......
MASTER NAGI IS HERE TO SAVE US!
THE ROGUE MASTER SLAUGHTERED ALL OF THEM!
ROGUE MASTER!
와아아
와아
와아
HOORAY!
와아아아아
HMPH, SIMPLE-MINDED PLEBEIANS.

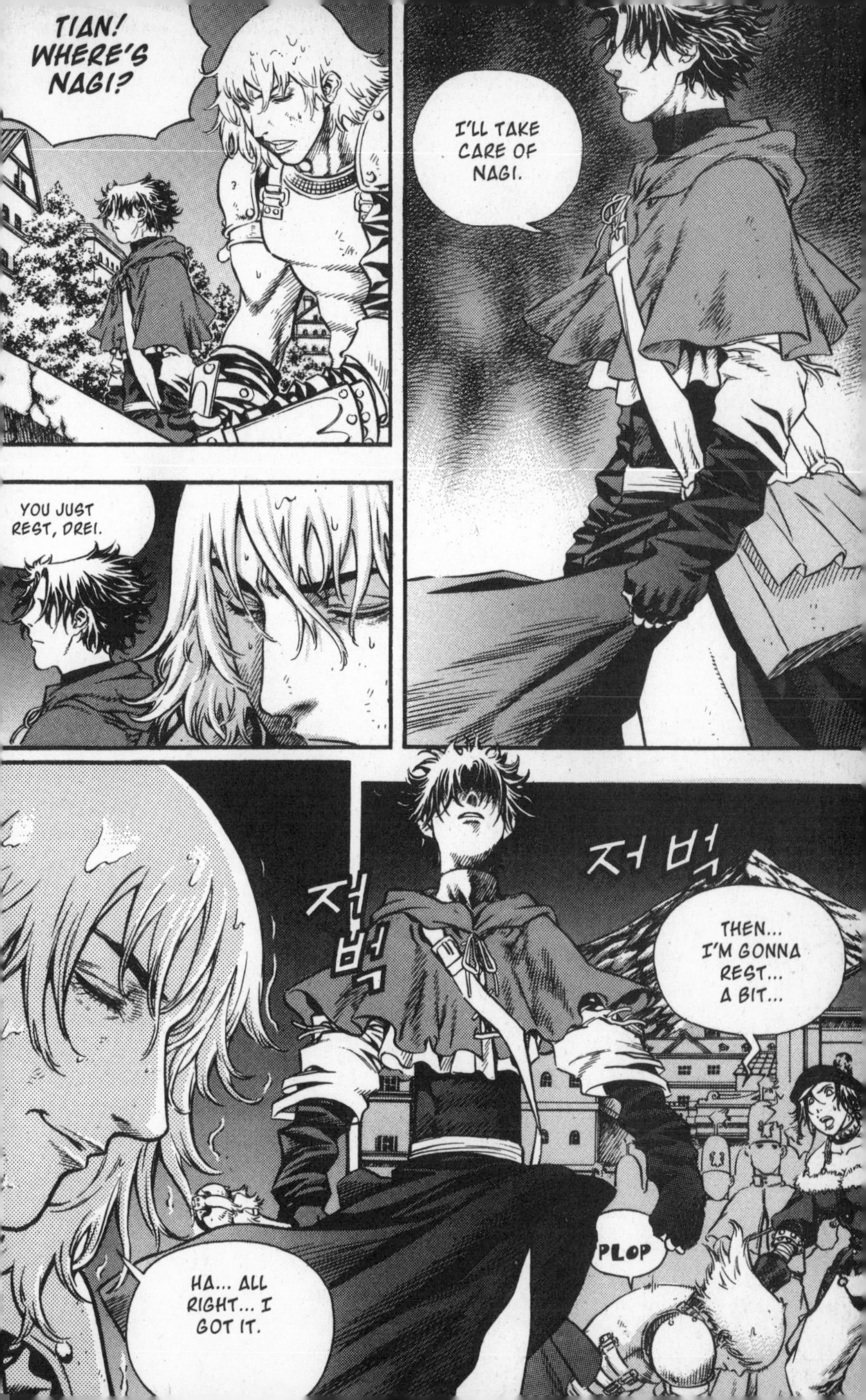
I'LL TAKE CARE OF NAGI.
TIAN! WHERE'S NAGI?
YOU JUST REST, DREI.
저벅
저벅
THEN... I'M GONNA REST... A BIT...
PLOP
HA... ALL RIGHT... I GOT IT.

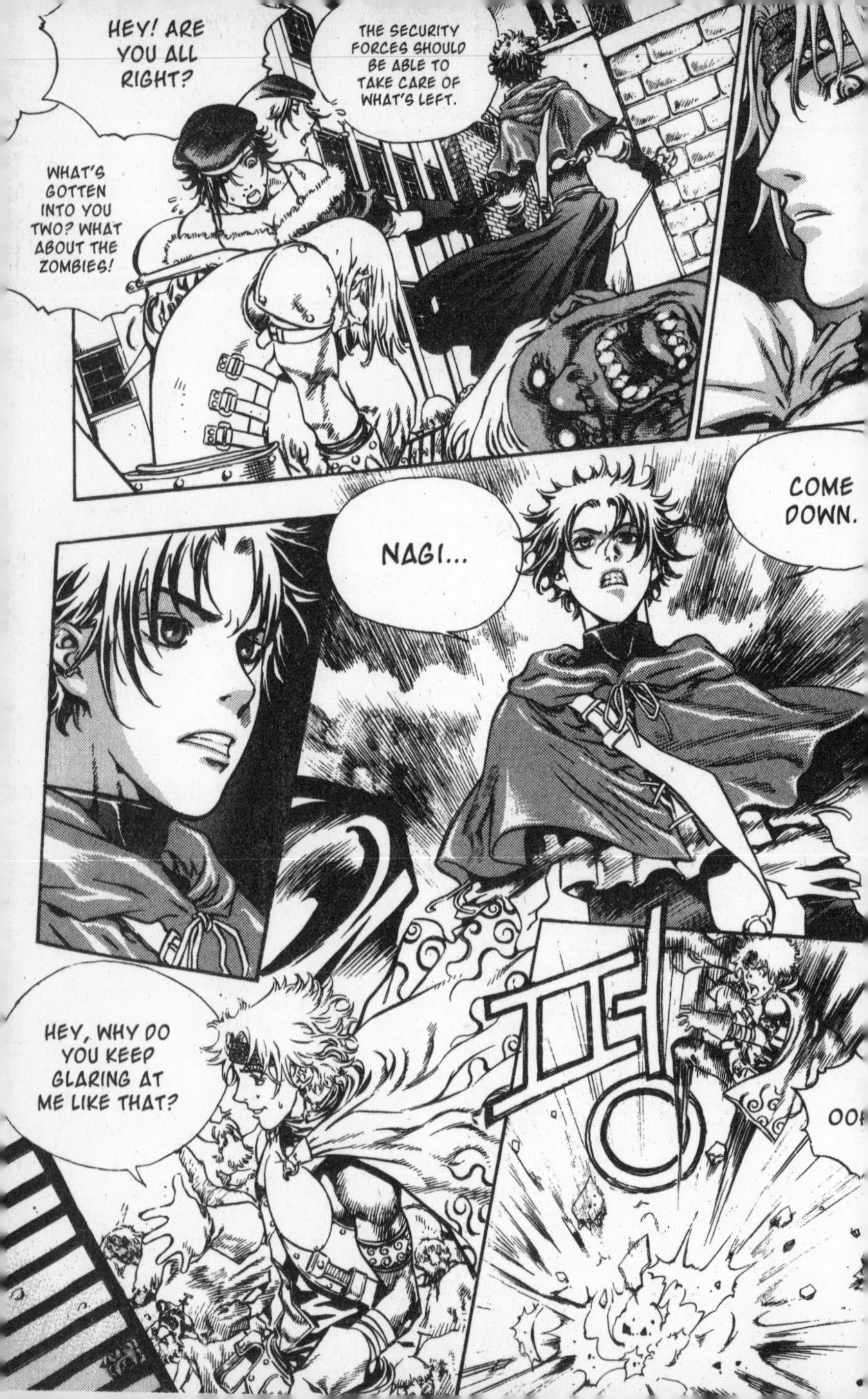
HEY! ARE YOU ALL RIGHT?
THE SECURITY FORCES SHOULD BE ABLE TO TAKE CARE OF WHAT'S LEFT.
WHAT'S GOTTEN INTO YOU TWO? WHAT ABOUT THE ZOMBIES!
COME DOWN.
NAGI...
HEY, WHY DO YOU KEEP GLARING AT ME LIKE THAT?
OO

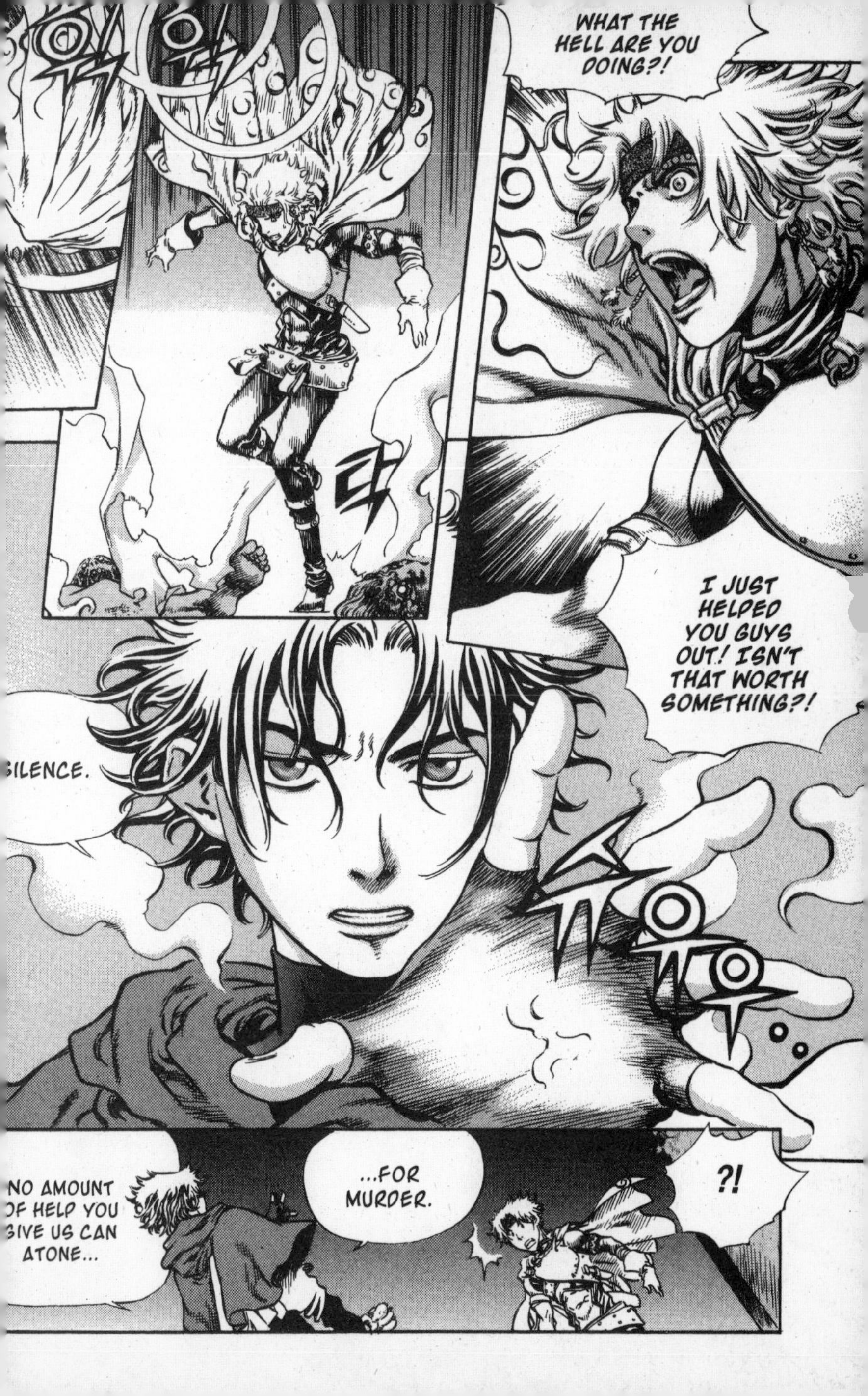
WHAT THE HELL ARE YOU DOING?!
I JUST HELPED YOU GUYS OUT! ISN'T THAT WORTH SOMETHING?!
SILENCE.
NO AMOUNT OF HELP YOU GIVE US CAN ATONE...
...FOR MURDER.
?!

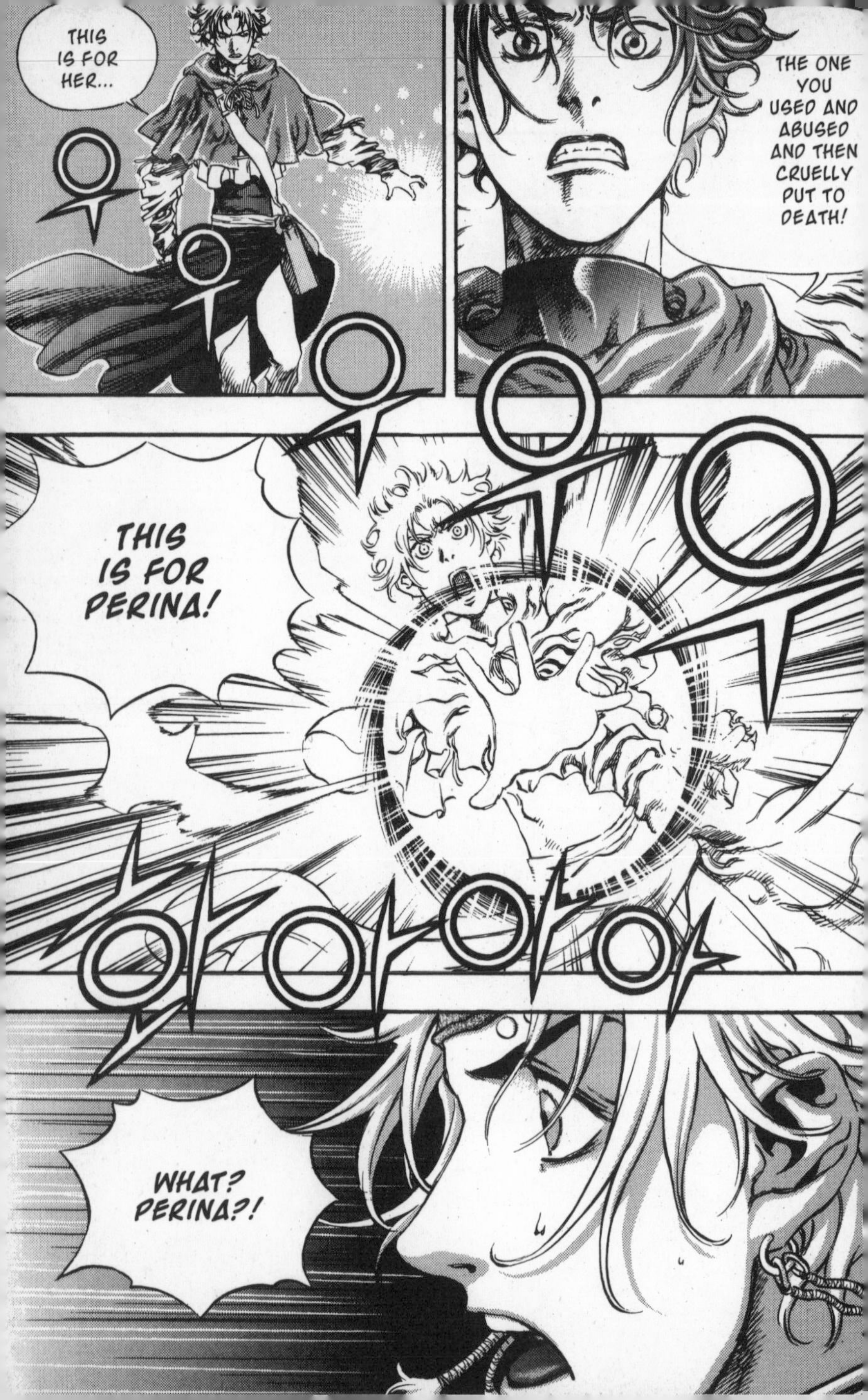
THIS IS FOR HER...
THE ONE YOU USED AND ABUSED AND THEN CRUELLY PUT TO DEATH!
THIS IS FOR PERINA!
WHAT? PERINA?!

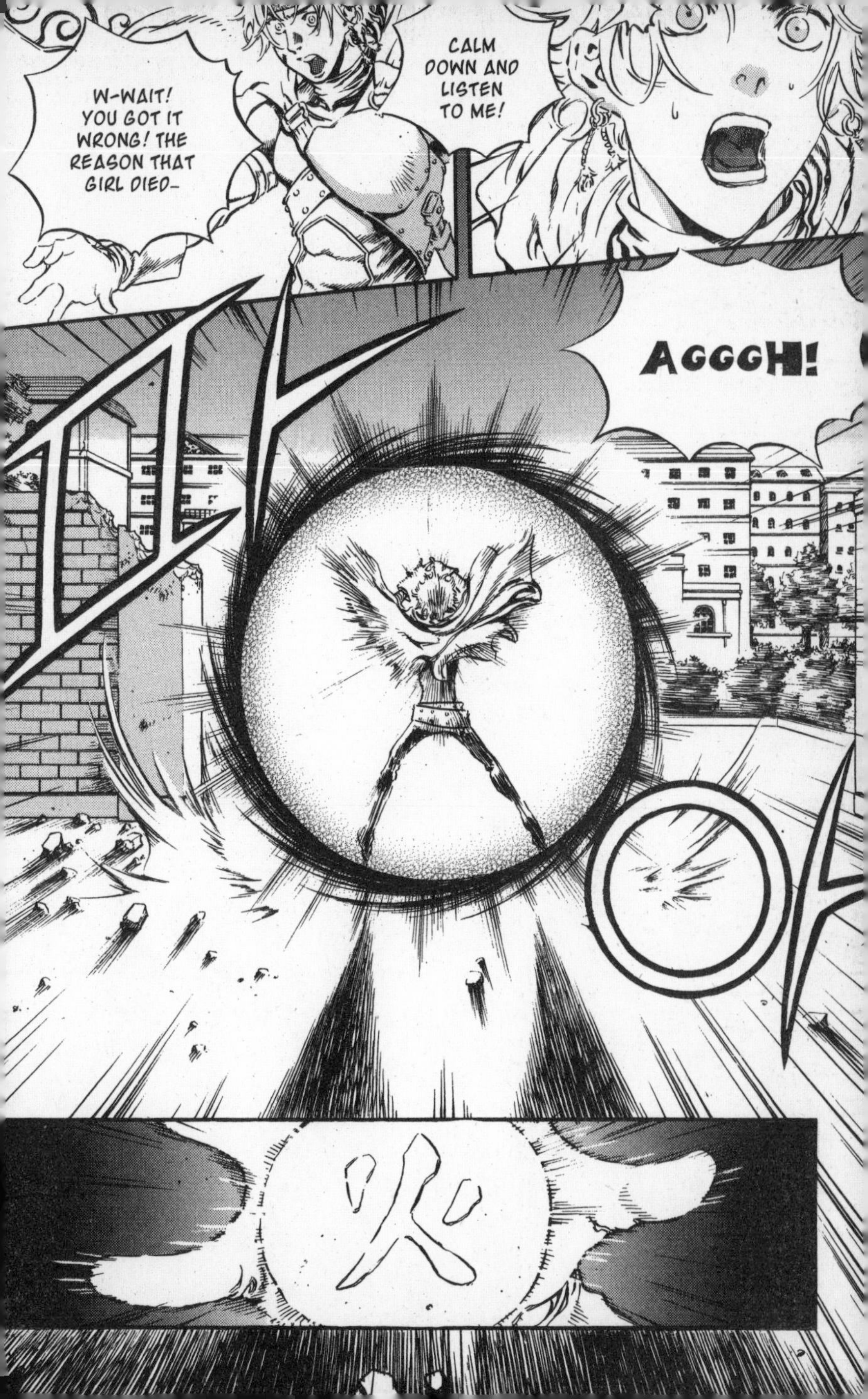
CALM DOWN AND LISTEN TO ME!
W-WAIT! YOU GOT IT WRONG! THE REASON THAT GIRL DIED-
AGGGH!
火

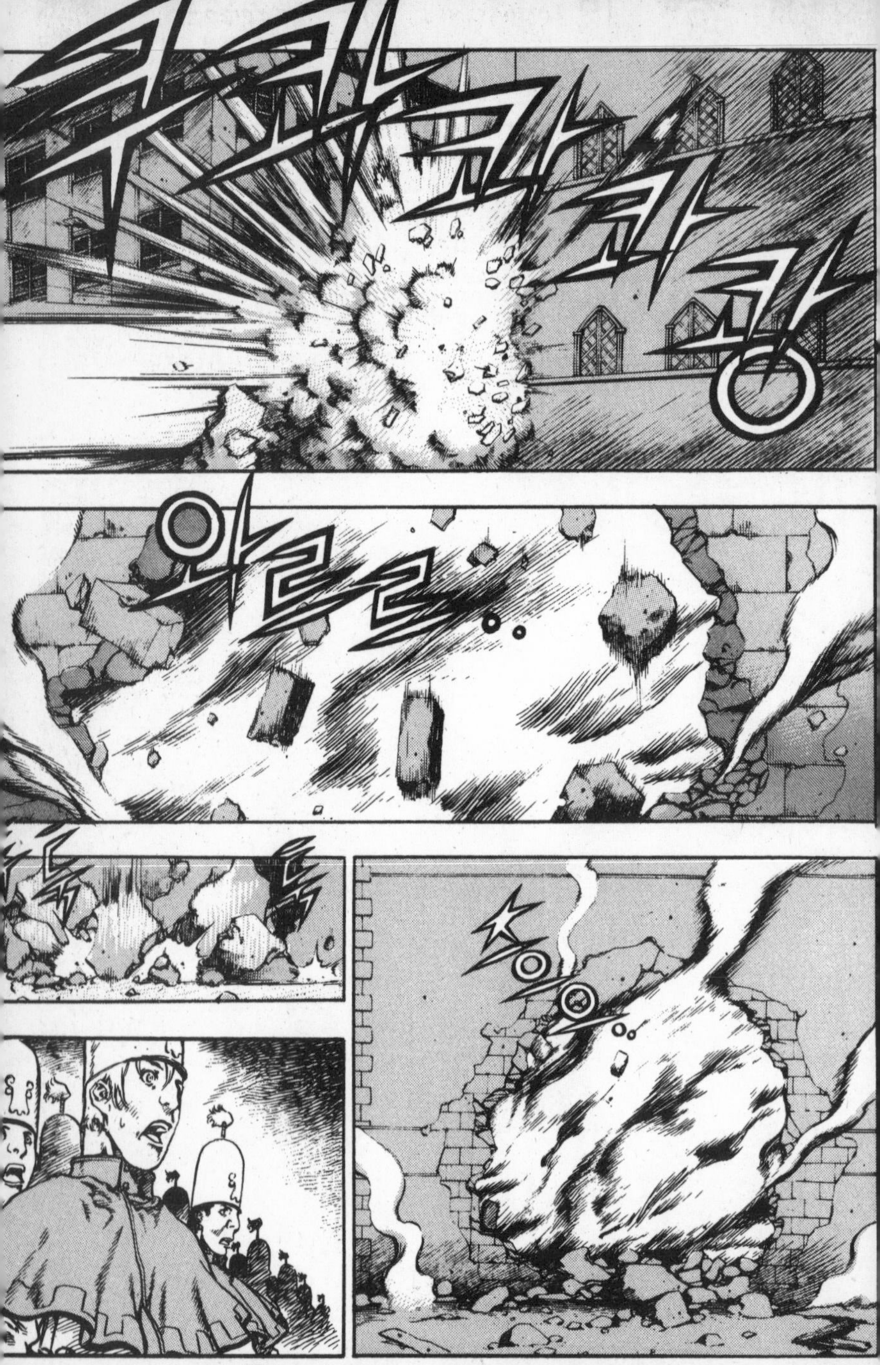

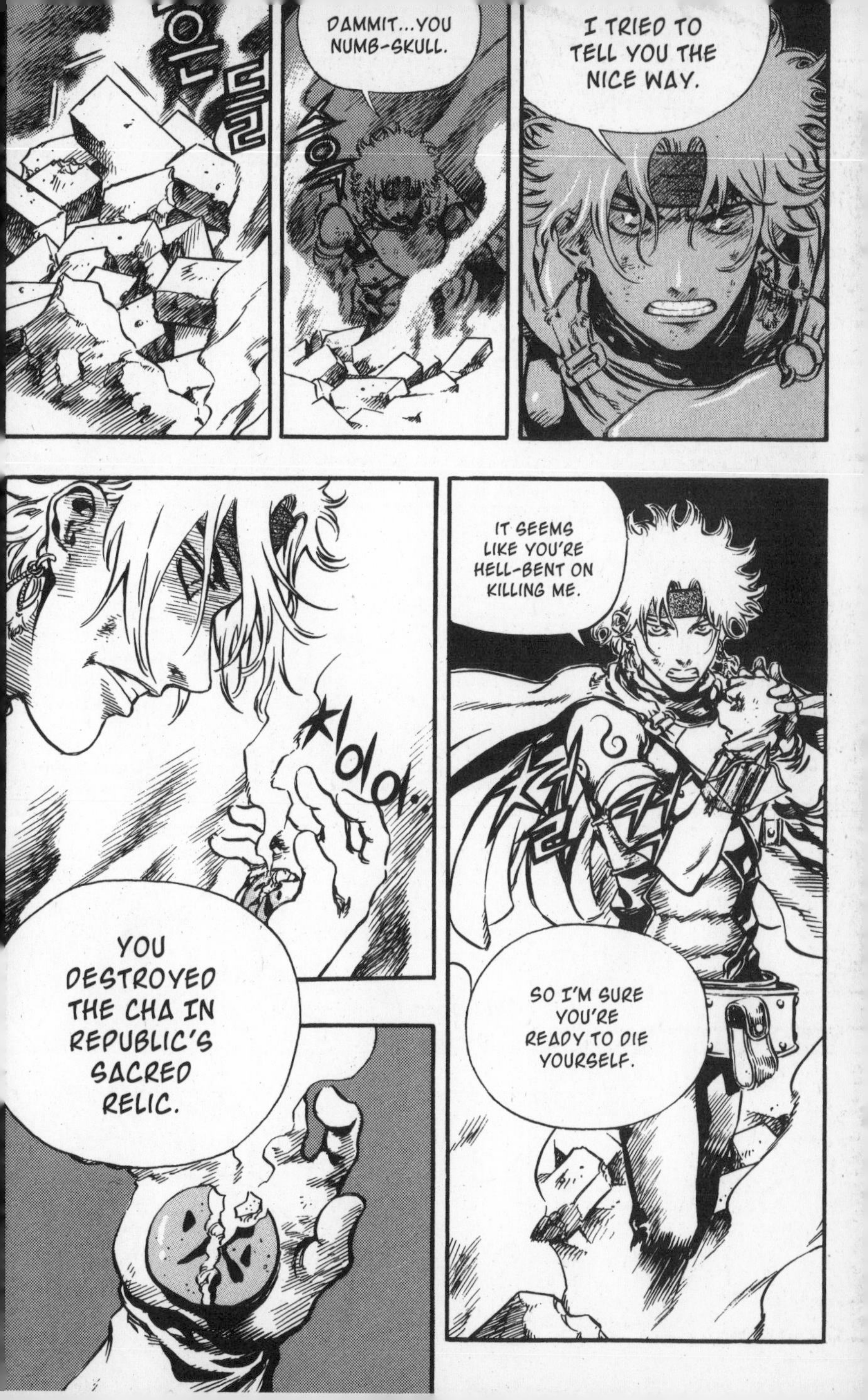
DAMMIT...YOU NUMB-SKULL.
I TRIED TO TELL YOU THE NICE WAY.
YOU DESTROYED THE CHA IN REPUBLIC'S SACRED RELIC.
IT SEEMS LIKE YOU'RE HELL-BENT ON KILLING ME.
SO I'M SURE YOU'RE READY TO DIE YOURSELF.

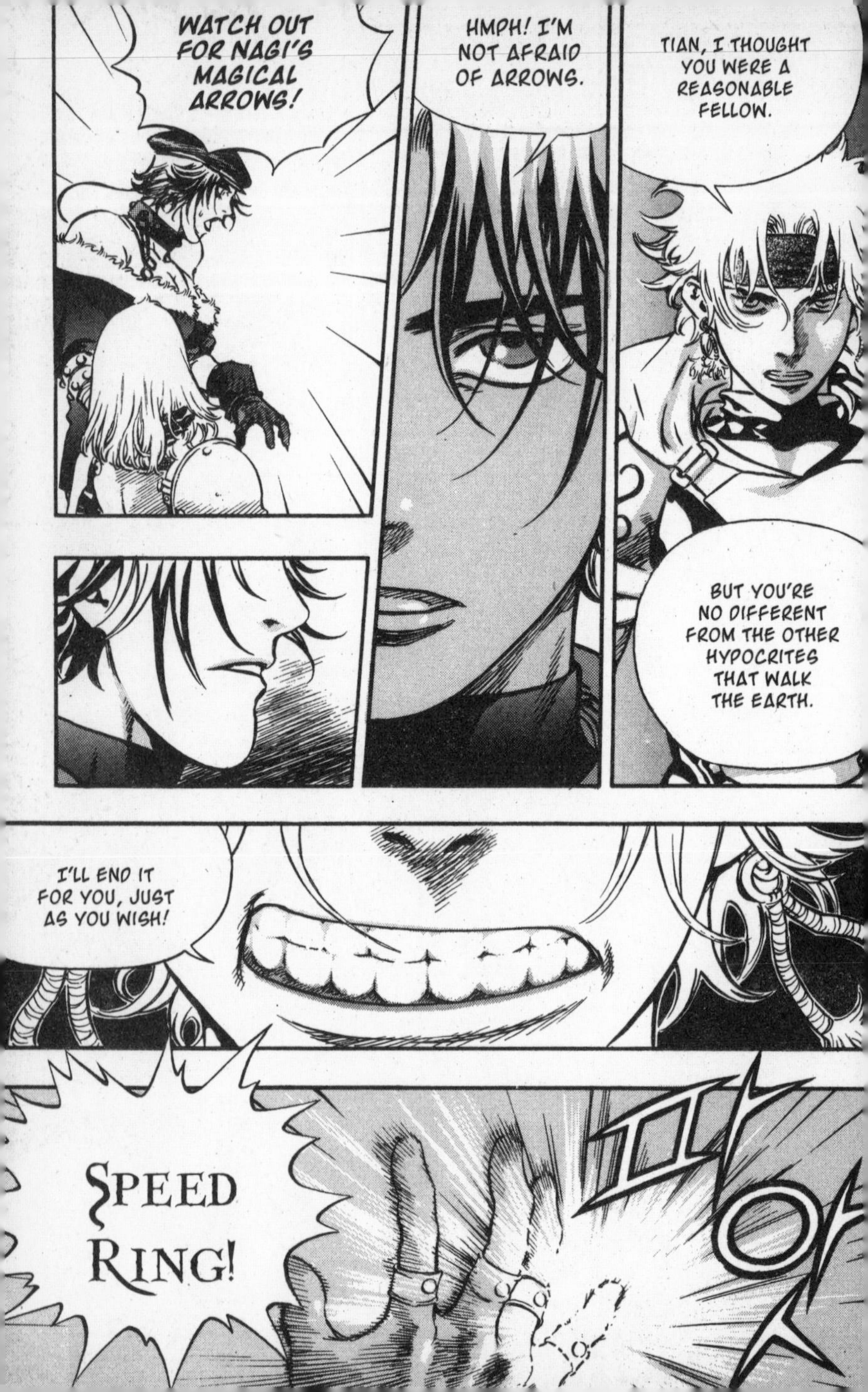
WATCH OUT FOR NAGI'S MAGICAL ARROWS!
HMPH! I'M NOT AFRAID OF ARROWS.
TIAN, I THOUGHT YOU WERE A REASONABLE FELLOW.
BUT YOU'RE NO DIFFERENT FROM THE OTHER HYPOCRITES THAT WALK THE EARTH.
I'LL END IT FOR YOU, JUST AS YOU WISH!
SPEED RING!

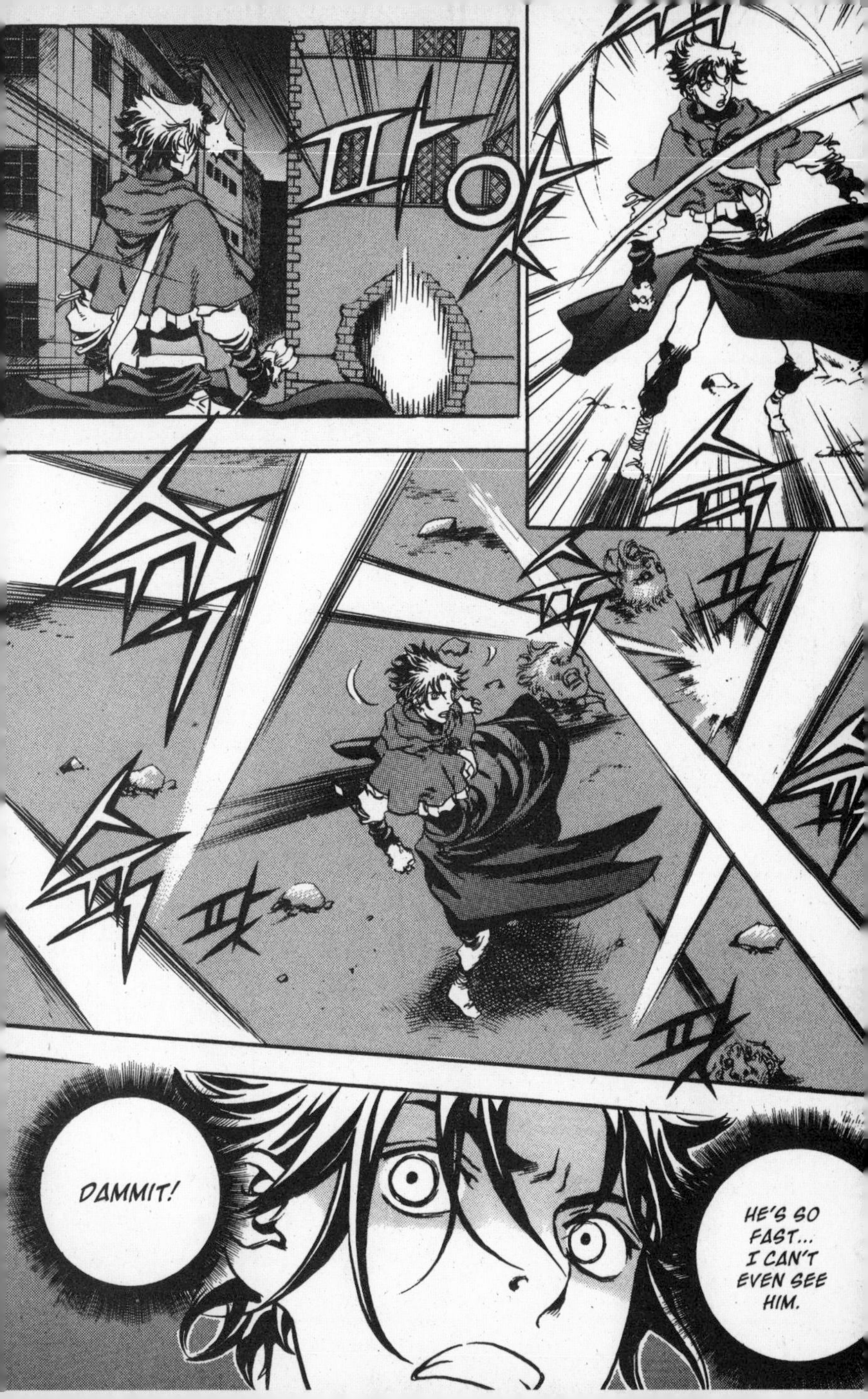
HE'S SO FAST... I CAN'T EVEN SEE HIM.
DAMMIT!

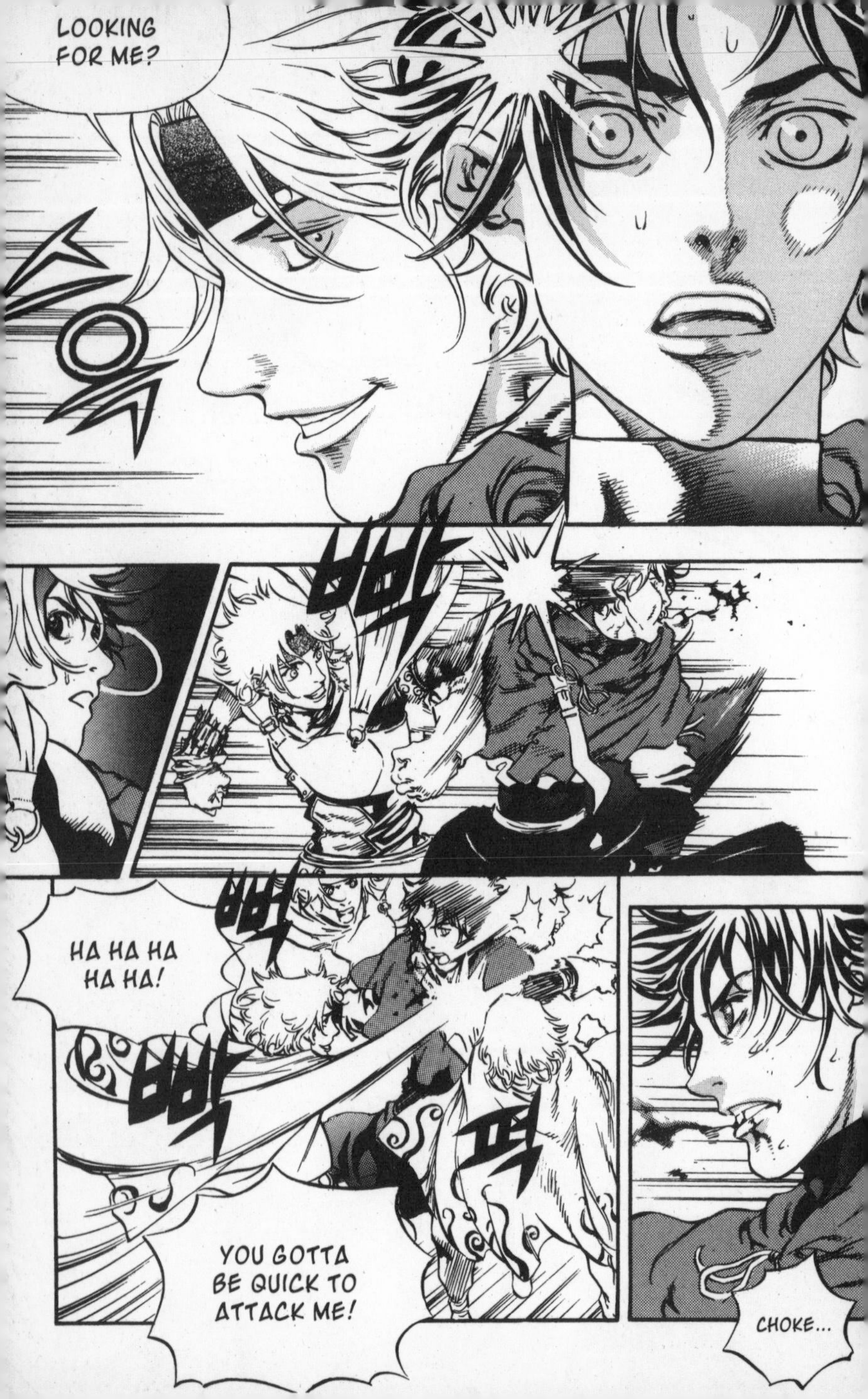
LOOKING FOR ME?
HA HA HA HA HA!
YOU GOTTA BE QUICK TO ATTACK ME!
CHOKE...

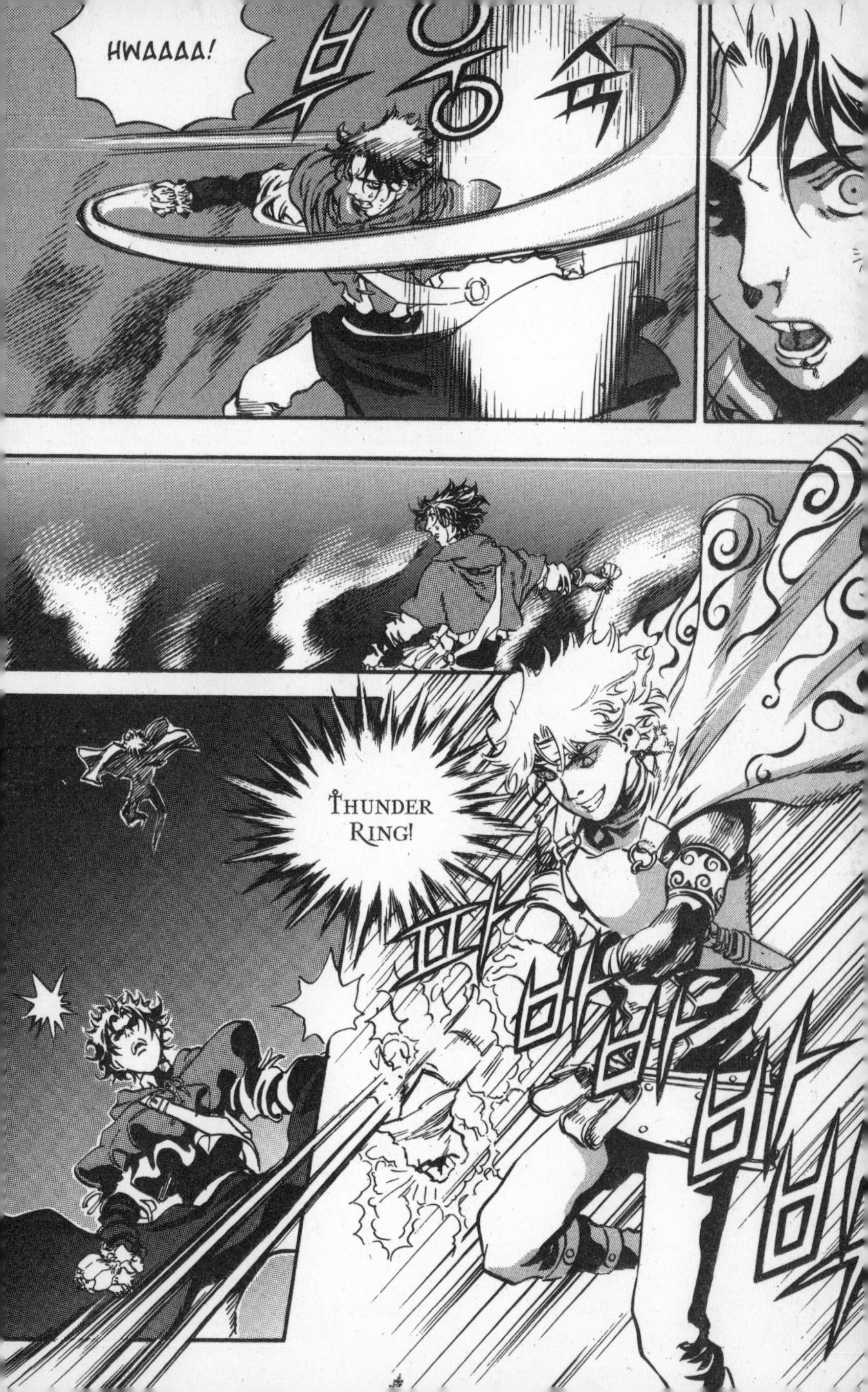
HWAAAA!
Thunder Ring!

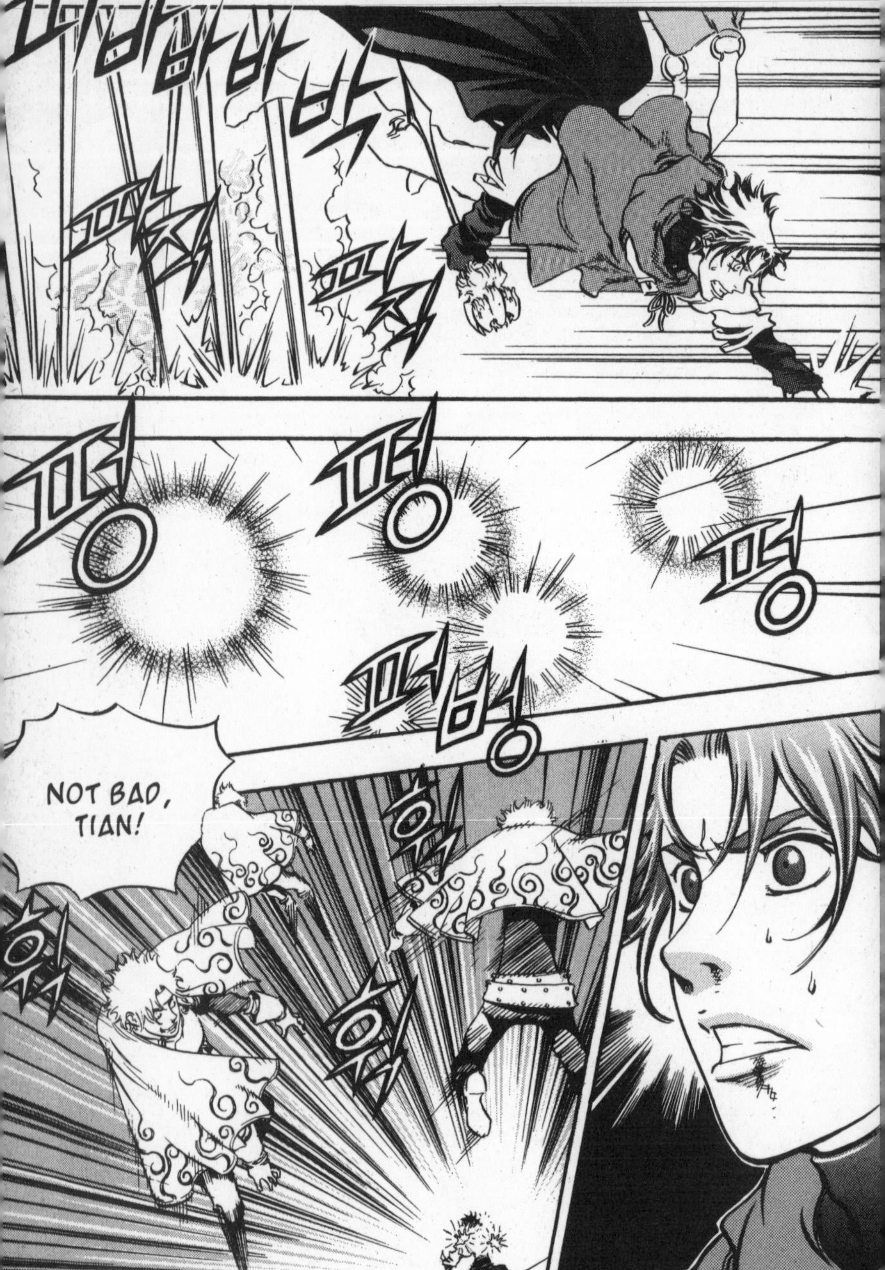
NOT BAD, TIAN!

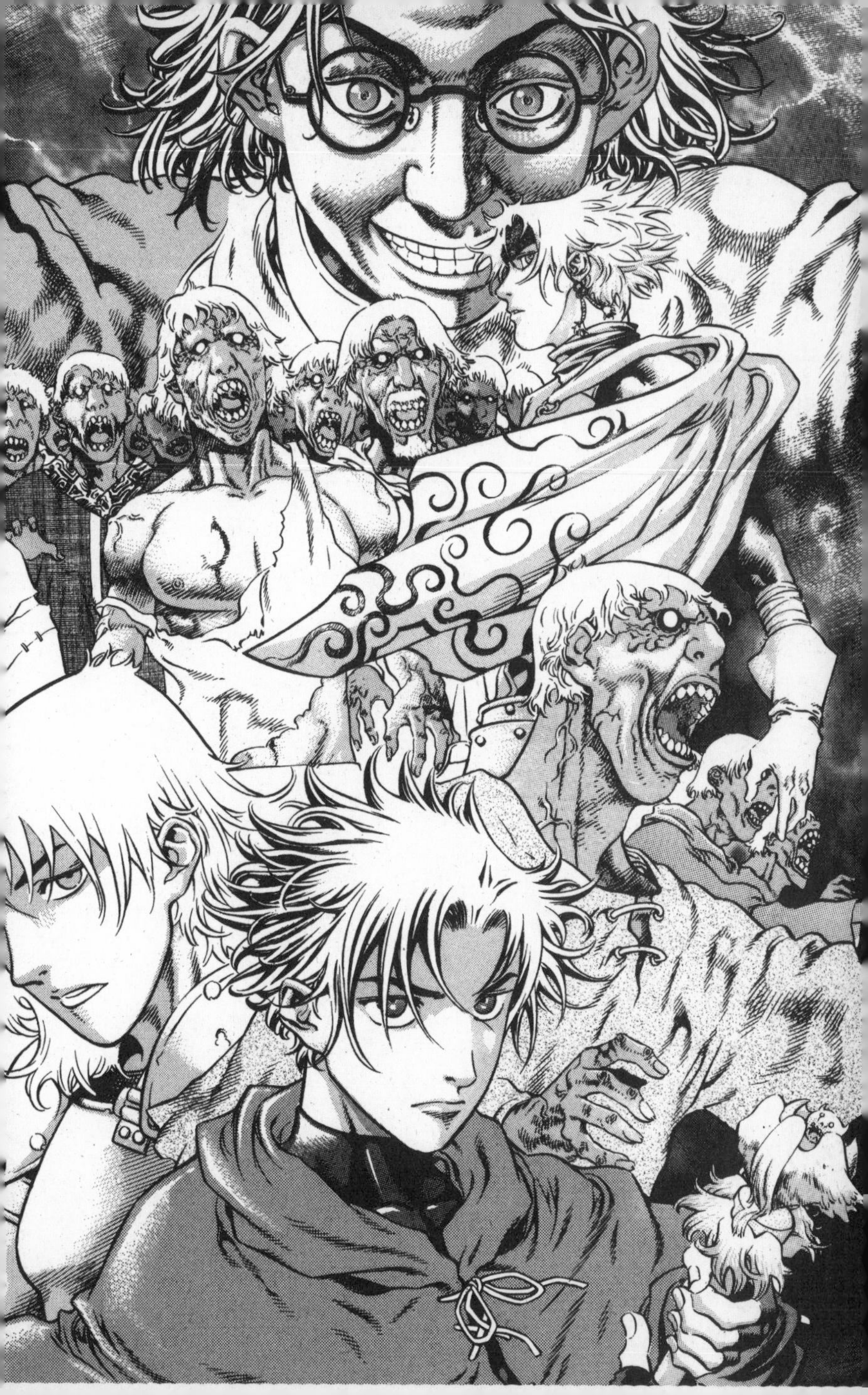

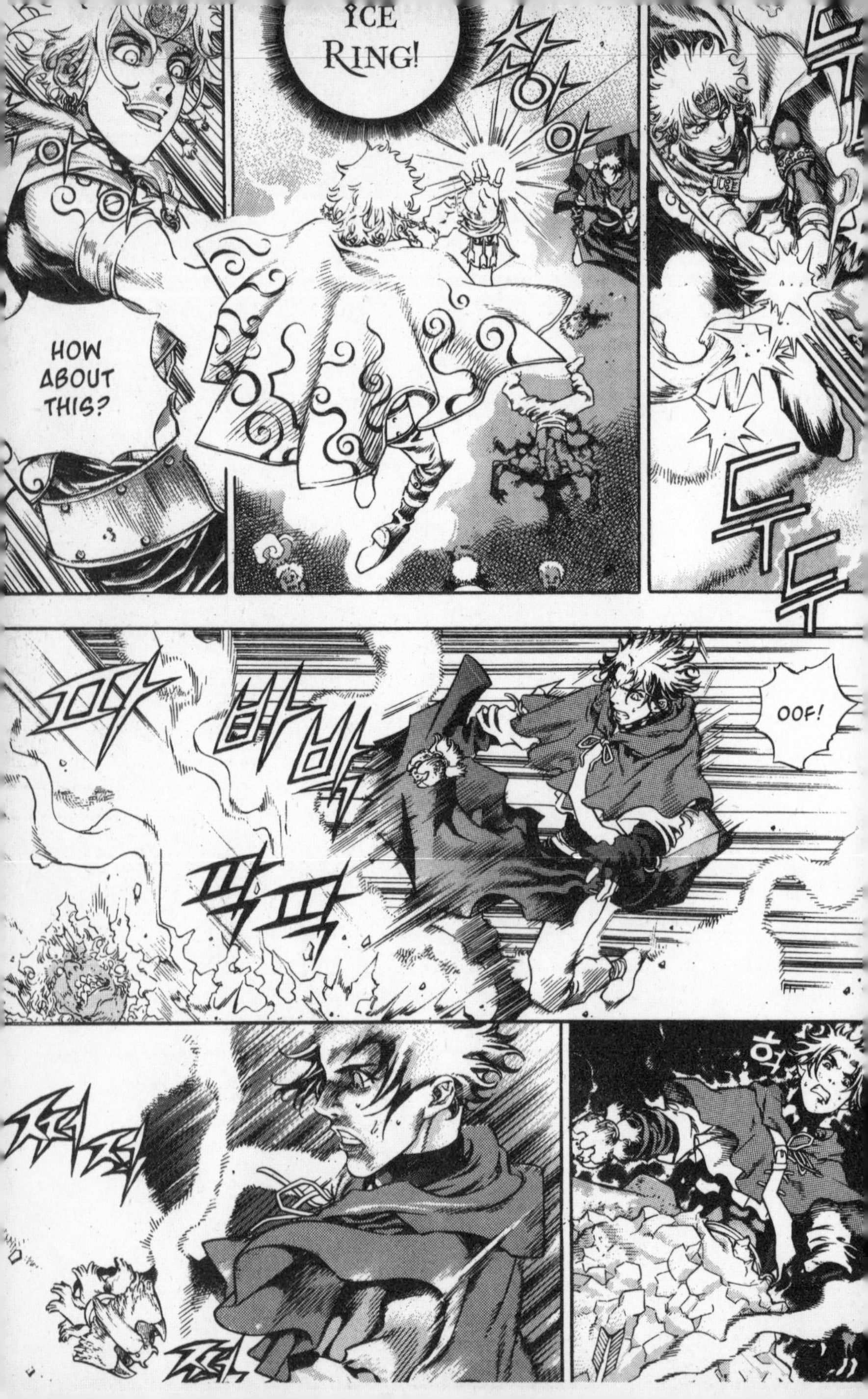
HOW ABOUT THIS?
ICE RING!
OOF!

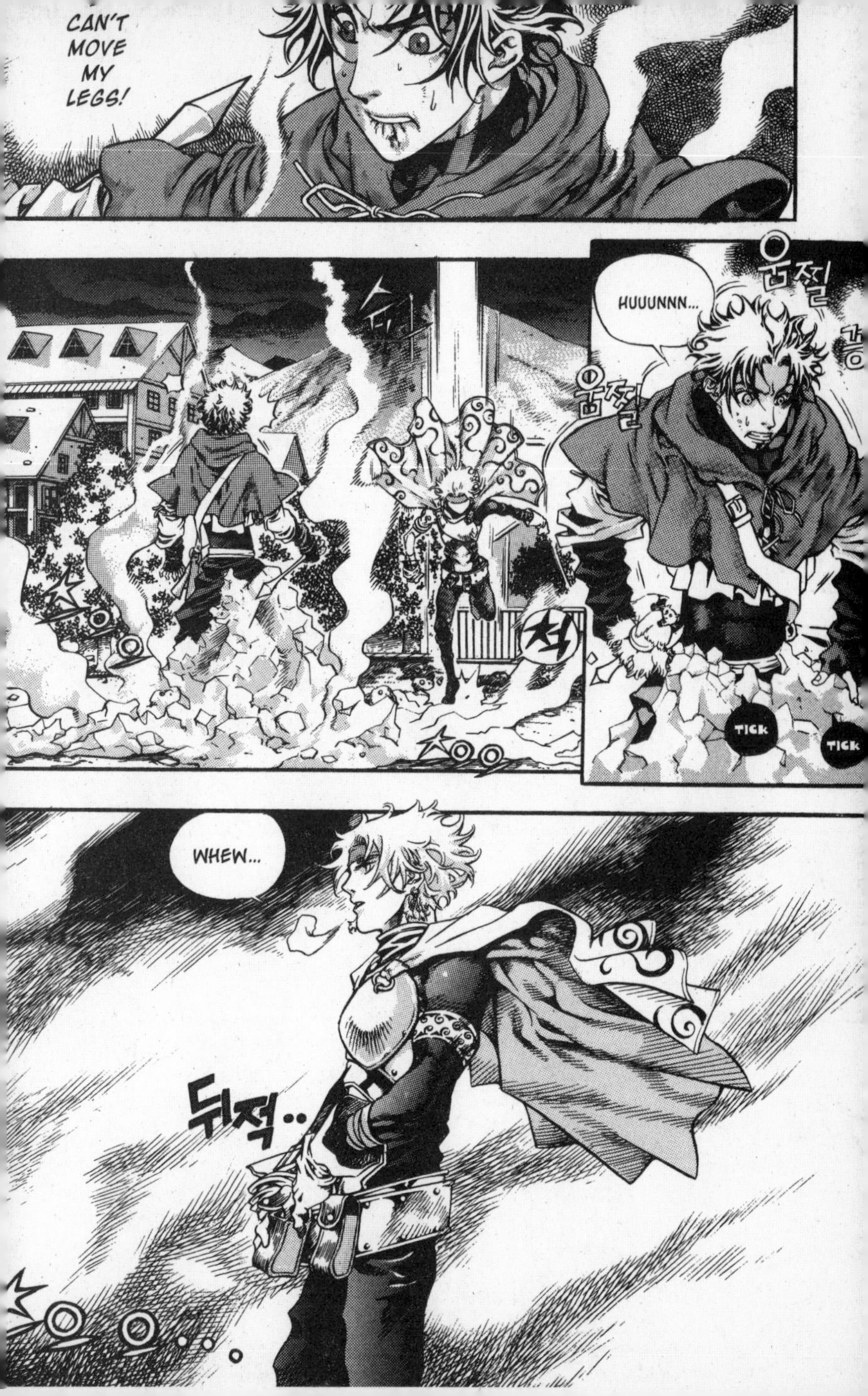
CAN'T MOVE MY LEGS!
HUUUNNN...
움찔
움찔
강
척
TICK
TICK
WHEW...
뒤적..

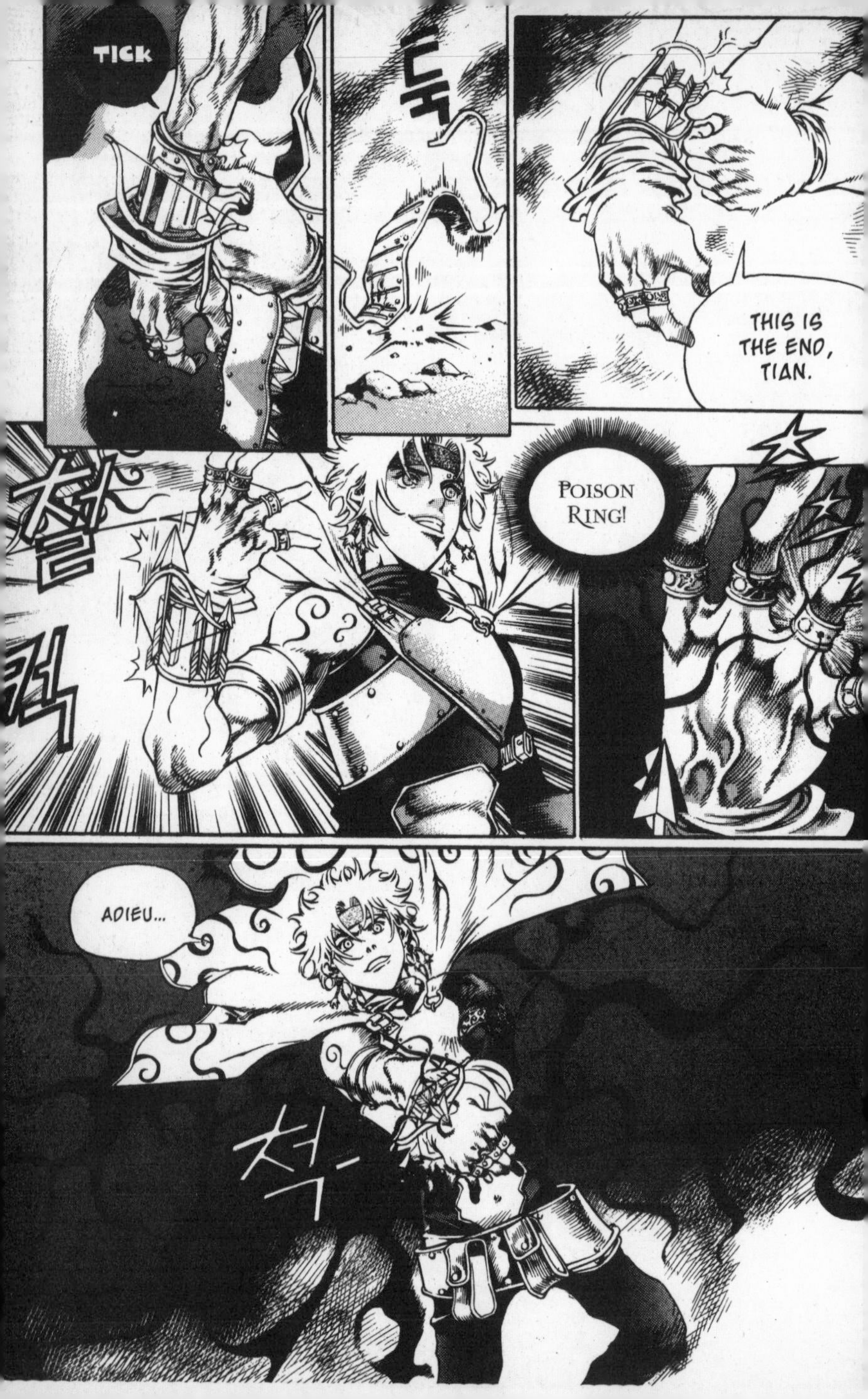
TICK
THIS IS THE END, TIAN.
POISON RING!
ADIEU...

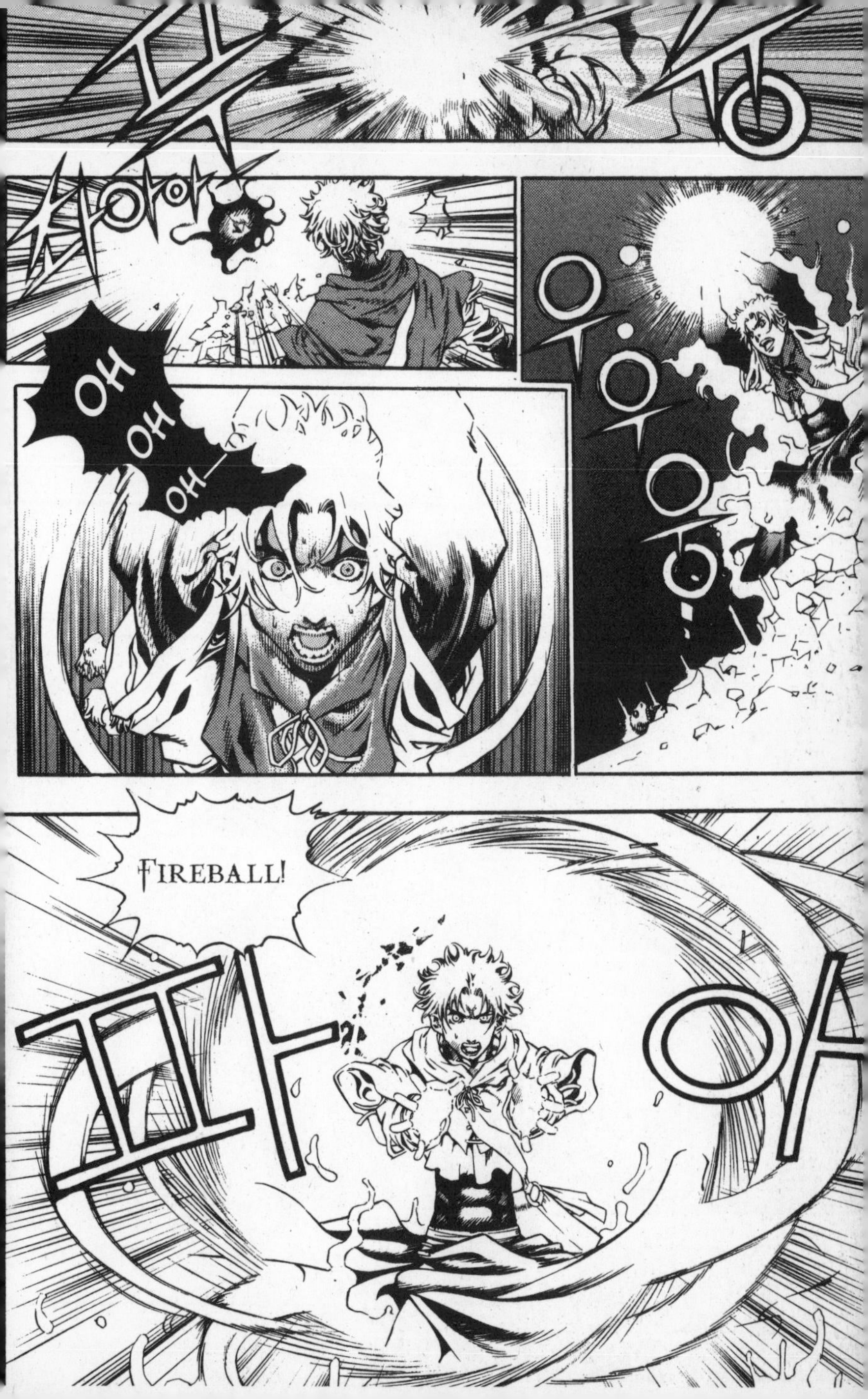

OH
OH
OH—
FIREBALL!

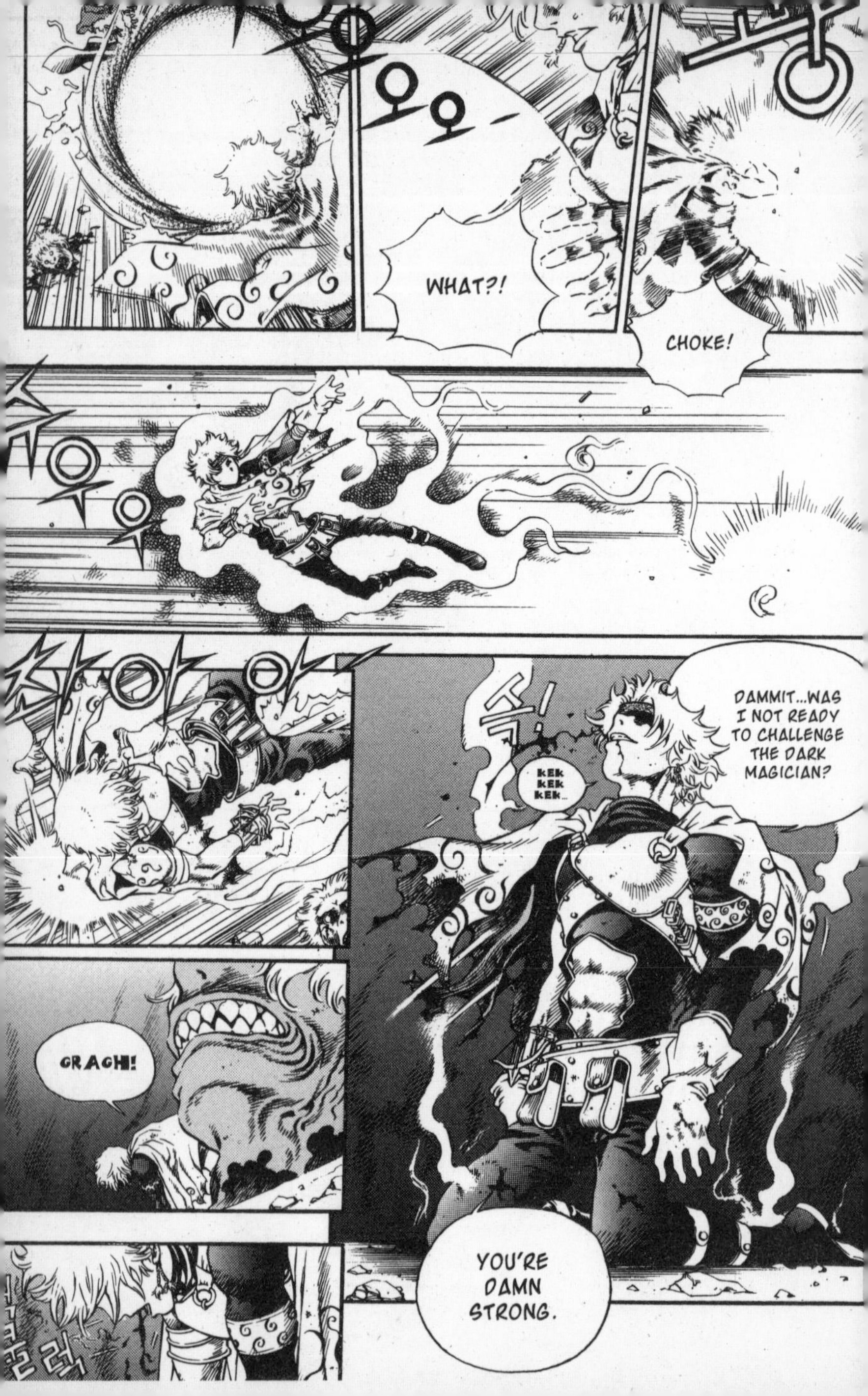
WHAT?!
CHOKE!
DAMMIT...WAS I NOT READY TO CHALLENGE THE DARK MAGICIAN?
KEK KEK KEK...
GRACH!
YOU'RE DAMN STRONG.

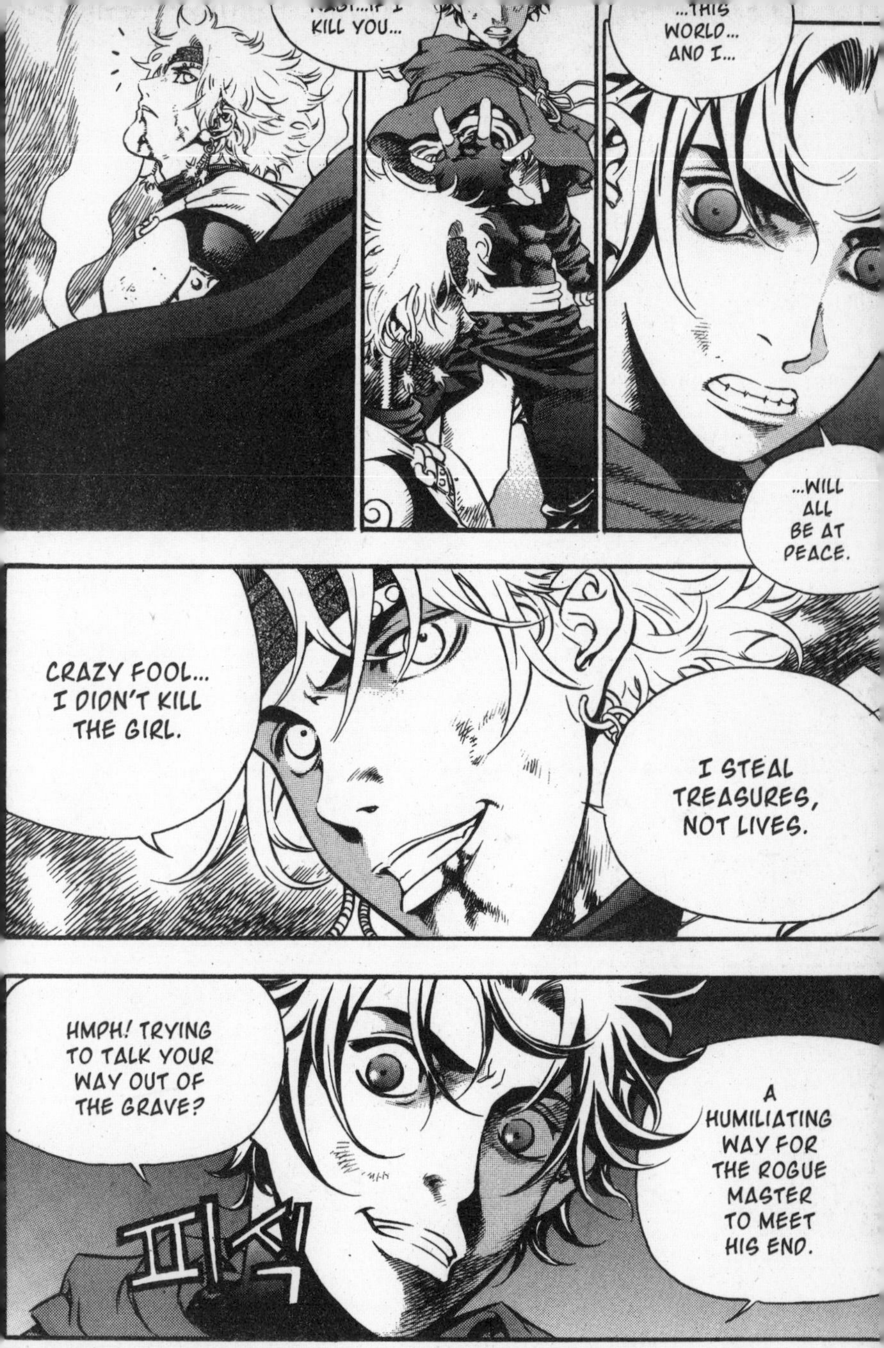
KILL YOU...
...THIS WORLD... AND I...
...WILL ALL BE AT PEACE.
CRAZY FOOL... I DIDN'T KILL THE GIRL.
I STEAL TREASURES, NOT LIVES.
HMPH! TRYING TO TALK YOUR WAY OUT OF THE GRAVE?
A HUMILIATING WAY FOR THE ROGUE MASTER TO MEET HIS END.

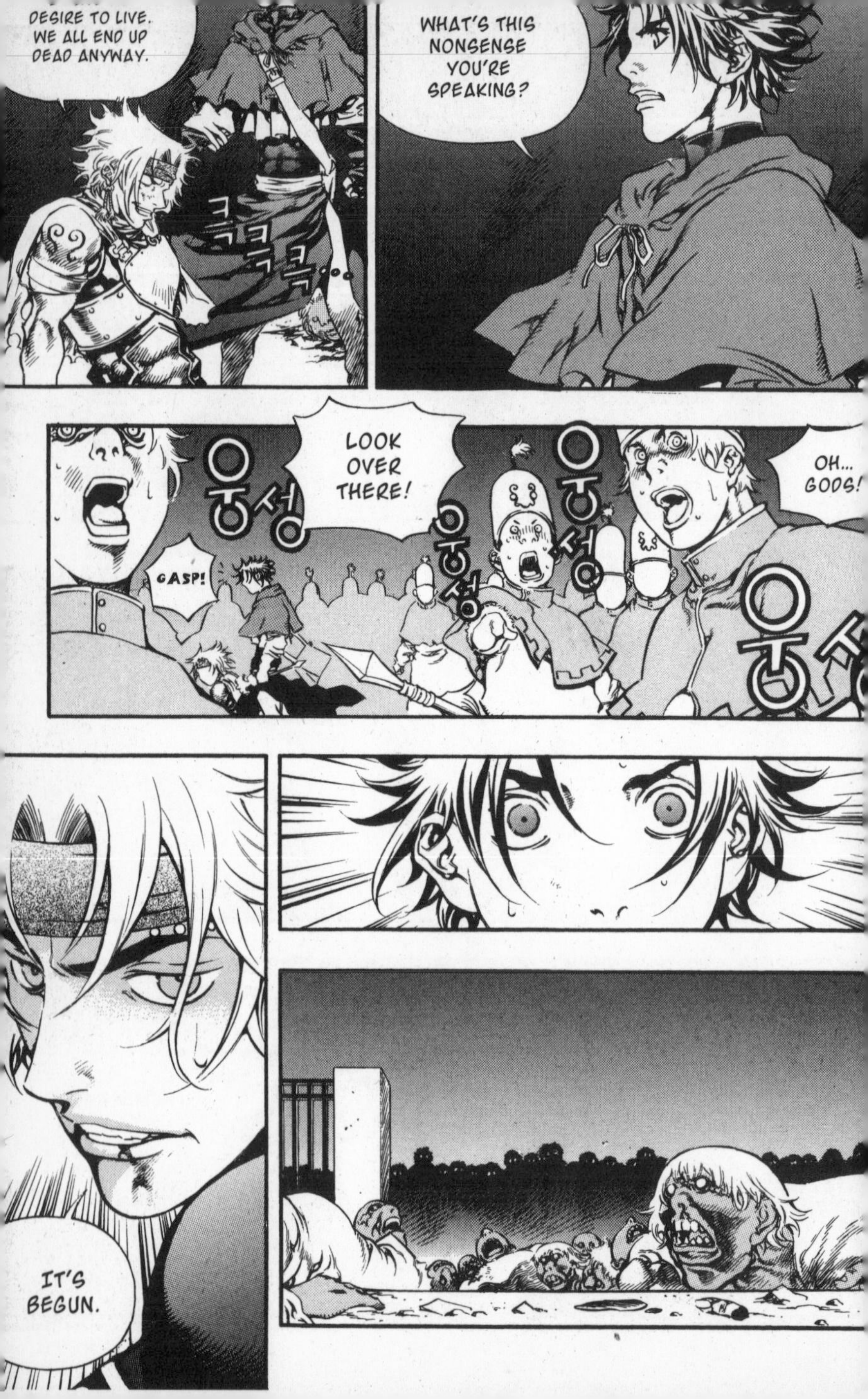

DESIRE TO LIVE. WE ALL END UP DEAD ANYWAY.
WHAT'S THIS NONSENSE YOU'RE SPEAKING?
LOOK OVER THERE!
웅성
웅성
웅성
웅성
GASP!
OH... GODS!
IT'S BEGUN.

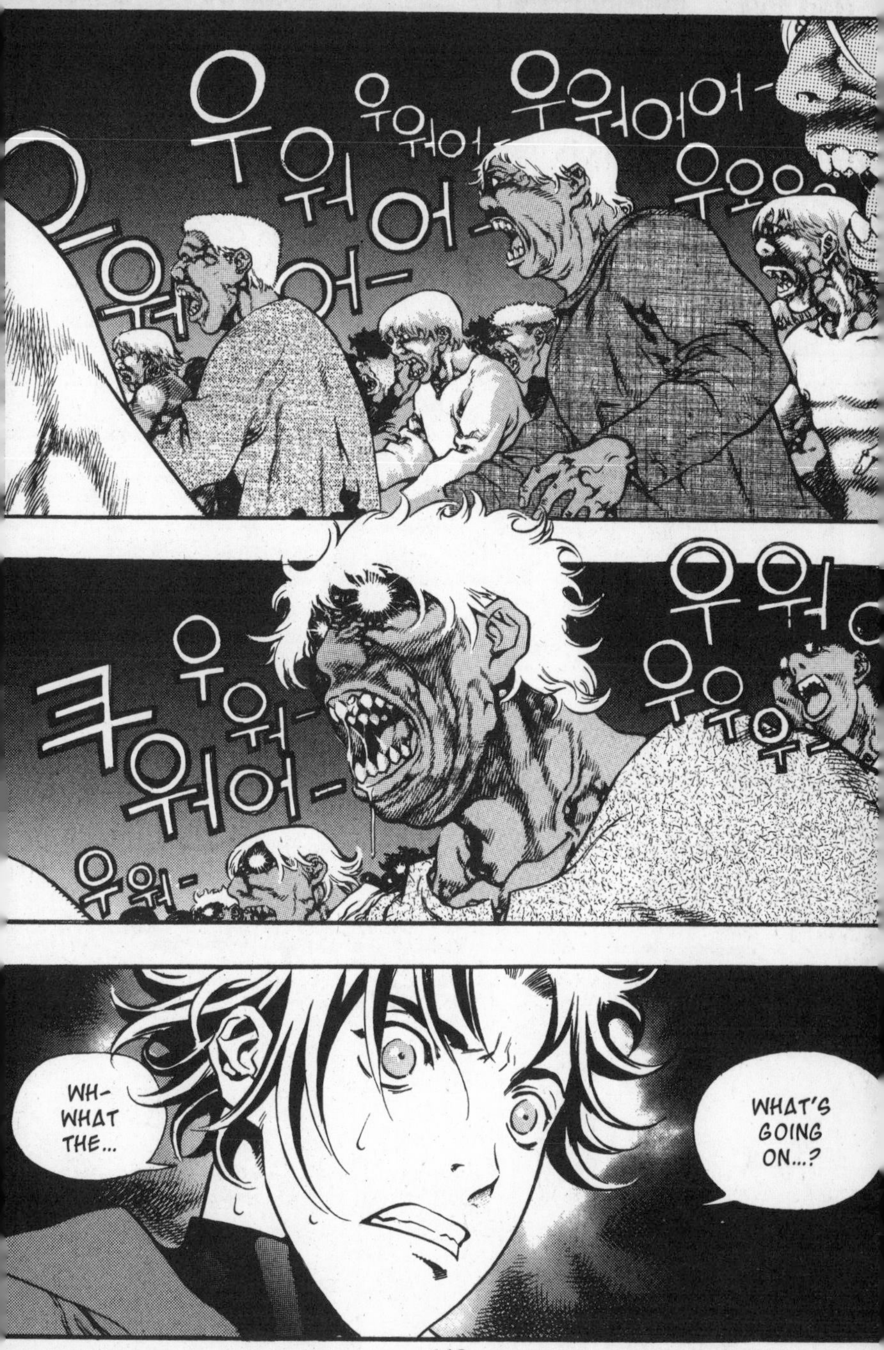
우워어-
우워어-
우워어어-
우워어-
우워-
쿠우워어-
우워-
WH-
WHAT
THE...
WHAT'S
GOING
ON...?

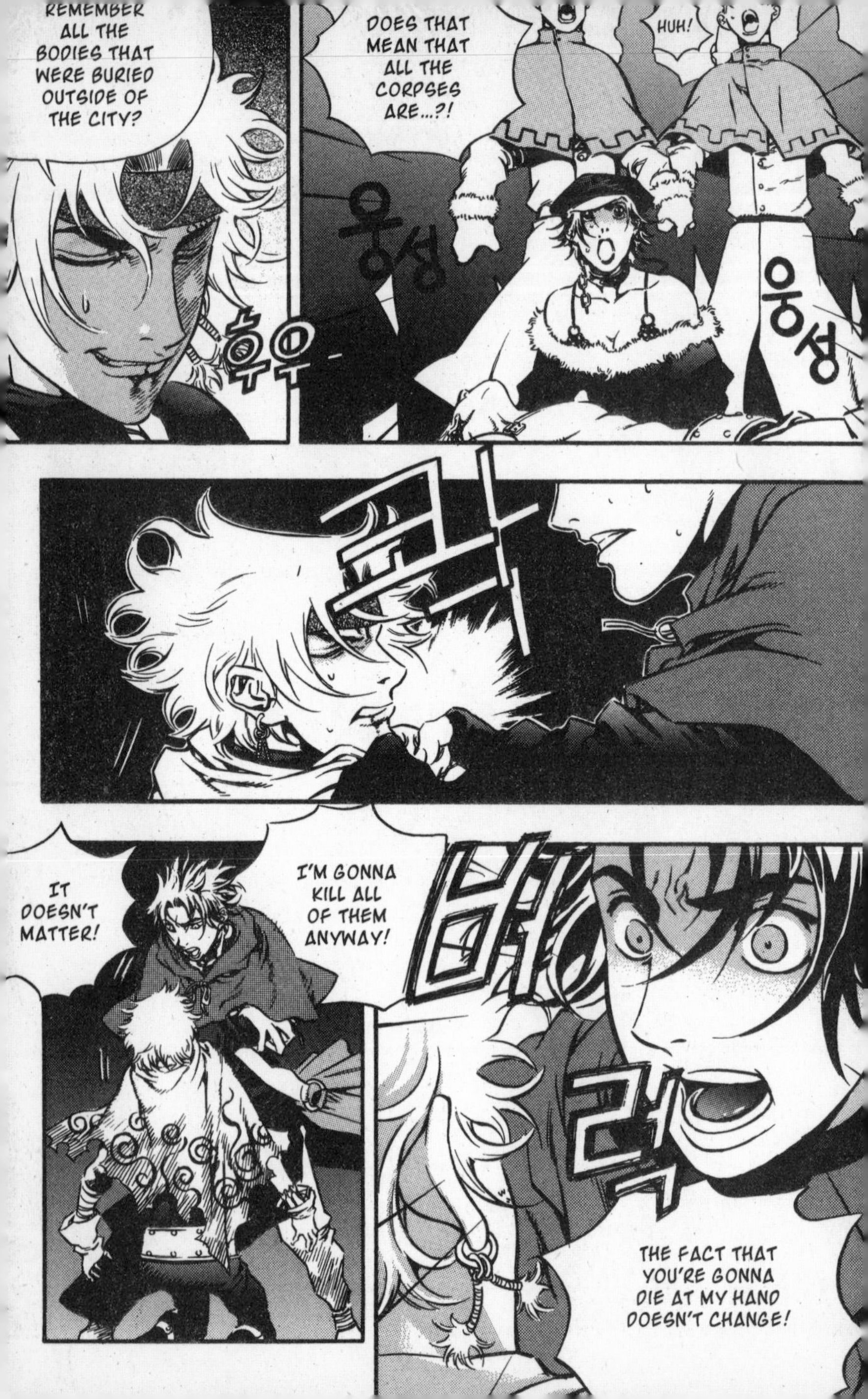
REMEMBER ALL THE BODIES THAT WERE BURIED OUTSIDE OF THE CITY?
DOES THAT MEAN THAT ALL THE CORPSES ARE...?!
웅성
HUH!
웅성
IT DOESN'T MATTER!
I'M GONNA KILL ALL OF THEM ANYWAY!
THE FACT THAT YOU'RE GONNA DIE AT MY HAND DOESN'T CHANGE!

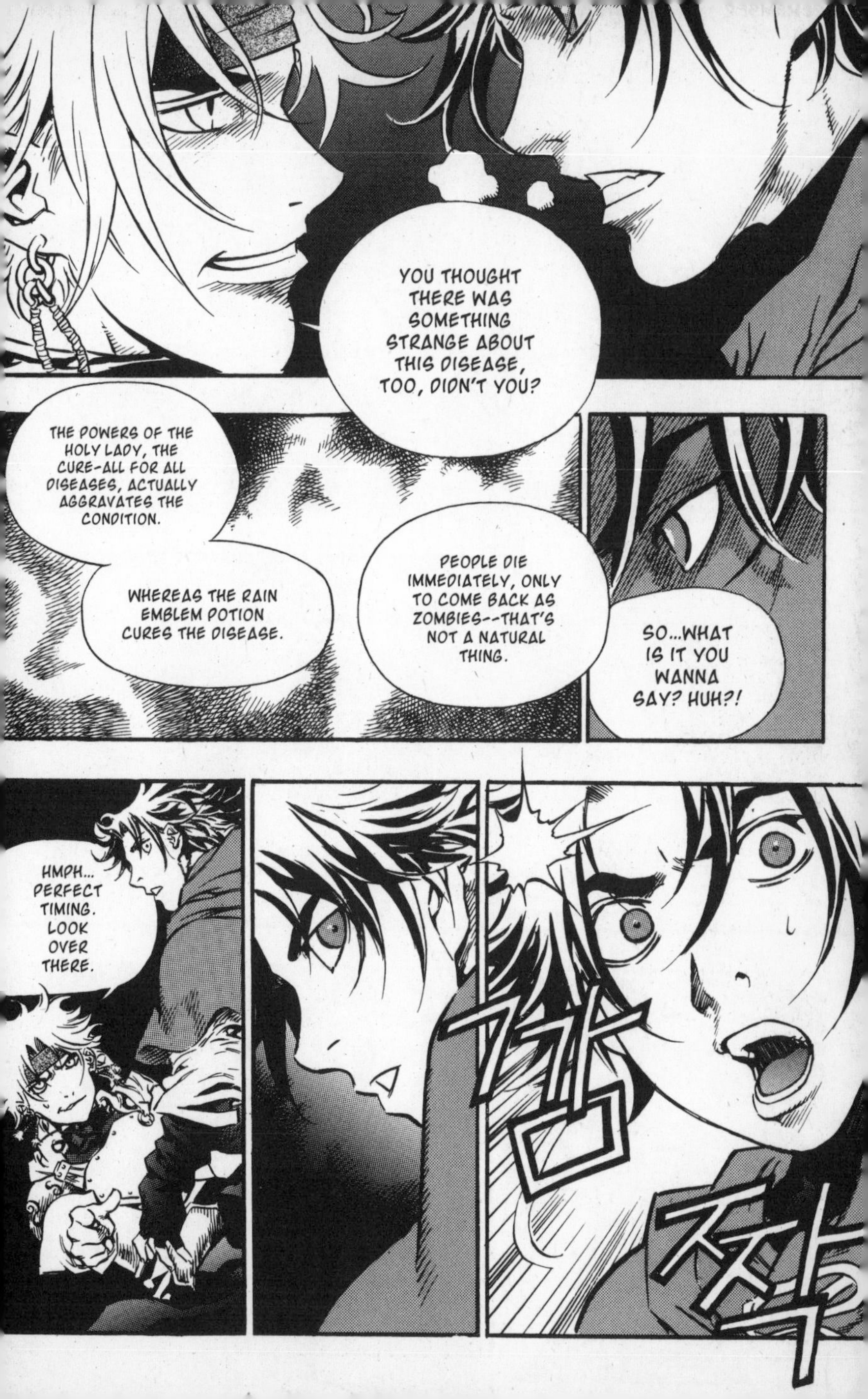
YOU THOUGHT THERE WAS SOMETHING STRANGE ABOUT THIS DISEASE, TOO, DIDN'T YOU?
THE POWERS OF THE HOLY LADY, THE CURE-ALL FOR ALL DISEASES, ACTUALLY AGGRAVATES THE CONDITION.
WHEREAS THE RAIN EMBLEM POTION CURES THE DISEASE.
PEOPLE DIE IMMEDIATELY, ONLY TO COME BACK AS ZOMBIES--THAT'S NOT A NATURAL THING.
SO...WHAT IS IT YOU WANNA SAY? HUH?!
HMPH... PERFECT TIMING. LOOK OVER THERE.

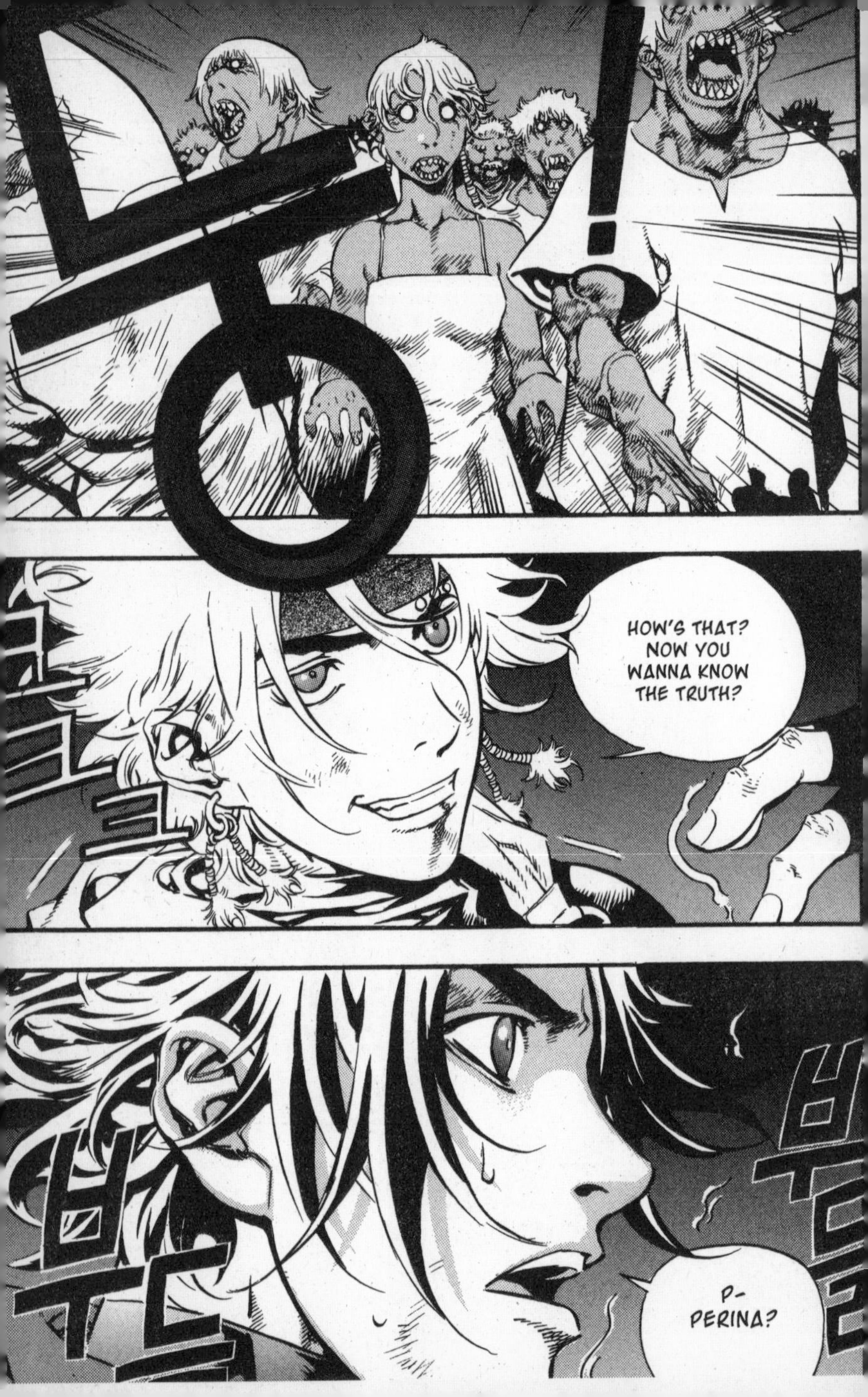
HOW'S THAT? NOW YOU WANNA KNOW THE TRUTH?
P- PERINA?

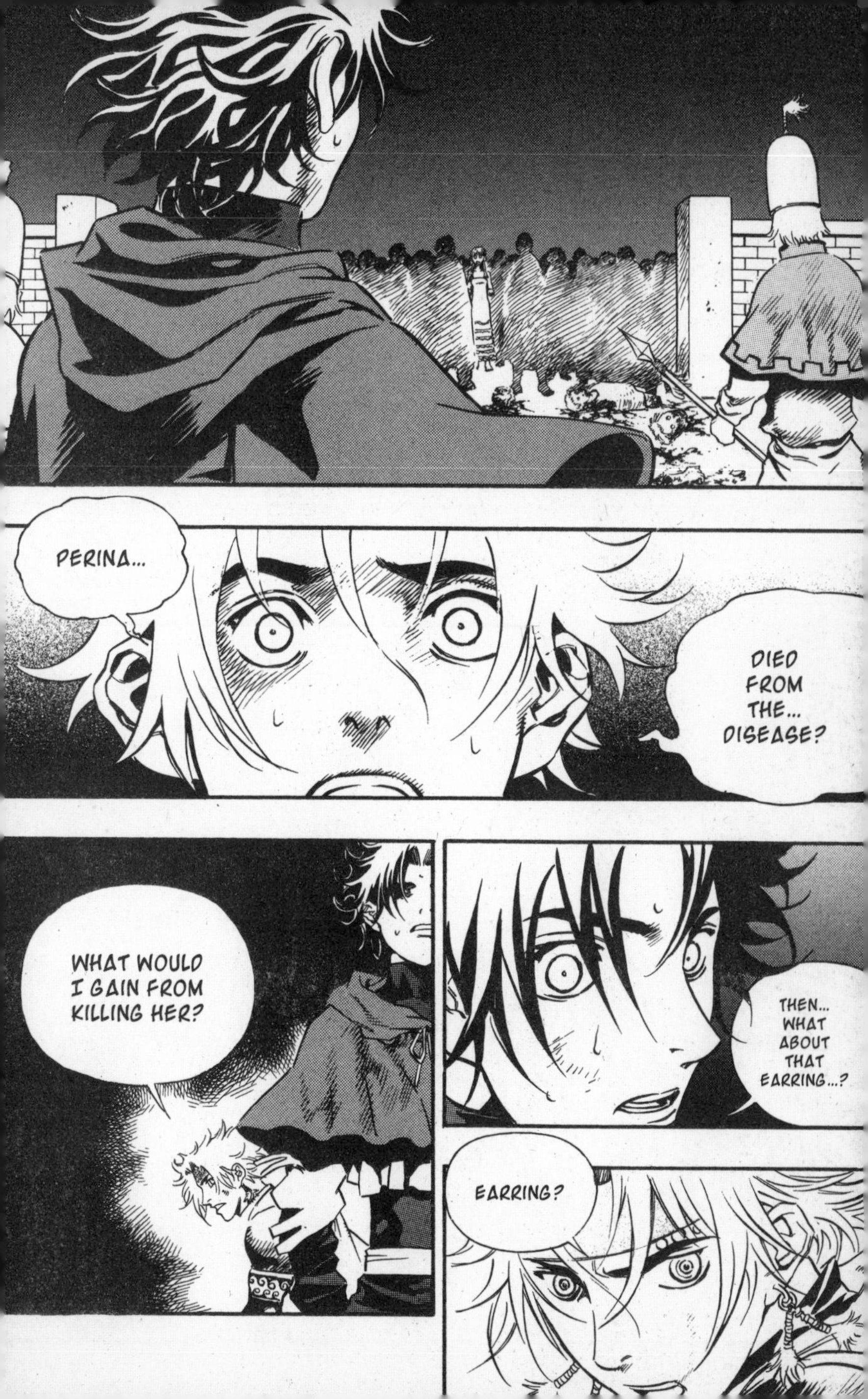
PERINA...
DIED FROM THE... DISEASE?
WHAT WOULD I GAIN FROM KILLING HER?
THEN... WHAT ABOUT THAT EARRING...?
EARRING?

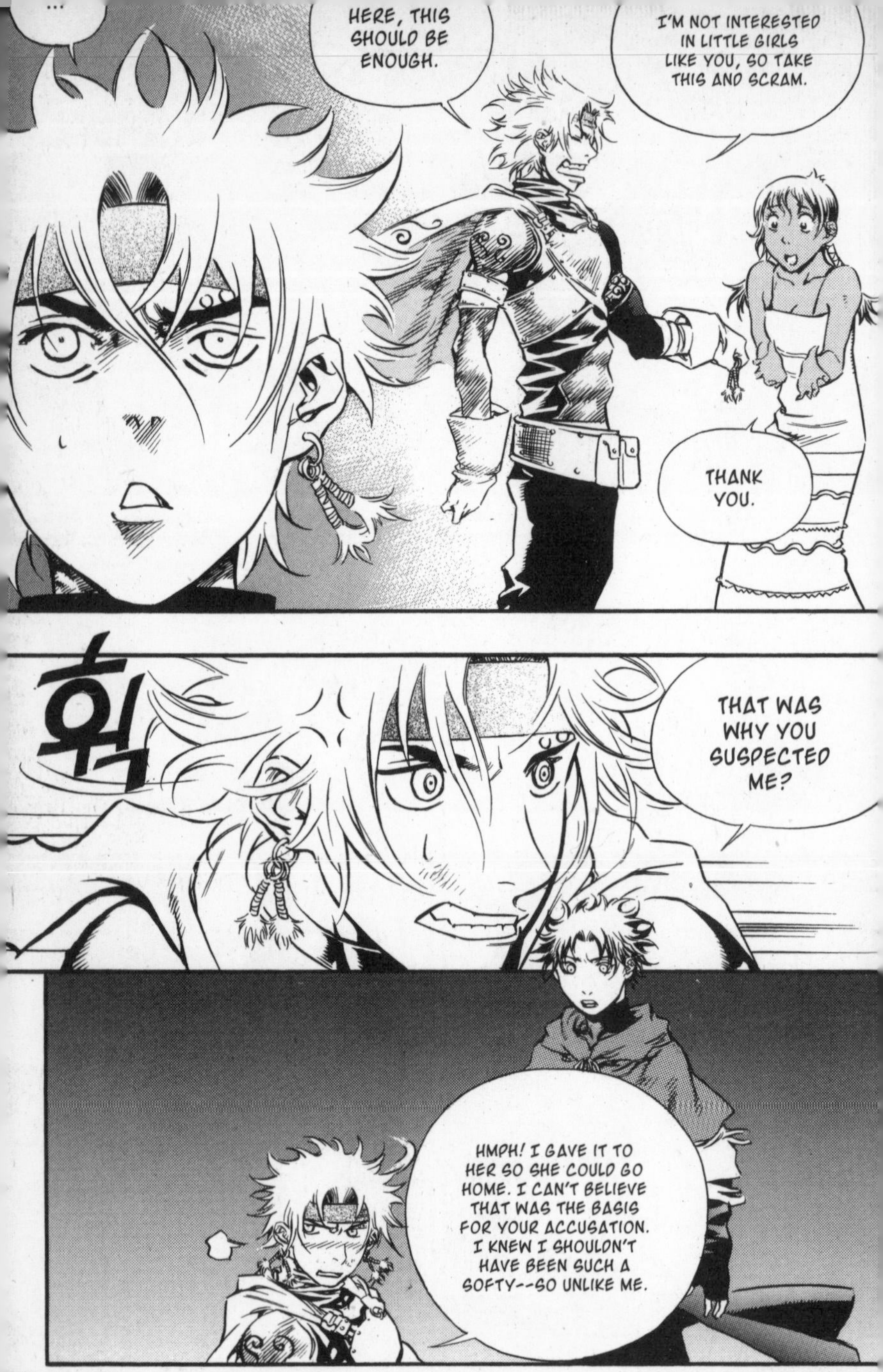
...
HERE, THIS SHOULD BE ENOUGH.
I'M NOT INTERESTED IN LITTLE GIRLS LIKE YOU, SO TAKE THIS AND SCRAM.
THANK YOU.
훽
THAT WAS WHY YOU SUSPECTED ME?
HMPH! I GAVE IT TO HER SO SHE COULD GO HOME. I CAN'T BELIEVE THAT WAS THE BASIS FOR YOUR ACCUSATION. I KNEW I SHOULDN'T HAVE BEEN SUCH A SOFTY--SO UNLIKE ME.

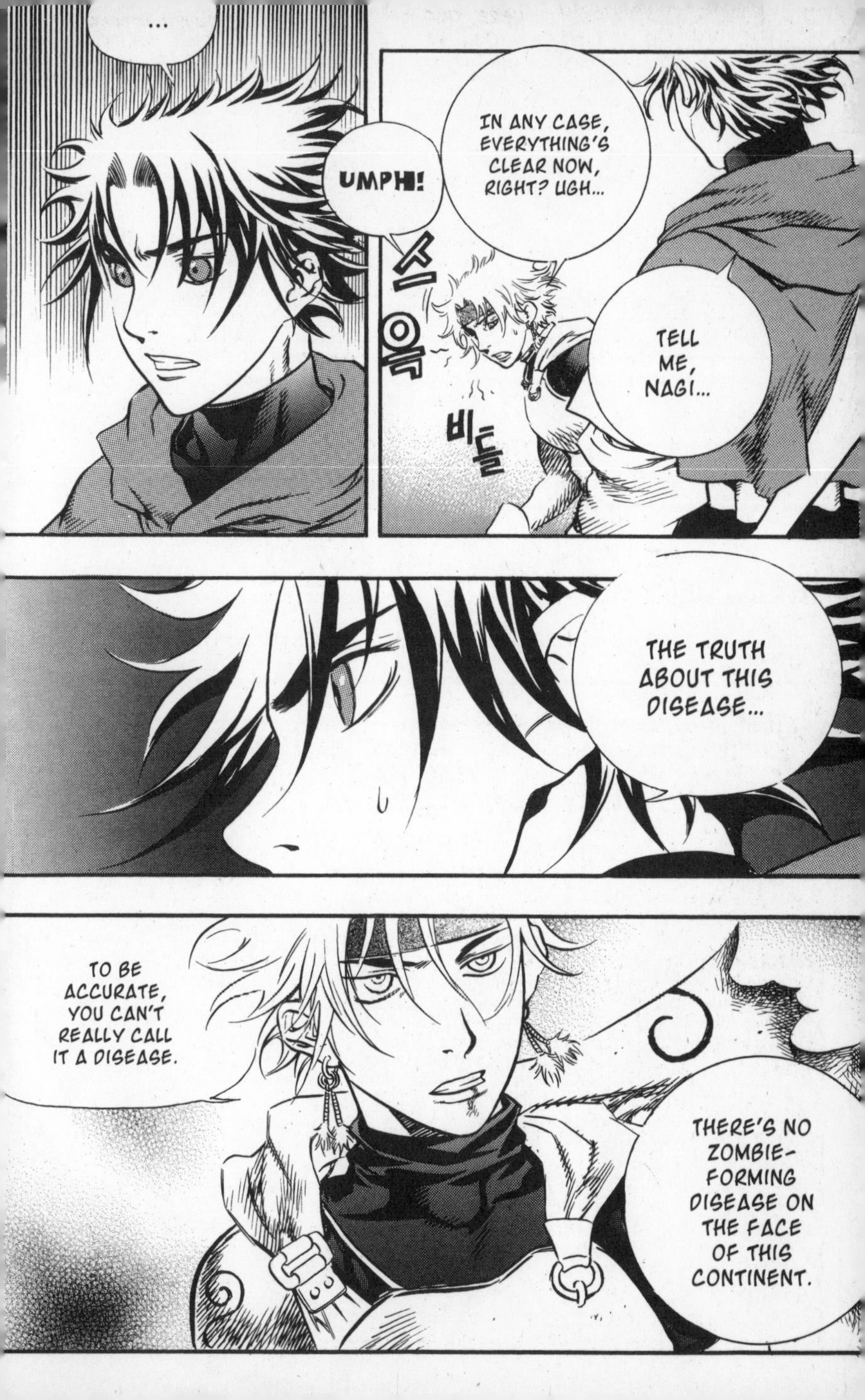
...
UMPH!
IN ANY CASE, EVERYTHING'S CLEAR NOW, RIGHT? UGH...
스윽
비들
TELL ME, NAGI...
THE TRUTH ABOUT THIS DISEASE...
TO BE ACCURATE, YOU CAN'T REALLY CALL IT A DISEASE.
THERE'S NO ZOMBIE-FORMING DISEASE ON THE FACE OF THIS CONTINENT.

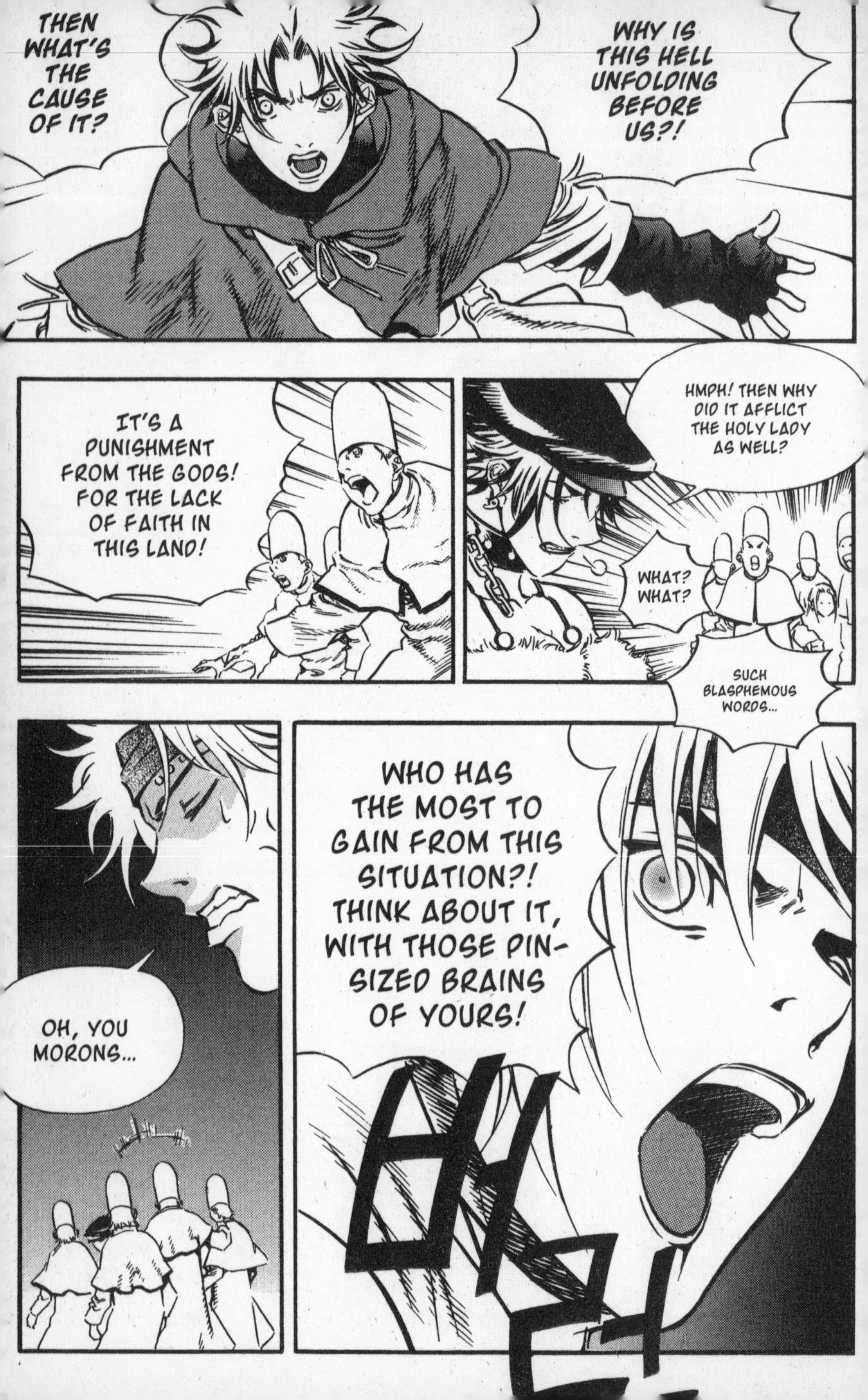
THEN WHAT'S THE CAUSE OF IT?
WHY IS THIS HELL UNFOLDING BEFORE US?!
IT'S A PUNISHMENT FROM THE GODS! FOR THE LACK OF FAITH IN THIS LAND!
HMPH! THEN WHY DID IT AFFLICT THE HOLY LADY AS WELL?
WHAT? WHAT?
SUCH BLASPHEMOUS WORDS...
OH, YOU MORONS...
WHO HAS THE MOST TO GAIN FROM THIS SITUATION?! THINK ABOUT IT, WITH THOSE PIN-SIZED BRAINS OF YOURS!

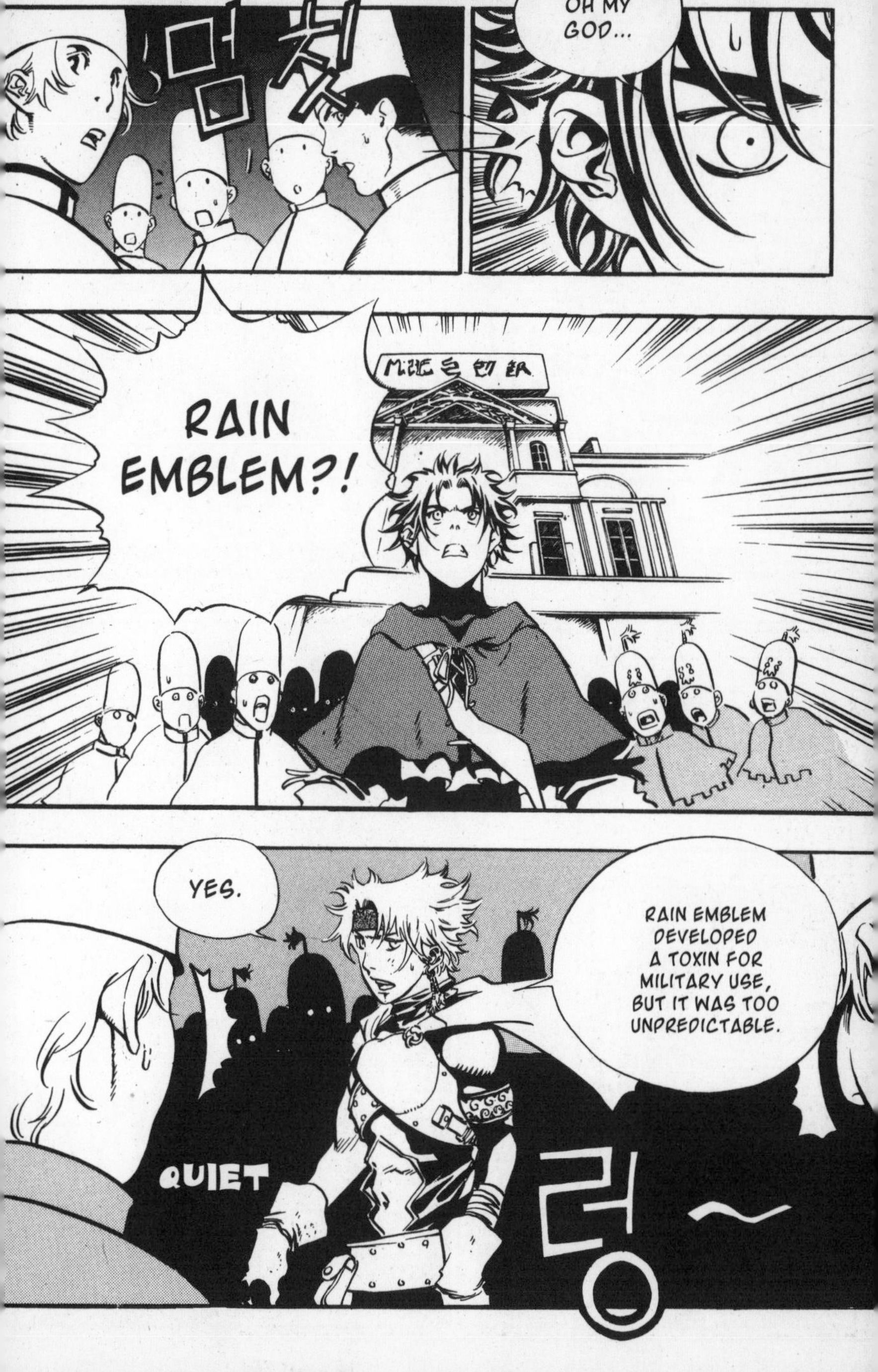
OH MY GOD...
RAIN EMBLEM?!
YES.
RAIN EMBLEM DEVELOPED A TOXIN FOR MILITARY USE, BUT IT WAS TOO UNPREDICTABLE.
QUIET

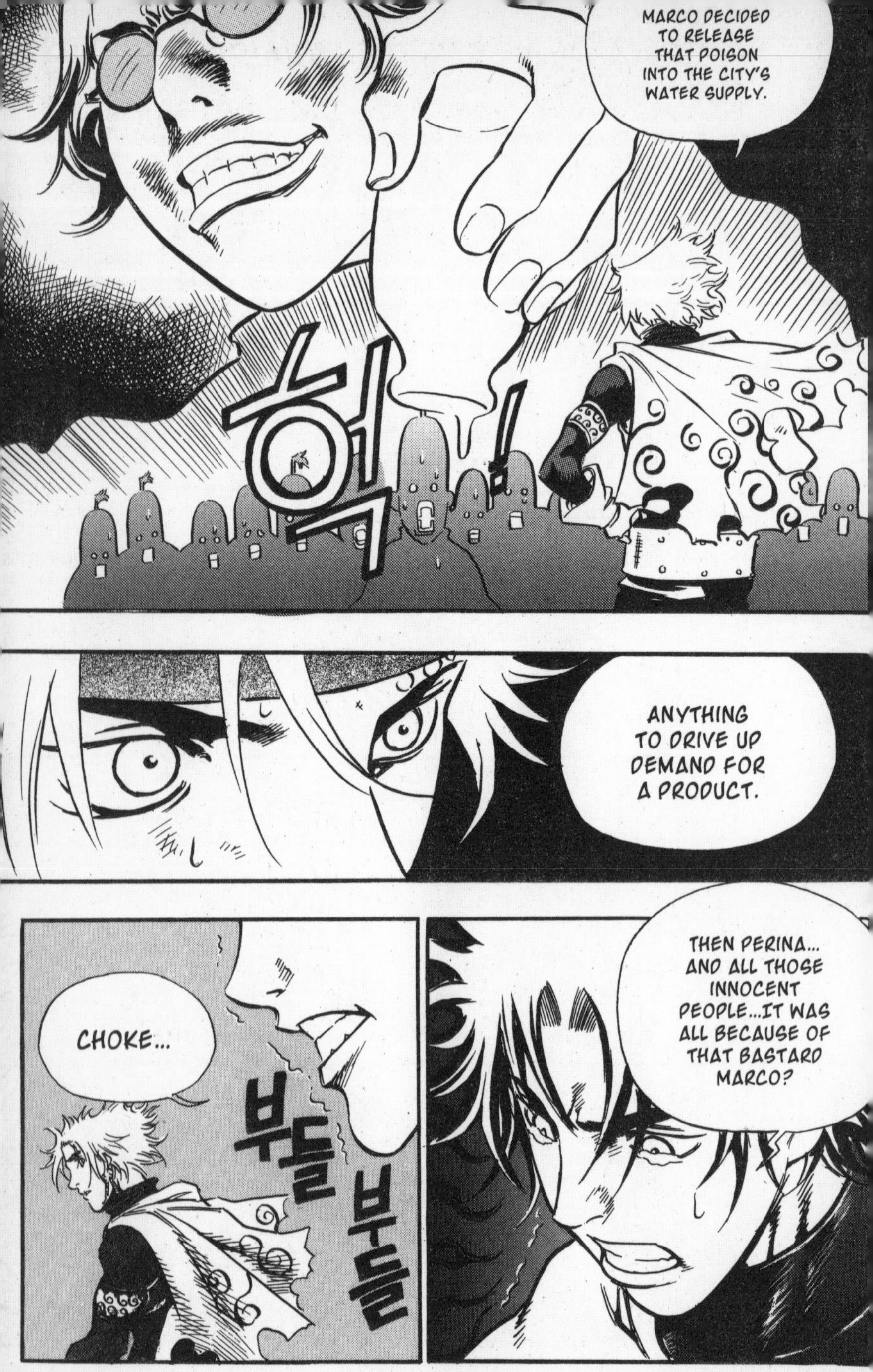
MARCO DECIDED TO RELEASE THAT POISON INTO THE CITY'S WATER SUPPLY.
헉!
ANYTHING TO DRIVE UP DEMAND FOR A PRODUCT.
CHOKE...
부들 부들
THEN PERINA... AND ALL THOSE INNOCENT PEOPLE...IT WAS ALL BECAUSE OF THAT BASTARD MARCO?

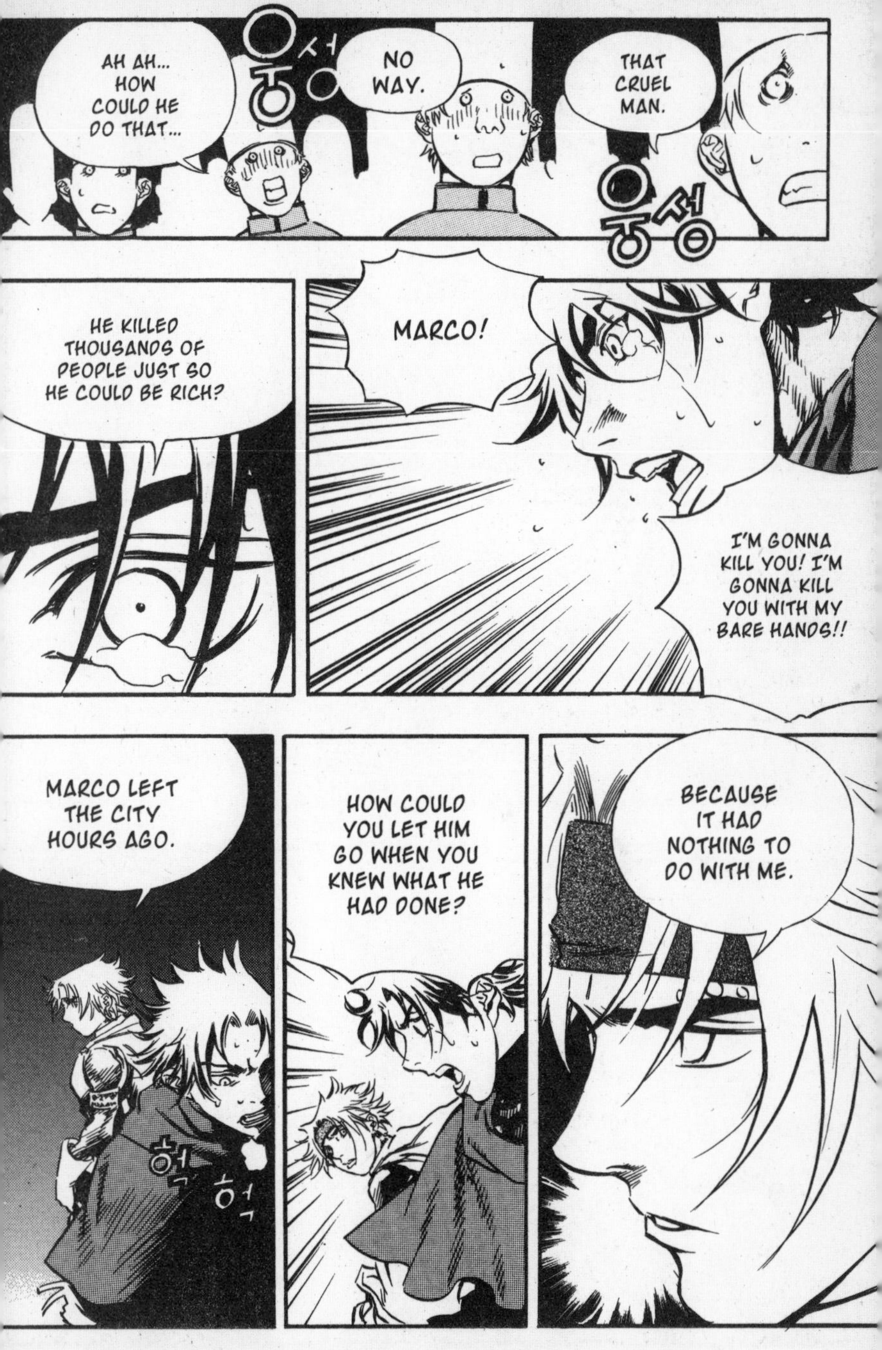
AH AH... HOW COULD HE DO THAT...
웅성
NO WAY.
THAT CRUEL MAN.
웅성
HE KILLED THOUSANDS OF PEOPLE JUST SO HE COULD BE RICH?
MARCO!
I'M GONNA KILL YOU! I'M GONNA KILL YOU WITH MY BARE HANDS!!
MARCO LEFT THE CITY HOURS AGO.
헉 헉
HOW COULD YOU LET HIM GO WHEN YOU KNEW WHAT HE HAD DONE?
BECAUSE IT HAD NOTHING TO DO WITH ME.

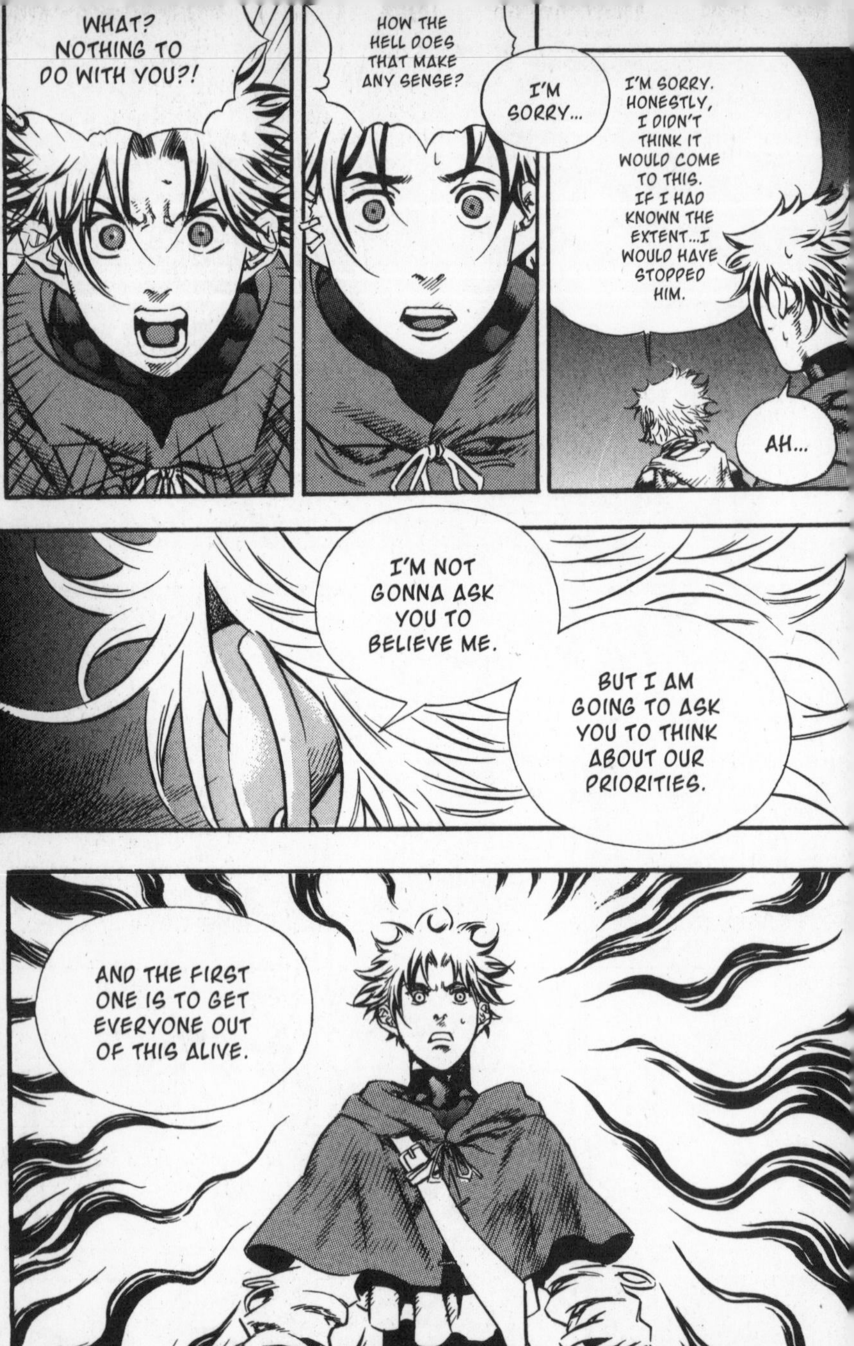
WHAT? NOTHING TO DO WITH YOU?!
HOW THE HELL DOES THAT MAKE ANY SENSE?
I'M SORRY...
I'M SORRY. HONESTLY, I DIDN'T THINK IT WOULD COME TO THIS. IF I HAD KNOWN THE EXTENT...I WOULD HAVE STOPPED HIM.
AH...
I'M NOT GONNA ASK YOU TO BELIEVE ME.
BUT I AM GOING TO ASK YOU TO THINK ABOUT OUR PRIORITIES.
AND THE FIRST ONE IS TO GET EVERYONE OUT OF THIS ALIVE.

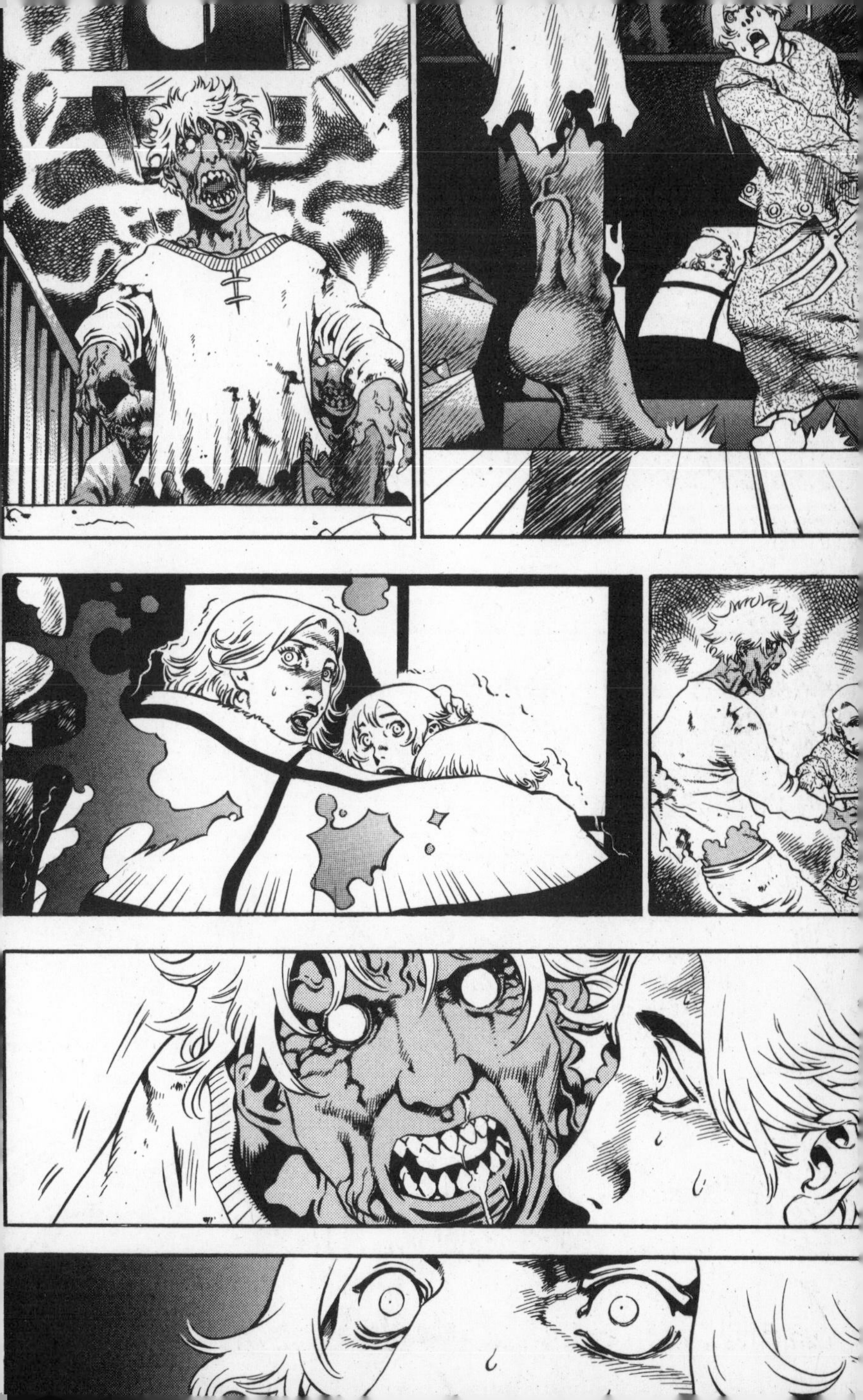

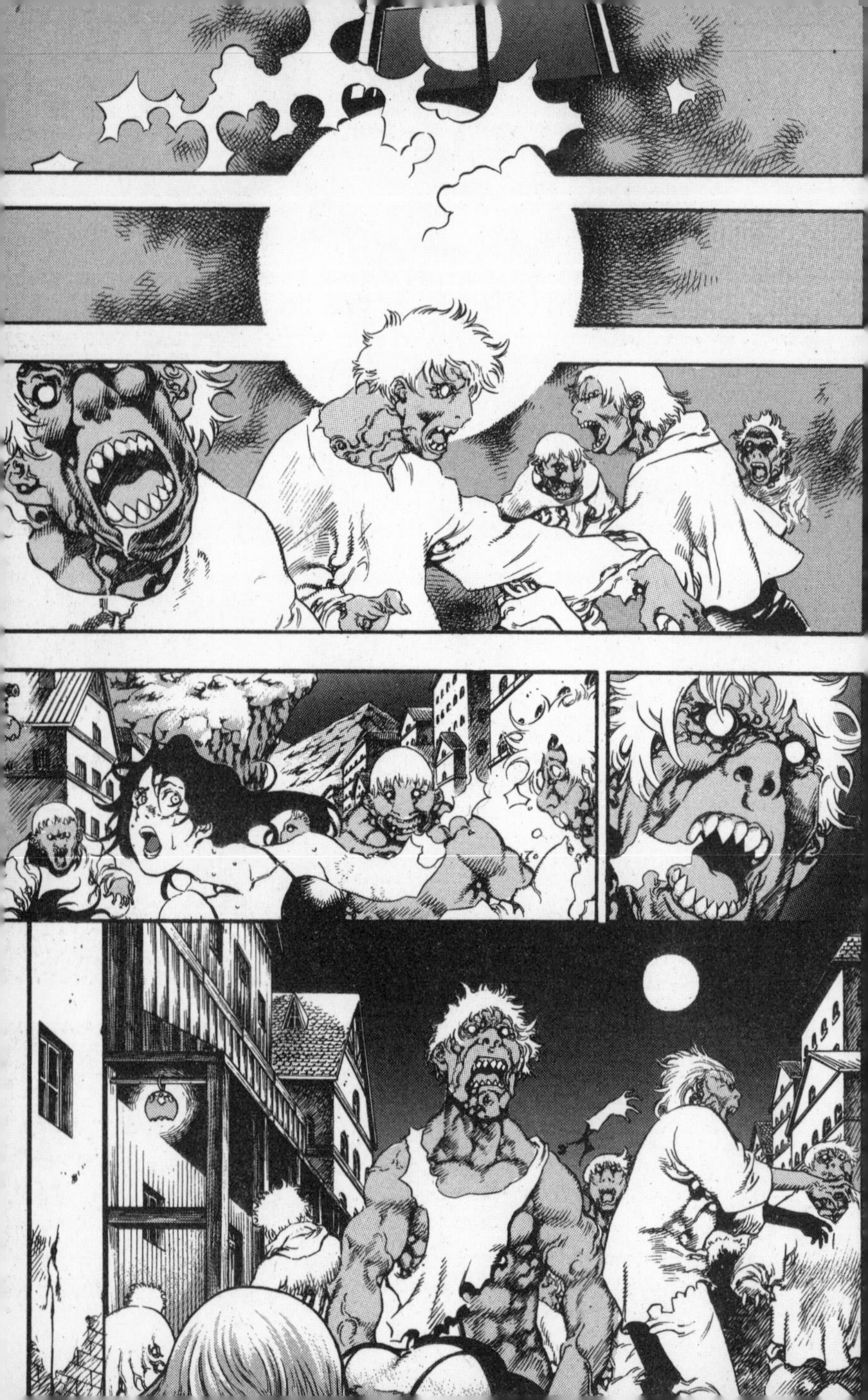

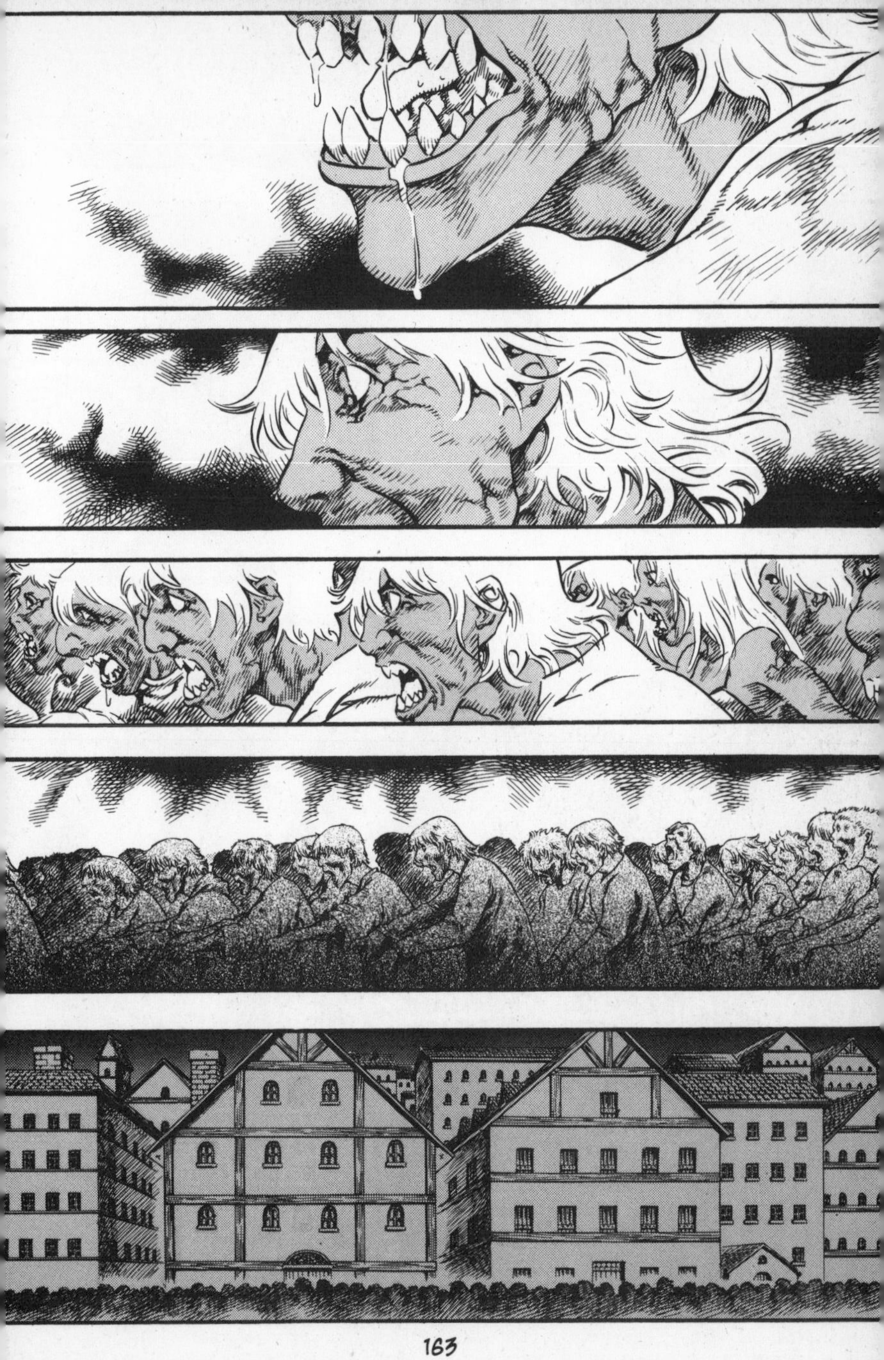

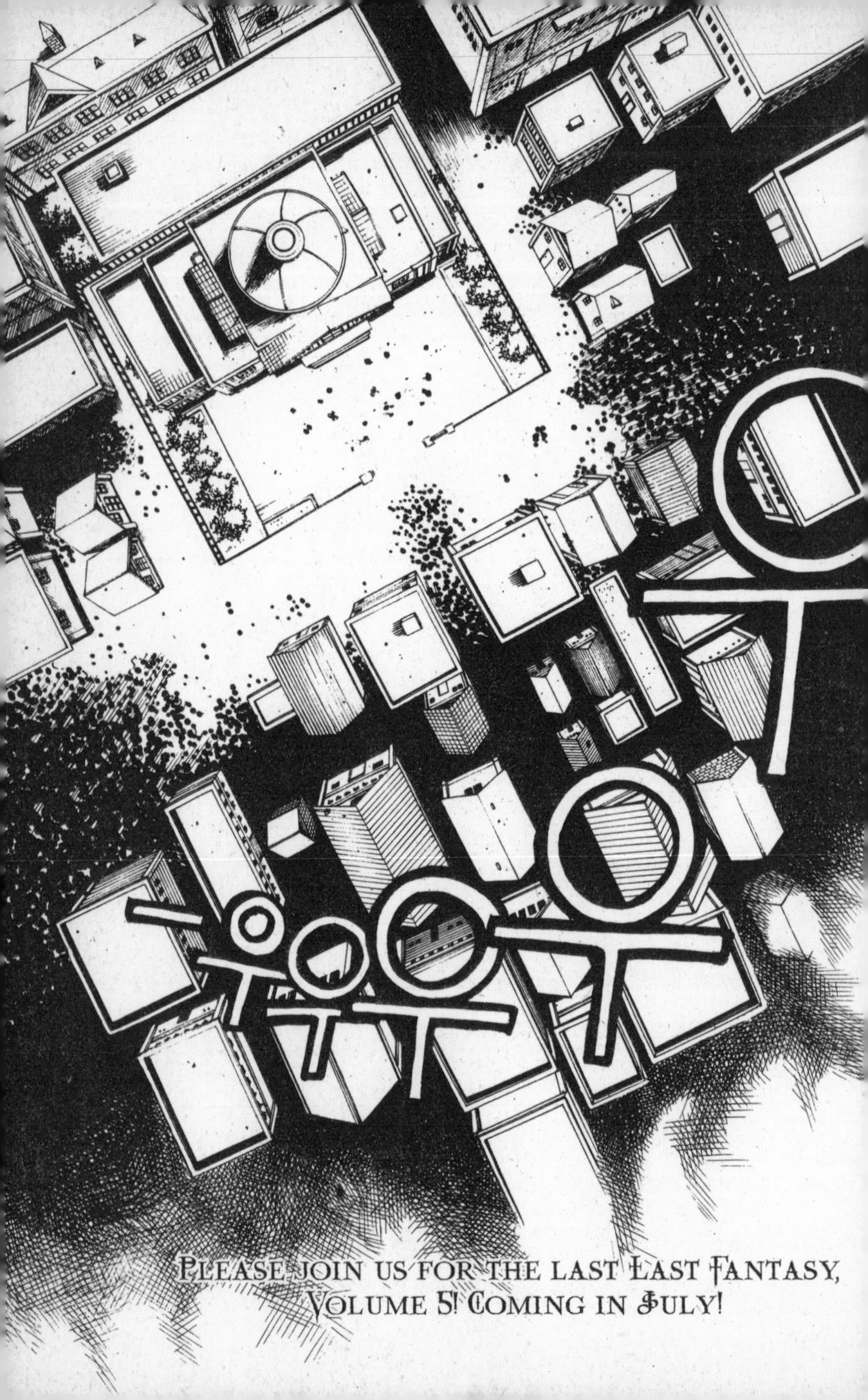
Please join us for the last Last Fantasy,
Volume 5! Coming in July!

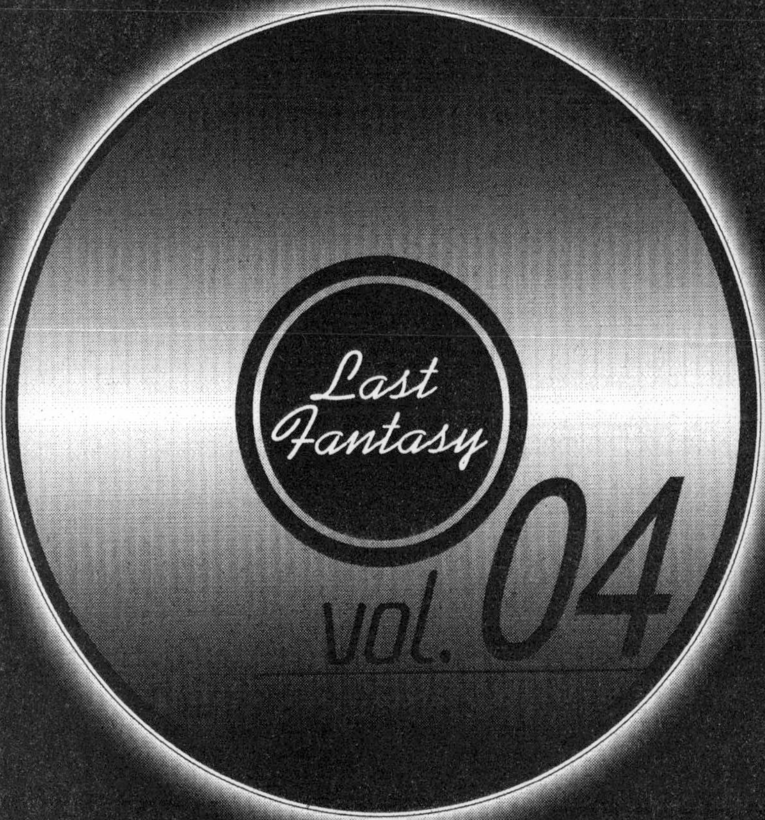
Last
Fantasy
vol. 04

BONUS TRACK

What Though Life Conspire To Cheat You

삶이 그대를 속일지라도

– Aleksandr Sergeyerich Pushkin –
푸슈킨

What though life conspire to cheat you,
삶이 그대를 속일지라도,
Do not sorrow or complain.
슬퍼하거나 노여워말라.
Lie still on the day of pain,
슬픈 날엔 참고 견뎌라,
And the day of joy will greet you.
이제 곧 기쁨의 나날이 오리니.

Hearts live in the coming day.
마음은 미래에 사는 것.
There's an end to passing sorrow.
현재는 한없이 우울한 것.
Suddenly all flies away,
모든 것이 하염없이 날아가버려도,
And delight returns tomorrow.
내일은 기쁨으로 돌아오리라.

JUST LIKE IN THE WORLD IN WHICH WE ARE LIVING, IN THE FANTASY WORLD OF TIAN AND DREI, LIFE CAN BE A BIT MUCH TO HANDLE. IT APPEARS THAT THIS LIFE, TOO, CANNOT BE LIVED BY THE INNOCENT DREAMS AND VIGOR OF YOUTH. TIAN AND DREI ARE A DEPICTION OF OUR OWN SELVES: THEY WORK HARD AND DILIGENTLY, ONLY TO REPEAT MISTAKE AFTER MISTAKE AND RUIN THEIR INTRICATELY LAID, IDEAL PLANS. AT TIMES, WE FALL INTO DESPAIR BECAUSE WE ARE UNABLE TO CARRY THE BURDENS AND THE RESPONSIBILITIES THAT HAVE BEEN LAID UPON US. AND THERE ARE TIMES AT WHICH WE IGNORE THEM AND RUN AWAY. HOWEVER, IF YOU HAVE THE STRENGTH TO STAND UP ONCE AGAIN, CLENCH YOUR FISTS, AND RUN TOWARDS TOMORROW, THEN YOU HAVE EVERY RIGHT TO BE CALLED A WARRIOR. ALTHOUGH LIFE MAY CONSPIRE TO CHEAT YOU, THIS WORLD IS ALSO IN DIRE NEED OF A YOUNG WARRIOR LIKE YOURSELF.